Health, 'Race' and Ethnicity

and Ethnicity

Making Sense of the Evidence

CHRIS SMAJE

King's
Fund
Institute

health and race - creating social change

share

©1995 King's Fund Institute

ISBN 1 870607 37 6

King's Fund Institute
14 Palace Court
London W2 4HT

Design & print: Intertype

Contents

Boxes, figures and tables

Foreword

Many of us working in the field of health and race are aware of the enormous literature which is available and of the debates which exist in relation to race, ethnicity and health.

There are many differing views on the health status of Black populations, on the sort of policies which should be implemented, and on what kinds of research should be carried out to address population health needs, either for specific communities or more generally.

This book is the first comprehensive review of the literature available on the health issues pertaining to Black populations. Its purpose is to bring together research findings on the health and health care of Black populations, along with a critical commentary on the formation of relevant policies.

We hope that the book will be useful for anyone working on health and race, be they academic researchers or purchasers and providers of health care, and that it will enable those in a position to make decisions about the provision of care to Black populations to make more informed choices about the issues.

Tahera Aanchawan
Project Manager
SHARE
King's Fund Centre

Acknowledgements

A number of people have provided me with invaluable assistance during the production of this book. First, I would like to thank Ken Judge and Julian Le Grand for encouraging me to undertake the project and for their support throughout. I am also indebted to Tahera Aanchawan and my other colleagues from the SHARE project at the King's Fund Centre, Kunbi Jones and Frances Presley, for their advice and assistance in assembling the research material and preparing the manuscript.

Waqar Ahmad, Raj Bhopal and Rory Williams provided extensive and extremely valuable comments on an earlier draft of the manuscript. Other helpful comments on all or part of earlier versions were provided by Tahera Aanchawan, Bernadette Alves, Veena Bahl, Michaela Benzeval, Sean Boyle, Seeromanie Harding, Ken Judge, Julian Le Grand, Bola Shoderu and Mike Solomon.

I am grateful to Bobbie Jacobson and her colleagues at East London and the City Health Authority for providing me with the MORI report on health in East London, and to Andrew Bebbington of PSSRU for providing me with the work on healthy active life expectancy in London.

Finally, my thanks are due to Jennifer Bew, Joy Cordwell, Karen Ho, Martyn Partridge, Kim Stirling, Roselyn Wilkinson and the library staff at both the King's Fund College and the King's Fund Centre, who all provided technical assistance of various kinds.

Any errors of fact or interpretation remain my own.

Chris Smaje

The author

Chris Smaje was a Research Officer at the King's Fund Institute from 1991 to 1994. He is now a lecturer at the University of Surrey.

Introduction

This book reviews the literature on the health of minority ethnic populations in Britain. People from these populations face the dual problems of racism and an increased likelihood of experiencing poverty and disadvantage, both of which may be expected to affect their health. As Chapter 1 shows, these factors have arisen historically and substantially interact. Nevertheless, the research evidence about ethnic patterns in health status and access to health care is complex, and not always consistent with the notion that poorer circumstances lead to poorer health and poorer access. To complicate matters still further, researchers have advanced many differing, and often competing, explanations for their observations.

The aim of the book is to summarise this research evidence in a format which is accessible to the general reader. It focuses principally upon current knowledge about the health status of minority ethnic populations in Britain and the use of health care resources made by them, as well as describing the suggested factors which underlie these patterns. It also provides a commentary on policy-making in the health sector which has been undertaken with specific regard to minority ethnic populations. In pursuing these themes, the book relates the health experience of minority ethnic groups to an understanding of their particular positioning in contemporary British society and its broader implications for the social patterning of health. To do so, it necessarily adopts a critical perspective on the material it summarises, while at the same time attempting to achieve some balance in the range of perspectives described.

The book is divided into seven substantive chapters. Chapter 1 provides essential background material. It first examines the meaning of terms such as 'race' and 'ethnicity', which are often used with little definitional precision; it shows how the complexity of these concepts leads to problems of both theory and method in health research. It goes on to outline how the concept of ethnicity has been operationalised in empirical research, and considers some of the problems that arise in doing so. Finally, it examines the ethnic composition of contemporary Britain, and provides some broad indicators of the social and economic position of different ethnic groups today.

Chapter 2 describes general indicators of health status among minority ethnic populations. It examines the findings of large national studies of mortality (deaths), and mainly smaller-scale studies of ethnic patterns in self-assessed morbidity (illness). It also looks briefly at the growing literature on ethnic patterns in the general health of women, children and elderly people. Finally, it summarises the available evidence about health–related behaviours among different ethnic groups.

Chapter 3 turns to an examination of the detailed research evidence on ethnic patterns in particular diseases. It covers the five key areas raised in the government's White Paper *The Health of the Nation* (Secretary of State for Health, 1992), as well as other diseases or groups of diseases for which particular concerns have been raised about their impact on minority ethnic groups. Nevertheless, as the chapter points out, it is often as appropriate to emphasise ethnic similarities in health as ethnic differences.

Chapters 2 and 3 also describe the main explanations which researchers have offered for their findings. These normally consist of searching for ethnic differences in the distribution of immediate or 'proximal' causes of specific diseases. Chapter 4 takes a step back from particularising explanations of this sort. Instead, it summarises the broader categories of explanation which have been invoked to account for the underlying causes of ethnic patterns in disease, providing a critical evaluation of their ability to account for the evidence described in the earlier chapters.

Chapter 5 examines the empirical evidence for ethnic patterns in access to and use of health care services. This evidence is restricted largely to analysis of utilisation rates for particular services by different ethnic groups. The chapter focuses on the utilisation of acute and GP services, and the uptake of preventive care.

Chapter 6 goes on to consider the factors that may underlie these observed patterns of utilisation. Such factors can conveniently be thought of in terms of, on the one hand, 'need' or demand side issues such as population age-structure or ethnic differences in attitudes to health care, and, on the other, 'provision' or supply side factors, such as the distribution of health care resources or racism among health care providers, all of which may affect either access to or utilisation of health services. The chapter describes the evidence for the effects of a variety of possible demand side and supply side factors.

Chapter 7 provides a commentary on policy-making which has attempted to address minority ethnic health needs. It first examines some broader issues about the significance of 'race' and ethnicity in public policy-making in order to provide a context within which to examine initiatives in the health sector. It goes on to describe some of the key questions that arise in designing the British health care system to meet the needs of minority ethnic populations. This is then illustrated through descriptions of a number of specific policy debates. A final section examines broader critical positions on the policy-making process.

Finally, a brief conclusion draws together the main arguments of the book. In particular, it attempts to look forward by highlighting some of the major gaps in existing knowledge and outlining the agenda for research and policy which is required in order to gain a better understanding of the health experience of minority ethnic groups and the appropriate means for addressing their health needs.

The reader seeking an overview of the health and welfare of minority ethnic populations in Britain can turn to a growing number of sources (Ahmad, 1993a; 1992a; Ahmad et al., 1989a; Atkin and Rollings, 1993; Balarajan and Raleigh, 1993; Cruickshank and Beevers, 1989; Department of Health, 1992; Donovan, 1984; Hopkins and Bahl, 1993; Mares et al., 1985; Rathwell and Phillips, 1986). This book aims to complement these sources by providing a broad structure for understanding and thinking about minority ethnic health issues – not restricted to particular populations, policy areas or theoretical positions – which can be supplemented by more detailed reading. Thus, although it aims at a reasonably thorough coverage of the key areas of interest, it is by no means comprehensive. It is based on published material primarily in the fields of sociology, epidemiology, health services research, social policy and race relations, derived largely from bibliographic databases but selected ultimately by the author's choice of work which informs either an empirical or a theoretical understanding of the issues. Again, where it informs discussion of the British research evidence, the book makes occasional reference to related literatures, such as those concerned with social and community care, voluntary sector initiatives and international – particularly US – research on ethnic patterns in health. However, the book is not intended as a summary of these areas, nor is it intended as a practical guide to those concerned directly with the health care of people from minority ethnic groups.

It is customary in publications of this sort to set out and justify the ethnic terminology adopted. Chapter 1 discusses in some detail the theoretical issues underlying such questions, since these have arguably received insufficient attention in the health literature. The generic term adopted in this book for those whose ethnicity differs from that of the majority of the population is 'minority ethnic' groups or populations. Although for some the word 'minority' has negative connotations, it is important in so far as it indicates that ethnicity is possessed by all human beings, not just those readily identifiable as belonging to some distinctive subpopulation.

The term 'white' is used somewhat interchangeably with 'majority ethnic population' throughout the text, although it is recognised that the former scarcely represents a unitary ethnic identity. Indeed, it must be conceded that the long-established white populations of Great Britain (used here to denote England, Scotland and Wales) themselves constitute a multiethnic and multinational population. The book does not dwell upon these distinctions, characterising the experiences of white populations in the three countries as that of an aggregate majority ethnic population. In fact, the provision of routine health and population statistics is such that often data for England and Wales alone are available, although many important research studies conducted in Scotland are reported in the text. Health issues in Northern Ireland arising from its ethnic-religious composition are important, but go beyond the scope of this book. On the other hand, considerable attention is paid to the health of populations living in Great Britain from both Northern Ireland and the Republic of Ireland (particularly the latter) and their descendants, since these constitute an identifiable ethnic population in Britain with a distinctive health profile. By contrast, little is said about other white minority populations, including 'internal' migrants such as those from Scotland. Although research among these populations is scarce, this omission is deliberate, whereas the sparing references to the health and health care of African, Chinese and Middle Eastern populations mainly reflects the lack of significant research attention to them.

'South Asian' is used to describe people who were born in the Indian subcontinent (ie. India, Pakistan or Bangladesh) or descended from those who were born there, although where possible distinctions are made between people according to their national and, occasionally, religious identities; see Bhopal *et al.* (1991) for further discussion. 'Caribbean' is used to describe people of primarily African descent who were born in one of the Caribbean islands, or who are descended from those born there. Similarly, the terms 'Irish', 'Chinese', 'African' etc. are used to describe people either born in those areas or descended from those born there, despite the unsatisfactory vagueness of terms such as 'African'.

It is important to distinguish between migrant and minority ethnic populations. The latter term is both broader – referring in addition to British-born individuals – and conceptually different. Unfortunately, the deficiencies of the data are such that reliance must often be placed on information about migrants alone to characterise the experiences of minority ethnic populations. The text specifies when data refer solely to migrants, but interpretive ambiguities are inevitable.

Where different terminologies are used on the basis of those adopted by other authors, these are normally placed in inverted commas. All terminologies are inevitably arbitrary and somewhat unsatisfactory, perhaps reflecting what Bonnett has called "that most elusive and contradictory of phenomena, an anti-racist form of 'racial' nomenclature" (1993, p.179). The one adopted here at least reflects current usage, and a specific rationale for adopting an 'ethnic' rather than a 'racial' focus is provided in Chapter 1.

A final point about the nature of the book should be made. A summary of the research literature can easily appear to suggest that the particular concerns of that literature are the uniquely valid ones. Clearly, this is not the case: the research agenda reflects the priorities and preoccupations of the academic and policy communities as much as those of the populations it seeks to examine. Its underlying assumptions are revealed both in the particular research questions which are chosen and in the way they are tackled. It is not a principal aim of this review to provide a critique of the research process itself (see Ahmad, 1993b; Pearson, 1983; Stubbs, 1993). Nevertheless, it does aim to provide a critical introduction to the literature, not only by commenting upon the approaches and methods of particular studies, but also by placing them in a broader analytical framework within which minority ethnic health can be examined.

1 Ethnicity in context

Introduction

This chapter begins by defining ethnicity and discussing some of the insights from social and biological science which have a bearing on the way the concept is used in health research. It goes on to examine how concepts of ethnicity have been operationalised in research, and considers some of the criticisms that have been made of this process. Finally, it describes the development of Britain's contemporary ethnic composition and the structure of the main ethnic groups in Britain today.

What is ethnicity?

In its original usage, to be ethnic was to be heathen. Deriving from the Greek word *ethnos* – nation – contemporary usage has often preserved the exclusionary sentiments implicit in this conflation of religion and nationality. To be ethnic is to be different, foreign and marginal: not 'one of us'. More recently, social scientists have extended the concept of ethnicity to encompass all of the ways in which people seek to differentiate themselves from others. In this sense, ethnicity has largely replaced 'race' – differentiation according to physical appearance – as the appropriate way to think of human difference.

The concept of race has a long and fairly dishonourable history in the biological and social sciences (Gould, 1981; 1977). It was at one time customary to distinguish between several broadly defined human races on the basis of physical traits such as skin colour, facial characteristics and so on, with the implicit or explicit assumption that members of each race had biological commonalities not shared with other races. Modern geneticists term the physical form of an individual their *phenotype*, which arises through the interaction of the environment with the organism's *genotype*, or heritable genetic makeup. Although phenotypic differences between human populations are self-evident, advances in genetics have shown that classifying such differences into 'races' constitutes neither a useful nor an accurate representation of the underlying genotypic variation. In fact, most genes occur identically in all human beings. Of the ones which do not – so-called *polymorphic* genes – a very small number underlie the phenotypic differences which are conventionally thought of as defining 'race'. Moreover, other polymorphic genes, such as those that determine particular blood types, cut across these conventionally defined races (Jones, 1981). There is insufficient correlation between polymorphisms for any discrete set of 'races' to be meaningfully defined. In fact, most genetic variation occurs at the individual level and, as Hill has suggested:

> the amount of variation within a racial group is considerably greater than the average genetic difference between races. Clearly the genes responsible for the morphological features that allow us to classify individuals into broad racial groupings are atypical and extremely unrepresentative of the true degree of interracial genetic difference

> (1989, p.26).

On the basis of such observations, Gould poses the following forceful questions:

Shall our approach to such variation be that of a cataloguer? Shall we artificially partition such a dynamic and continuous pattern into distinct units with formal names? Would it not be better to map this variability objectively without imposing upon it the subjective criteria for formal subdivision that any taxonomist must use?

(1977, p.234).

In fact, most biologists have long since abandoned racial taxonomies and adopted more sophisticated multivariate techniques for analysing genetic differences between populations. The persistence of racial taxonomies owes more to their sociopolitical significance than to an underlying biological reality. In analysing 'racial' patterns in health, the significant agents are therefore usually more likely to relate to the social meanings people attach to phenotypic differences than to any particular genetic trait.

This observation returns the argument to the realm of ethnicity. Phenotypic difference is just one of the characteristics which people can use to differentiate themselves from others, albeit a particularly powerful one. Although, for historical reasons, current ethnic distinctions in Britain are strongly identified with an ideology of 'race' which constitutes physical appearance – and particularly skin colour – as the fundamental marker of ethnicity, distinctions can and have also been made around language, religion and historical or territorial identity, as well as more diffuse notions such as culture, or what Wallman (1986) has called 'symbolic identifications', such as dress, diet, kinship systems and so on. As Wallman puts it:

Once it is clear that ethnic relations follow on the social construction of difference, phenotype falls into place as one element in the repertoire of ethnic boundary markers

(1986, p.229).

Thus, the particular characteristics with which people choose to emphasise differences between themselves are essentially arbitrary. Although factors such as language, phenotype and religion usually demarcate social differences of importance to the individuals concerned, there is no logical reason why they should inevitably become ethnic markers with strong exclusionary implications. For this reason, the notion of 'race' or phenotypic difference is here subsumed into the concept of ethnicity.

Two major objections to discussing ethnicity in this way have been raised. First, a number of writers have pointed out that although the term 'ethnicity' is now generally preferred to 'race', explanations for ethnic difference are still routinely sought in genetic terms (Lock, 1994; Senior and Bhopal, 1994). In this sense, ethnicity can become little more than a euphemism and its supposed emphasis on social rather than biological causation undermined. Strictly speaking, it is of course possible that there may be *some* correlation between the frequency of particular genetic traits with a bearing upon health and socially ascribed ethnic identity, as with sickle cell disorders (see Chapter 3). Nevertheless, the general thrust of the argument is a sound one and provides a useful caution about the unthinking use of 'ethnic' terminologies.

Second, it is sometimes suggested that a concept of ethnicity defined in terms of arbitrary ethnic markers ignores the political and historical factors by which these markers are given concrete social meaning. For this reason, several writers prefer to retain a distinction between ethnicity and race (Gilroy, 1990; 1987; Weissman, 1990), constituting race as a "precarious discursive construction"

(Gilroy, 1990, p.72). Whether such a distinction is retained or not is perhaps less important than recognising the broader point that, although the characteristics used to define ethnic boundaries may be arbitrary, the circumstances in which they are used are not. Typically, ethnic distinctions are most forcefully made when political or economic power is at stake. Indeed, the recent history of minority ethnic groups in Britain has been shaped fundamentally by the incorporation of migrant labour into subordinate sectors of the economy (Miles, 1982). Moreover, although a particular historical concept of 'race' casts a long shadow over European thought (Allen, 1994), ethnic boundaries are not immutable but can change according to historical and political circumstances. Drawing these arguments together, Wallman suggests:

> *Differences between groups of people turn into ethnic boundaries only when heated into significance by the identity investments of either side*

> (1986, p.230).

Thus, the meaning of Catholicism and Protestantism as ethnic markers is very different in Belfast compared with Bristol. Similarly, 'Caribbean' ethnic identity in the Caribbean itself, if it indeed exists, is a rather different phenomenon from such an identity in Britain (James, 1993).

It is the task of sociology and history to explain how the nexus of migrations, ethnic markers and economic relations has come to create ethnic identities in Britain and impart social meaning to them. However, this task is not without relevance to health studies. One important conceptual issue which has found its way into the health field – via the arguments of Miles (1982) and Phizacklea (1984) in the sociology of race – is the point that if race and ethnicity are social inventions, what does it mean to talk of 'ethnic differences' in health experience? Indeed, some commentators believe that the analytical status of these concepts is so questionable that they should not be used in health research:

> *if public health workers continue to use the term 'race' because people act as though race exists, they are guilty of conferring analytical status on what is nothing more than an ideological construction*

> (Sheldon and Parker, 1992, p.105).

A counter-argument to this position is that it is precisely because people *do* act as though race exists that race or ethnic status have social consequences, not least in terms of health experience. As Marmot has argued:

> *The vagueness of the term 'ethnic'... does not invalidate this area of study. If two groups, however defined, have different rates of disease, productive aetiological investigations may follow*

> (1989, p.13).

The differing emphases of these positions reflect the current lack of consensus about the status of ethnicity in public health research which, according to Cooper and David (1986), demands urgent debate. Neither position disputes that health experience is determined by factors associated with ethnicity rather than ethnicity itself. However, the danger which Sheldon and Parker are concerned to highlight is that a focus on ethnicity rather than these associated factors can lead easily to the inference that it is ethnicity itself which causes poor health (since it is poor rather than good health which is generally the object of interest). Examples of such 'victim blaming' abound in the literature on the health of minority ethnic populations, and are usefully summarised by Donovan (1984). It follows from Sheldon and Parker's argument that the proper strategy should be to examine the determinants of health directly. On the other hand, ethnic distinctions have concrete social meanings which, as Cooper and David (1986) point out, are antecedent to the experience of these direct determinants. In other words, it is not simply that people from particular – socially defined – ethnic groups happen to be exposed to particular health determinants more (or less) commonly than other groups. Rather, the concrete implications for social and economic position of the 'ideological construction', race, substantially govern these exposures. It might therefore be appropriate to preserve an analytic role for ethnicity, rather than reducing it simply to the experience of various kinds of disadvantage.

These points demonstrate the complexity of ethnicity as a category in health research, and underscore the need for further debate emphasised by Cooper and David. Clearly, important theoretical ambiguities exist in the concept of ethnicity which are of relevance to its use in research. Some comments on the sociology of ethnicity may help to illustrate this point.

As the discussion above suggested, one useful way of thinking about ethnicity is as an indicator of the process by which people create and maintain a sense of group identity and solidarity which they use to distinguish themselves from others. But ethnicity also refers to the external creation of categories which people impose on others, and with which the people so categorised do not necessarily identify. Mason (1990) has usefully addressed this distinction between ethnicity as *identity* and ethnicity as *category*, developing the arguments of Jenkins (1986), who suggested that ethnicity is generally associated with the creation of identity – an 'us' statement – while 'race' is associated with categorisation – a 'them' statement. In such a scheme, identity is a positive process of group formation, categorisation a negative consequence of cultural power.

However, Mason points out that a process of identification is impossible without categorisation. Moreover, as a large anthropological literature attests, the flexibility of the concept of ethnicity lies in people's ability to change its meaning over relatively short periods of time and to use externally imposed categories to create internal identity (see, for example, Comaroff, 1985; Dominguez, 1977; Jayawardena, 1980). Historically, the unequal relationship between Europe and its colonies allowed European definitions of the exotic and the primitive – the 'not one of us' referred to above – to prevail (Said, 1978). This process is still in evidence today in common representations of minority ethnic culture in Britain (Sivanandan, 1982). At the same time, the people so defined produce their own conceptions of ethnicity, both in relation to the categories imposed upon them and autonomously.

What, then, are the implications of this partial distinction between category and identity for health research? As Mason (1990) points out, the debate about the meaning of ethnicity generally takes place in circumstances where the relationship between category and identity is unclear. There is an empiricism implicit in the position cited above of Marmot (1989) which, in suggesting that 'ethnic' status may be a useful dimension for research, however it has come to be ascribed, accepts the validity of regarding ethnicity as an externally imposed category. This position is not without merit. It may well be that in examining the factors which bear upon health and health care utilisation, an individual's self-ascribed identity is of less significance than how they are categorised by others, and the resulting social roles they must occupy. Nor must such an approach inevitably neglect the importance of ethnicity as identity, where this does not coincide with externally imposed ethnic categories.

Nevertheless, it is scarcely surprising that the uncritical acceptance of external ethnic categorisation makes some analysts uncomfortable. For Ahmad (1993b), such an approach betrays a falsely non-political stance. Moreover, in common with the deficiencies of an 'objectivist' social science which seeks explanations beyond those of everyday common sense reality, such an approach may often deny analytical significance to the accounts produced by the relevant populations themselves (Bourdieu, 1977).

It should not be assumed, however, that a concept of ethnicity based on ethnic identity is any less problematic. At what level of identity should ethnicity be conceptualised? As Mason suggests, both analysts and activists sometimes seem to suggest that:

> because 'black' people share a common experience of racism and exclusion, they **ought** to pursue a political strategy founded on the unity of the oppressed

> (1990, p.125).

Clearly, however, many people who experience racism do not necessarily embrace a unitary 'black' identity, or believe that such an identity is appropriate (Modood, 1988). In fact, the construction of a unitary 'black' identity may betray an equally high-handed objectivism. One of the difficulties is that ethnicity has a situational aspect, in which people 'use' their ethnicity in different ways at different times. For example, a Punjabi Sikh living in Britain may in some circumstances constitute themselves as 'black' to identify their experience of racism, at other times as 'Asian' to distinguish themselves from people of other geographic origins, and at other times as 'Sikh' to identify their particular set of beliefs and practices and to emphasise politically their distance from an 'Indian' identity. In an important sense, then, any identified ethnic group is an artifice abstracted from a more complex set of social relationships. Ethnic groups are 'imagined communities' (Anderson, 1991) and ethnicity itself is a property of individuals which emerges in particular circumstances through their social practice, and that of others (Bourdieu, 1977).

These points help to explain some of the problems which are encountered when concepts of ethnicity are deployed in health studies. A 'black' identity forged in the context of political opposition to racism may not be welcomed when applied as a category of assumed cultural identity by predominantly white social scientists. But from the researcher's point of view, it may be appropriate to think of 'black' people as a category, since the common experience of racism and disadvantage may be a common factor underlying their health experience. On the other hand, it may be better to think in terms of the ethnic identity of different groups, since their different beliefs, behaviours and lifestyles may affect their health experiences in singular ways.

Such differing approaches are reflected in the continuing debate between multiculturalism and anti-racism. Although both terms lack precise meaning, multiculturalism can broadly be characterised as an attempt to emphasise both the existence and the validity of different cultural traditions in contemporary Britain, and to promote tolerance and understanding of these traditions between ethnic groups. By contrast, anti-racism places a much more political emphasis on the forces that structure social relationships and determine access to power in society. For anti-racists, dominant social ideologies are inherently 'racialised', and racism is identified as a pervasive instrument of social control which marginalises people from minority ethnic populations (Solomos, 1989; Stubbs, 1993).

This debate has been conducted most fiercely in social policy fields such as education (Rex, 1989; Solomos, 1989), although – as it is argued in Chapter 7 – the issues raised are also highly relevant to health policy. However, elements of the multiculturalist and anti-racist positions are also to be found in the contrasting approaches of social researchers. Those writing in a broadly anthropological tradition, with its emphasis on patterns of cultural practice, typically subscribe to the former (Khan, 1979a; Watson, 1977), whereas the failure of these writers to emphasise both racism and the material constraints facing minority ethnic populations has led to strong criticism from the anti-racist position (Lawrence, 1982a). Anti-racism has in turn been criticised for contributing to a view of minority ethnic populations as little more than passive victims of racism, forever trapped behind immutable racial difference (see, for example, discussions in Ballard, 1992; Gilroy, 1990; Goering, 1993; Stubbs, 1993; Werbner, 1987). There is no easy resolution to the debate, as some of the best writers in each tradition recognise. However, it provides an important background to much of the material in the chapters which follow, since – depending upon the position adopted – most researchers tend to emphasise either cultural or sociopolitical explanations in examining both health policy-making and the health experience of minority groups themselves.

Clearly, however, from a research point of view, no *a priori* assumptions should be made about either the interaction between ethnicity and health or the appropriate situational level at which to hypothesise any putative interaction. Nor do any easy answers emerge as to how ethnicity can usefully be theorised in a universally acceptable manner. Nevertheless, Mason's thoughtful comments are worth quoting at some length:

> *The use of categories which stand in varying degrees of coincidence with the identities of those who are placed in them is … unavoidable in … sociological analysis … Only a social science free to develop categories and modes of analysis which are different from those embraced by everyday actors can have any claim to be more than common sense … Social scientists cannot claim to know more about, say, racial discrimination than those who are its victims … What they can offer is different kinds of knowledge … we should not be afraid to use categories which are not embraced by actors themselves if these can illuminate patterns of disadvantage and domination. We must, however, be clear when we are doing so and not imply that these categories coincide with the identities of those to whom they refer*

(1990, p.128).

To summarise, all human 'races' share substantial biological continuity, but ethnic groups in Britain, though not necessarily elsewhere, are characterised by marked social discontinuities, albeit that their boundaries are inevitably unclear. It may therefore be useful to examine ethnic patterns in health experience, but if these are to be properly understood it is important to pay careful attention to the nature of such boundaries and the interests their maintenance serves. If, then, there is a role for examining ethnic patterns in empirical health research, there is clearly a need to be able to analyse population health data in ethnic terms. How this can and has been done is the subject of the following section.

Operationalising ethnicity

This section falls into three parts. It begins by outlining briefly how the concept of ethnicity has been operationalised in health and social studies in the last twenty years or so. It then examines some criticisms of these approaches. Finally, it offers a brief critical conclusion which evaluates the preceding arguments.

The development of ethnic statistics

The most authoritative source of demographic information in Britain is the decennial census. Until 1971, the only question relevant to ethnicity asked by the census was nationality. The 1971 Census asked for country of birth and mother and father's country of birth. In view of the relatively recent migrations which had substantially constituted the formation of contemporary ethnic distinctions, this question picked up the majority of respondents from most, but by no means all, minority ethnic populations. However, the increasing numbers of people from such populations born in Britain made apparent the need for a question on ethnicity rather than country of birth. This was a major departure from the established practice of asking only 'objective' questions (Leech, 1989), and it required considerable effort to choose a question which satisfied both the needs of the official users of the information and the concerns of the respondents. In fact, pilot studies leading up to the 1981 Census failed to resolve these problems and the census of that year consequently included a question only on birthplace.

More generally, most research on the health of minority ethnic populations has been dependent upon birthplace data, as recorded in censuses or death certificates. Although knowledge of migrant health is often used as a proxy for the health experience of minority ethnic groups as a whole, there are clear deficiencies in such an approach. To rectify them, one of two broad strategies could be adopted. Research could:

- Extend the approach adopted in the 1971 Census, asking for country of birth and parents'/ grandparents'/great grandparents' country of birth; or,

- Abandon a direct focus on migration and devise an acceptable ethnic taxonomy from which individuals can indicate their preferred identity.

Despite their differences, both strategies require essentially arbitrary choices to be made about the appropriate demarcation of either geographic areas or ethnic categories. The attraction of the former is that country of birth is a much simpler and less conceptually muddled descriptor than ethnicity. It can be justified with reference to the fact that the presence of most commonly identified minority ethnic groups in Britain is a relatively recent phenomenon to which the approach is sensitive; that it elicits information much less likely to suffer from respondent bias; and that it better conforms to the epidemiological emphasis on establishing the cause of disease by tracing variations in its incidence across time, place and person (Marmot, 1989). Indeed, the approach has been used with considerable success to illuminate changing patterns of disease across populations (Syme *et al.*, 1975). On the other hand, its objectivity can be overstated. For example, as well as requiring arbitrary choices about geographic aggregation, further value judgments must be made about how to allocate according to parents' country of birth when this is not congruent, a problem which has arisen with regard to parents' ethnicity in routine US health statistics (Cooper and David, 1986).

By contrast, the emphasis on ethnicity as opposed to migration stems from the recognition that systematic social forces exist in the 'host' country which lead to the reproduction of social differences persisting beyond the migrant generation into its indigenous offspring. These differences lead to inequalities in access to resources which may affect health experience, among other things. Thus, the argument runs, it is not the fact of migration but of the continuing emphasis of difference which should be the appropriate object of enquiry, particularly since the continuing focus on immigration may succour racist notions of the 'alien' threat from abroad. This argument is rarely made in these explicit terms, but some version of it underlies the position of most advocates for the focus on ethnicity as opposed to migration (Nanton, 1992). It provides a more explicitly political rationale for research to grasp the social realities of ethnic plurality, notwithstanding the debate about how that plurality can best be described by empirical research and what the true motives for such research might be (Ahmad and Sheldon, 1991; Ohri, 1988).

Some researchers have combined elements of both approaches. For example, Hazuda *et al.* (1986) constructed an algorithm to allocate 'Mexican–American' ethnicity among subjects of an epidemiological study in Texas which employed self-reported ethnicity and grandparental ethnicity, parental birthplace and concordance of parental surnames as a proxy for ethnic identity. Although the investigators may well be correct in arguing that in this particular case their method yields the optimum results, the algorithm ultimately reflects only a more stringent set of inclusion criteria which still rest upon *a priori* judgments about ethnic identity. It would seem that, however complex the method, arbitrary choices must be made. Thus, although plausible justifications can be offered for adopting a variety of possible methods for assigning ethnicity, no 'gold standard' can be defined against which their validity can be measured.

Whatever the merits of the various approaches, measures of self-reported ethnicity from a predefined list appear to have gained the upper hand in official British statistics. From 1979 onwards, surveys such as the *Labour Force Survey,* the *National Dwelling and Household Survey* and the *General Household Survey* began to ask respondents to identify their ethnic group. The most commonly used list of groups from which respondents were asked to choose is illustrated in Figure 1.1.

Figure 1.1 **Ethnic origin in the *Labour Force Survey* and *General Household Survey***

'To which of the groups listed do you consider you belong?'

White

West Indian or Guyanese

Indian

Pakistani

Bangladeshi

Chinese

African

Arab

Mixed Origin

Other

Although these surveys provide rich data in different areas, the fact that they are household surveys of relatively small size makes them less useful as sources of overall summary statistics. Throughout the 1980s, therefore, the Office of Population Censuses and Surveys (OPCS) experimented with a variety of ethnic questions, eventually settling for the one illustrated in Figure 1.2, which was included in the 1991 Census. Despite some apparent conceptual limitations, this format for the question proved to be the most acceptable and least ambiguous to the public (Teague, 1993).

The inclusion of this question will undoubtedly help to move ethnic statistics from the realm of immigration to broader issues, but it is too early to assess its impact so far, since the data are only just becoming available. In the absense of such information, researchers at the local level have used other techniques to focus on the health of minority ethnic groups. Of special note are 'name searches' of records such as death certificates and FHSA or electoral registers in order to identify particular ethnic populations. Clearly, this approach requires populations with names distinctively different from the majority population and with a high degree of endogamy (ie. marriage within the ethnic group). Although the precise methodologies employed are rarely made explicit, the technique has been used with apparent success in studies of South Asian populations and has been shown to yield accurate and reliable results (Coldman et al., 1988; Ecob and Williams 1991; Nicoll et al., 1986). However, since naming systems among South Asians relate largely to religion (Henley and Taylor, 1981), they do not provide foolproof information on ethnic origin in the absence of more detailed local knowledge. For example, it is difficult to distinguish widely varying Muslim populations from name alone. Moreover, the reliability of the technique is likely to wane with diminishing endogamy (Senior and Bhopal, 1994). Although the potential exists to extend the technique beyond South Asian populations (Harland et al., 1994), the accuracy of the method in groups with names less distinctively different from the majority population is clearly questionable, an observation confirmed by recent research in Bristol (Pilgrim et al., 1993).

Figure 1.2   1991 Census question on 'ethnic group'

'Ethnic group - please tick the appropriate box'

White

Black - Caribbean

Black - African

Black - Other (please describe)

Indian

Pakistani

Bangladeshi

Chinese

Any other Ethnic Group (please describe)

'If the person is descended from more than one ethnic or racial group, please tick the group to which the person considers he/she belongs, or tick the 'Any other ethnic group' box and describe the person's ancestry in the space provided'.

The critique of ethnic statistics

A number of writers have criticised the construction and use of ethnic statistics on varying grounds and with varying degrees of severity (see, for example, Ahmad and Sheldon, 1991; Booth, 1988; Leech, 1989; Nanton, 1992; Ohri, 1988; Sheldon and Parker, 1992). Their arguments concern both problems which are intrinsic to the construction of ethnic taxonomies and problems which arise in specific circumstances on the basis of the choices which are made. The main arguments can be summarised as follows:

- Ethnic statistics deflect attention from racism by focusing on 'race'

- They ignore the fact that people do not always classify themselves the same way

- They are inflexible to changes in ethnic identity over time

- They conflate conceptually distinct categories in their construction

- They do not provide data refined enough to be useful.

Some brief comments will be made on each of these points in turn.

In their evidence to the Home Affairs Committee in 1983, a number of bodies representing minority ethnic groups suggested that it was inappropriate to start with the ethnic group as the object of study rather than the problem of discrimination itself (see Nanton, 1992). There is a strong argument that, for practical purposes, 'race' only matters because racism matters. Thus, in keeping with the arguments of Sheldon and Parker (1992) outlined above, there is a danger that, in isolating ethnicity as a focus of attention, it is ethnicity itself which appears to be the 'problem', rather than the actions and meanings people place upon it. The tendency to make a problem out of ethnicity or race rather than racism, and thus to define the minority as deviant, is only too evident in both academic and popular contexts (Lawrence, 1982a, 1982b).

These issues have been debated most energetically in the field of ethnic monitoring. For writers like Bhrolchain:

Ethnicity statistics are needed to document the level of discrimination and disadvantage, to take action to combat these and to establish how far policies having this objective are succeeding

(1990, p.545).

For Bhrolchain, 'statistical invisibility' can lead to a political invisibility which prevents the development of an appropriate policy agenda. Other commentators working within a similar framework point out the beneficial force of ethnic statistics:

It was census data that revealed unemployment rates among black teenagers to be twice the national average. It was census data that was used to show how racial minorities had been concentrated in the most derelict, overcrowded and least secure sectors of inner-city housing ... It was census data that helped demonstrate that, far from racial minorities making disproportionate demands on social services, the opposite was in fact the case

(quoted in Leech, 1989, p.16).

Other analysts are less convinced that ethnic statistics can, in themselves, significantly help to combat ethnic disadvantage:

The lack of political will on the part of government has long been accepted as the framework ... within which data are produced ... The real need is thus not for better definitive data but for a new framework of political will aimed at reducing and eradicating racial disadvantage and discrimination. It is only within this context that appropriate data can be instrumental in reaching that aim

(Booth, 1988, p.263).

These arguments form an important backdrop to the use of ethnic statistics in health research, but they are engaged with a slightly different set of problems, concerned with devising appropriate strategies to tackle racial discrimination. By contrast, the imperative in health research is to describe and explain ethnic patterns in health experience. Clearly, racism in its direct or indirect forms is likely to be an extremely important factor in that experience. However, as it was suggested in the first part of the chapter, a focus purely on racism arguably contains *a priori* assumptions about the determinants of that experience which are no less questionable than the ones the approach seeks to avoid.

From a research point of view, then, a strong case remains for collecting ethnic statistics, very much along the lines suggested by Mason (1990), quoted on page 18. Clearly, however, tackling racism in health service provision need not depend upon first producing immaculate research evidence. Nor can researchers escape the "deep suspicion which surrounds any claim that the collection of [ethnic] statistics is a neutral tool of policy-making" (Ohri, 1988, p.12). In using such statistics, then, there is a need to be aware of the assumptions underlying them, the uses to which they will be put and the stake in them that different social groups may hold. Echoing the critical sentiments of writers such as Booth, Bhopal (1989) makes a good case on this basis for a 'back to basics' approach in research, whereby analysts ask themselves hard questions about the likely impact of their work upon an understanding of the health of minority ethnic groups.

Turning to the issue of changes in self-classification, Leech (1989) cites US research in which it was found that in consecutive years 35 per cent of a population sample classified themselves by a different ethnic or racial descriptor than in the first year. Results from the Validation Survey for the 1991 British Census show that only about 1 per cent of white and South Asian respondents subsequently indicated a different ethnic group from that they had chosen in the Census. Among 'black' (ie. Caribbean and African) respondents the figure was 12 per cent, and, perhaps expectedly, among those who had originally indicated their ethnicity as 'other' it was 22 per cent (Storkey, 1994). Are such changes a problem? For many contemporary researchers, the only valid measure of an individual's ethnicity is one provided by the person concerned, albeit that it might be chosen from categories which are not of their own making (Karmi and Horton, 1992). If this is the case, changes in self-classification are unproblematic since no other legitimate categories exist against which the choice can be evaluated.

On the other hand, measurement reliability is a key principle of epidemiological investigation (Alderson, 1983). One of the aims of careful question design is precisely to maximise reliability. Indeed, the rather odd mixture of categories in the 1991 Census question partially arises as the result of consumer testing on precisely this issue (Teague, 1993). However, if reliability cannot be assured and no external categories exist against which responses can be validated, difficult theoretical choices must be made. Should the sovereignty of individual self-classification be respected above all else, or could variables such as externally perceived ethnicity or family origins be more useful descriptors in uncovering patterns of health experience? The choices here resemble those implicit in the divergent positions of Marmot (1989) and Sheldon and Parker (1992) examined above. Again there is no easy resolution. The extent of the problem can only be judged in terms of the theoretical status accorded to the ethnicity variable and the type of research question which is being addressed.

A third issue is the question of larger-scale changes in ethnic identity over time. Clearly, censuses and surveys which collect ethnic statistics can only attempt to reflect ethnic identities extant at the time of their completion. They are therefore inflexible to change. Although this is certainly true, it is worth pointing out that censuses and surveys themselves change. An ethnic question in the 1891 Census might have given the options 'Irish' and 'Jewish'. In 1971, country of birth seemed an appropriate way to identify most of the key minority ethnic populations. In 1991 a new approach was devised, while in 2001 further changes may be necessary.

The real problem, perhaps, is in the detail of the choices which are made. Here, the obverse of Bhrolchain's (1990) point about statistical invisibility becomes relevant for, as Nanton (1992) has argued, the categories chosen in ethnic statistics can hinder the detection of discrimination and disadvantage. This is evident in the invisibility of Irish people and new migrants from eastern Europe in the 1991 Census. Moreover, official classifications require the invention of fixed, discrete and mutually exclusive ethnic categories. It is therefore unlikely that they will be either as subtle or as sensitive to changing social norms as everyday ethnic concepts. As the discussion above suggested, there is therefore a danger that their routine use will reinforce stereotypes of a disadvantaged and unchanging ethnic separateness (Anwar, 1990).

A practical example is the case of 'mixed' ethnic origin. The question on ethnic origin in the *Labour Force Survey* includes a 'mixed' ethnic category, to which some 11 per cent of the 'non-white' population in the years 1987-89 indicated they belonged. This group, largely composed of children from inter-ethnic unions, is significant both in that it is likely to grow considerably in the future and in that it displays different patterns of geographical, and possibly social, distribution (Nanton, 1992).

'Mixed' and 'other' ethnic categories indicate the limit of official taxonomies. The problems created by the former have been avoided in the 1991 Census question by providing no 'mixed' category, but rather two write-in categories for those who do not perceive their ethnicity to conform to any of the other seven pre-existing categories. However, the coding frame for the census largely re-allocates the write-in categories to the pre-existing ones. Nevertheless, some 10 per cent of the non-white population is still consigned to the residual 'other' category (OPCS, 1992).

A further objection to classifications such as the 1991 Census question is that they conflate unacceptably notions of race, ethnicity and nationality. This is perhaps most evident in the contrast between the 'black' categories, – 'black Caribbean' and 'black African', for example – which betoken ethnic identity, and the Asian ones – 'Indian', 'Pakistani', 'Bangladeshi', 'Chinese' – which apparently refer to national identity. Moreover, although the 'white' category was adopted largely to minimise respondent confusion (Haskey, 1993), it scarcely represents a homogeneous ethnic identity. Indeed, a major shortcoming of the debate on ethnic terminology has been the failure to examine the problems associated with the use of the term 'white' (Allen, 1994; Bonnett, 1993).

Given the arbitrary nature of ethnic boundary formation discussed above, it is a moot point whether such categories are indeed conceptually flawed. It could be argued that a combination of skin colour, national origin and presumed cultural identity are precisely constitutive of most everyday concepts of ethnicity in contemporary Britain. Inevitably, however, the exact format of any particular classification is open to question, and OPCS has offered nothing more than a pragmatic rationale for the mixture of characteristics chosen in the 1991 Census (Teague, 1993).

The final criticism of ethnic statistics is that they do not provide data which are refined enough to be useful. Categories such as 'white' and 'Indian' encompass an extremely broad range of ethnic identities: Irish, English, Turkish Cypriots and Jewish people originally from East and Central Europe, along with, among others, Sikh Punjabis, Hindu Gujaratis and Muslim Bengalis, are all encompassed in two terms. As Ahmad and Sheldon (1991) point out, a health authority's knowledge of the number of 'Indians' in its local population is of little use in planning appropriate meals, interpreting services and religious provision. Nor do they necessarily provide categories which are refined enough to be really useful in epidemiological research, particularly as research moves from observing ethnic patterns towards attempting to explain them (Senior and Bhopal, 1994). Clearly, there is no substitute for detailed local knowledge and clear hypotheses about the nature of the 'ethnic' effect. A pragmatic defence of classifications such as the 1991 Census might be that they are a distinct improvement upon gross categories such as 'non-white' (LaVeist, 1994; Benzeval et al., in press). Nevertheless, there is a legitimate fear that they might confuse rather than clarify if the over-simplified categories they inevitably adopt are used without sufficient caution.

Conclusion

Ethnic statistics are a pervasive feature of contemporary research and policy-making. They are often justified, most notably by bodies such as the Commission for Racial Equality, in terms of the role they can play in highlighting discrimination and thus helping to improve the lot of minority ethnic populations. Nevertheless, their collection has been vigorously criticised on political, theoretical and practical grounds.

Health researchers cannot ignore the political dimensions of their work. Arguably, however, they must first confront a more practical set of problems, raised in the preceding sections, about how to use statistics appropriately in order to illuminate ethnic patterns of health experience. Many analysts appear to have thought more carefully about ethnic terminology than about the social significance of ethnicity itself. A growing critical literature nevertheless reminds us of the need to look beyond 'ethnic differences' to establish exactly which are the relevant social and economic forces behind such empirical findings (Bhopal, 1989; LaVeist, 1994; Senior and Bhopal, 1994; Sheldon and Parker, 1992; D. Williams et al., 1994). In short, research needs to be driven by sensible hypotheses which can inform choices about the type of ethnic statistics which are relevant.

Unfortunately, researchers are not always free to make those choices. Often, they must rely on routine statistics such as the 1991 Census in which ethnic taxonomies were not designed with the requirements of health research in mind. One option is to lobby for appropriately refined classifications. Although momentarily attractive, devising one which is adequate for both general and specialist purposes, universally acceptable and concise enough for use in surveys resembles the search for the holy grail. Indeed, Mason comments that "it is an illusion to think we can come up with any classification scheme which is valid for all times and places" (1990, p.127), arguing that the problem of category and identity fundamentally underlies the difficulties of assembling ethnic taxonomies which are both universally acceptable and conceptually clear. Moreover, sub-division into further categories could only reify ethnicity still more, while probably introducing notions of relative 'whiteness', 'blackness' or 'Asianness' which would be both unacceptable to many people and an inappropriate representation of the nature of ethnic boundaries in Britain (Nanton, 1992).

These problems need not lead analysts to reject entirely the use of routine ethnic statistics. Although such statistics may provide few clear answers, by enabling researchers to generate further questions they can greatly illuminate the way forward, and at the same time stimulate the kind of debate which Cooper and David (1986) have demanded. Perhaps the key point to emerge is the need to use ethnic statistics carefully, paying explicit attention to the assumptions about the nature of ethnicity that they entail.

The ethnic composition of Britain's population

Having devoted considerable attention to the theoretical questions underlying ethnicity and the use of ethnic statistics, we now turn to a brief empirical account of what ethnicity 'looks like' in contemporary Britain. In fact, neither the existence of a multiethnic society nor the presence of 'black' people are new phenomena in Britain. Indeed, as Fryer (1984) somewhat polemically points out, a black presence in the ranks of Roman battalions was recorded in Britain before the arrival of the Anglo-Saxon peoples who supposedly define indigenous ethnic identity.

More significantly, Jews, Gypsies, Irish and African people have made their homes in this country in the face of varying degrees of hostility as far back as mediaeval times. Moreover, indigenous ethnic identity has been complicated by regional loyalties, most strongly evident in the Celtic traditions of Scotland, Wales and Cornwall. This is not the place for a historical account of migration to Britain, but a brief sketch of some of the major points has some bearing on contemporary studies of health. This section therefore begins with a brief outline of the key historical events, derived largely from the accounts of Fryer (1984), Solomos (1989), Robinson (1986) and Walvin (1984). It is followed by a description of the contemporary distribution of Britain's minority ethnic populations, and concludes with a summary of the evidence for the existence of social disadvantage among minority ethnic groups. The significance of this for the health experience of such groups is outlined in subsequent chapters.

Migration to Britain

The contemporary ethnic character of Britain's population was forged largely in the 19th and 20th centuries, and largely as a result of British governments' own policies. The 19th century witnessed large-scale migration of Irish people especially after the famines of the 1840s – and of Jews, mainly working class, fleeing persecution in Eastern Europe. As colonial trade between Africa, Britain and the Caribbean developed in the latter part of the century, increasingly large black populations settled, particularly in the ports of Cardiff and Liverpool. Small populations of Chinese and South Asian people, originally composed mainly of 'lascar' seamen, also took root. However, by far the most significant migrant populations numerically were from the 'Old Commonwealth' countries of Australia, New

Zealand and Canada, as well as from elsewhere in western Europe and the USA.

During and after the two world wars, despite restrictions enforced under the Aliens Order of 1920, Britain experienced considerable migrations of European peoples, particularly Poles and German and Austrian Jews, as well as continued Irish migration and small numbers of Chinese people, mainly from rural Hong Kong. The buoyant economy of the 1950s and early 1960s led to labour shortages which Britain filled by either allowing or actively encouraging migration from its former colonies, the so-called 'New Commonwealth'. These migrations were not numerically the largest in British history, but in important respects they were definitive of the ethnic composition of Britain today. Although Jewish, Gypsy and Irish populations have all been subjected to explicit 'racial' stereotyping and discrimination in Britain at various times – illustrative, if nothing else, of the shifting terrain of 'racial' meanings – it was the arrival of large numbers of people of different skin colours in postwar Britain that ignited colonial ideologies of 'race'. Hence, increasingly from the 1950s, the 'problem' of immigration has been characterised largely in terms of race, or skin colour.

Most of the early migrants came from the British Caribbean, especially Jamaica, and from India and Pakistan. Indian migrants were mainly Muslim Bengalis, Hindu Gujaratis and Sikh Punjabis, the latter two groups generally comprising moderately well-off people with merchant backgrounds. Pakistani migrants tended to come from more impoverished rural areas in the Punjab and Kashmir, including many people from the Mirpuri area displaced by the Mangla dam project. Many Pakistani migrants were *Muhajirs*, people who had previously migrated from India after Partition (Anwar, 1979). Migrations also occurred from Sri Lanka (then Ceylon) and Cyprus.

The Immigration Act of 1962 effectively marked the end of large-scale primary immigration from the New Commonwealth. Subsequent legislation passed by both Conservative and Labour governments has made it successively more difficult for people from these countries to gain entry, although migration from the Old Commonwealth has been largely unaffected. Bangladeshis and people of Indian origin who left or were expelled from East Africa in the late 1960s and early 1970s (the latter again largely from moderately well-off professional or mercantile backgrounds, whereas the former were mainly from the more impoverished rural Sylhet region) have settled in Britain in more recent years, along with Cypriots fleeing the Turkish invasion of 1974, but most migration in the last thirty years or so has consisted of the families of the earlier, predominantly male, South Asian migrants coming to join their relatives. As the following section indicates, such patterns of migration have engendered particular demographic structures which are of some relevance in examining health.

The contemporary distribution of minority ethnic populations

The numbers of people in each ethnic group in Great Britain, as recorded in the 1991 Census, are displayed in Table 1.1. Overall, about 94 per cent of the population described themselves as 'white'; this included some 770,000 people born in Ireland, as well as people of Greek, Turkish, Cypriot, other European and 'mixed white' origins. The next largest group was Indian (including those of East African origin), comprising some 840,000 people, followed by the black Caribbean and Pakistani groups, which were a little over half that size.

Table 1.2 displays the proportion of each ethnic group resident in Britain which was born there. Less than half of the black Caribbean and Pakistani populations were born abroad, and even among

Table 1.1   **Resident population by ethnic group, Great Britain 1991**

Ethnic Group	Number (thousands)	Proportion of total Population (%)
White	51,874	94.5
Black – Caribbean	500	0.9
Black – African	212	0.4
Black – other	178	0.3
Indian	840	1.5
Pakistani	477	0.9
Bangladeshi	163	0.3
Chinese	157	0.3
Other – Asian	198	0.4
Other – non Asian	290	0.5

Source: 1991 Census, Local Base Statistics, OPCS Crown Copyright

the group with the lowest proportion of British-born people – the Chinese – nearly a third were born in this country. Overall, marginally less than a half of all minority ethnic populations are British born. From a methodological point of view, this indicates that reliance on country of birth as a broader indicator of ethnicity is no longer appropriate. Perhaps more significantly, it also indicates the necessity of a shift in policy focus from questions surrounding migrants and the issues they face in adjusting to a new environment, towards a more enduring concern with ethnic plurality.

Table 1.2   **Proportion of people resident in Britain who were born there, by ethnic group, 1991.**

Ethnic Group	Proportion British Born (%)
White	95
Black – Caribbean	54
Black – African	36
Black – other	84
Indian	42
Pakistani	50
Bangladeshi	37
Chinese	28
All other	44

Source: 1991 Census, Local Base Statistics, OPCS Crown Copyright

Table 1.3 **Ethnic group by age, Great Britain, 1991**

Ethnic group	Proportion of group in age-group (%)					
	0 – 15	16 – 44	45 – 64	65 – 74	75+	All ages*
White	19	42	22	9	7	100
Black – Caribbean	22	48	25	4	1	100
Black – African	29	59	10	1	0	100
Black – Other	51	43	5	1	0	100
Indian	30	50	17	3	1	100
Pakistani	43	43	12	1	0	100
Bangladeshi	47	38	14	1	0	100
Chinese	23	59	14	2	1	100
Other	35	50	12	2	1	100

Figures may not sum exactly due to rounding errors.

Source: 1991 Census, Local Base Statistics, OPCS Crown Copyright

Table 1.3 displays the age structure for each of the main ethnic groups, as enumerated by the 1991 Census. It is immediately apparent that the structure of all the minority ethnic groups is younger than that of the white group. For example, nearly 50 per cent of the Bangladeshi group is aged under 15, compared with around 20 per cent of the white group. Unremarkably perhaps, the groups identified by the census which have been longest resident in Britain are the ones whose age structures most resemble the white population. Nevertheless, 70 per cent of the 'black Caribbean' group – and 80 per cent of the Indian – are under 45, compared with only 60 per cent of the white group. The 'black other' group also has a strikingly young age structure, although this is largely for artefactual reasons. As Table 1.2 demonstrated, this category tended to be chosen by UK-born black people who, inevitably, are likely to be relatively younger.

The differences in age structure have a number of implications for the health sector. First, from a research point of view, they demonstrate the need to take age into consideration when making comparisons between groups. Second, they indicate that the relative demand for services by minority ethnic populations will at present tend to be dominated by the needs of children and younger adults. On the other hand, they emphasise that there is likely to be a large increase in demand for services in the future by older people.

Finally, it is important to note that most minority ethnic groups are highly concentrated residentially. Nearly 70 per cent of the people who described their ethnic group as other than 'white' in the 1991 Census live in just forty local authority boroughs where less than 20 per cent of the white population lives (OPCS, 1992), and these crude figures conceal greater segregation at the local level. For example, 67 per cent of the population in Northcote ward, Ealing, indicated their ethnicity as 'Indian', whereas less than 10 per cent indicated it as 'white'. In Spinney Hill ward, Leicester, the corresponding figures were 61 per cent and 16 per cent (OPCS, 1992). Moreover, residential concentration often occurs on the basis of ethnic identity at a level to which national statistics are insensitive. In the examples above, the 'Indians' in Southall are largely of Punjabi Sikh origin, while many of those in Leicester are Hindus of Gujarati origin who migrated from East Africa.

Ethnicity and disadvantage

Recent analyses have provided useful summaries of current patterns of socioeconomic experience among minority ethnic populations (Amin and Oppenheim, 1992; Jones, 1993; Owen and Green, 1992), using data from the *Labour Force Survey*, the *General Household Survey,* the Policy Studies Institute survey of 1982 (Brown, 1984) and from a variety of local studies. Some of the key findings of these studies – which refer to the experiences of both migrants and British-born individuals – are set out below.

- *Unemployment* rates for most minority ethnic groups – the principal exceptions being the Chinese and East African Indians – are considerably higher than those for whites, and the gap has widened throughout the 1980s. The differential is even wider among the young, and rates of long-term unemployment are greater among most minority ethnic groups.

- *Low-paid occupations* such as distribution, catering and manual labour employ a disproportionate number of people from minority ethnic populations. Brown (1984) found that, on average, Indian and East African Asian men earned less than whites, Caribbean men less still, and Pakistani and Bangladeshi men least of all. Moreover, Pirani *et al.* (1992) have argued that income differentials persist even after adjusting for differences in human capital, suggesting the existence of direct discrimination in the labour market. Ethnic differences in women's earnings are not as large, and indeed Caribbean women tend to earn more than white women. However, Bruegel (1989) has argued that these latter findings arise partly because women are concentrated in similar – and lower-paid – sectors of the workforce, and are also confounded by ethnic differences in the proportion of women working full-time as compared with part-time and by regional differences in earnings.

- *Poor working conditions* such as shift work, night work and homeworking are experienced by a greater proportion of people from minority ethnic groups than whites.

- *Poverty,* defined in various ways, is also experienced by a greater proportion of people from minority ethnic groups, including Irish populations.

- *Housing tenure* exhibits marked ethnic patterns. A greater proportion of people of Indian and Pakistani origin are home owner-occupiers than whites, whereas Bangladeshi and Caribbean populations rent disproportionately from local authorities. Moreover, the quality of housing in each tenure category tends to be poorer.

In attempting to explain these differences, Amin and Oppenheim (1992) emphasise the multi-faceted historical and structural nature of poverty and disadvantage among minority ethnic populations in Britain. In particular, they highlight the four interrelated areas of immigration policy, social security policy, the 'racial' division of labour and inner-city residence. Some brief comments on these points are appropriate.

As shown above, government encouragement of postwar migration of black people to Britain was to do with the increasing demand for unskilled labour, principally in the manufacturing sector. This structural inequality has largely persisted. Moreover, immigration policy has interacted with social security legislation to deny benefits to migrants.

There is considerable evidence of both direct and indirect discrimination against people from minority ethnic groups in social security (Amin and Oppenheim, 1992; Gordon and Newnham, 1985). The prohibition of certain categories of migrants from resort to 'public funds', greater levels of unemployment, residence abroad and other interruptions in work history and the weakening of the state earnings-related pension scheme, often disproportionately reduce the amount of benefit that can be claimed by people from minority ethnic populations. Such inequalities have been compounded by the decline of the manufacturing sector, in which many people from minority ethnic populations traditionally found employment. New service industry jobs have enabled some gains to be made during the 1980s among the Chinese and Indian populations, but rapid economic change in many urban centres of minority ethnic residential concentration have had a negative impact on labour market position, particularly for Caribbean, Pakistani and Bangladeshi populations (Owen and Green, 1992). From the little evidence available, it seems that the restructuring of public sector employment may have further disadvantaged minority ethnic populations in particular, as did the weakening of employment rights and the 'casualisation' of labour during the 1980s (Amin and Oppenheim, 1992).

Perhaps the simplest summary of these points is provided by Oppenheim, who suggests that:

Every indicator of poverty shows that black people and other ethnic minority groups are more at risk of high unemployment, low pay, shift work, and poor social security rights. Their poverty is caused by immigration policies which have often excluded people from abroad from access to welfare, employment patterns which have marginalised black people and other ethnic minority groups into low-paid manual work, direct and indirect discrimination in social security and the broader experience of racism in society

(1990, p.91).

The residential segregation of minority ethnic populations described in the previous section also has implications for patterns of disadvantage. In a useful review of the literature, Robinson (1987) cites evidence that segregation arises from three sources: local and central government policy, majority prejudice and the strategies adopted by minority ethnic groups themselves. Smith (1987) emphasises the significance of the former, arguing that, paradoxically, the very 'race neutrality' of central government housing policy has enabled the poor housing options faced by earlier migrants (Rex, 1989) to be reproduced.

Residential concentration may have some benefits in increasing access to political power and creating opportunities in local 'ethnic' economies (Robinson, 1987). On the other hand, research has shown that these opportunities rarely provide a route to economic independence (Aldrich *et al.*, 1986), and residential segregation is widely seen as being restrictive of social opportunities. As

Robinson argues:

> *The spatial distribution of ethnic groups produces inequalities in access to services, employment, desirable housing and ultimately life chances; it shapes patterns of social interaction...and it contributes to the development of attitudes and stereotypes*

(1987, p.193).

Robinson (1990) has also examined patterns of social mobility among migrants between 1971 and 1987, as measured by social class. He found there to be quite complex effects within and between ethnic groups and genders. However, in essence he showed that only among people born in India was there a clear tendency for upward mobility, and he argued that this must be seen in the light of downward mobility consequent upon migration. Robinson's work testifies to the complexity of the interaction between discrimination, residence and socioeconomic status, but the conclusion he draws is fairly straightforward:

> *if the best that our society can offer after thirty years is selective parity only for the most successful black group, then our efforts to ensure equality of opportunity have been far from adequate*

(1990, p.285).

In many respects, patterns of inner-city concentration, residential segregation, political empowerment and material and social disadvantage among minority ethnic populations mirror the situation in the USA, although they are clearly not as pronounced. US research has begun to document the impact of residential segregation and area of residence on minority ethnic health (Haan *et al.*, 1987; LaVeist, 1993). With the notable exception of Ecob and Williams (1991), few similar attempts have been made in this country.

Conclusion

This chapter has shown that ethnicity is a complex social phenomenon for which little definitional consensus exists. It argued that ethnicity is best understood in historical terms as the articulation of social differences between groups of people on the basis of attributes such as physical appearance, language and 'culture', often in circumstances of political or economic competition. Ethnic conflict is not a new phenomenon in Britain, but the key ethnic divisions in contemporary British society relate to 'black' postwar migrants from the New Commonwealth, and also to migrants from Ireland. Although this point commands fairly widespread agreement, all attempts to operationalise definitions of ethnicity for the purposes of research are open to criticism. It would nevertheless appear that classifications based upon a notion of enduring ethnic identity among these migrant groups are gaining increasing currency, albeit that this identity may be predicated largely upon the persistent 'racialised' concerns of the majority population. From a more practical standpoint, it was shown in the light of this 'racialisation' of society that conventionally defined minority ethnic populations tend to experience greater levels of discrimination and disadvantage.

Against this background, the following chapters examine the consequences of these manifest social differences in terms of the health experience of minority ethnic groups. Often, the research cited pays little attention to the difficulties of defining ethnicity, treating categories such as 'Asian' and 'Caribbean' as if they were self-evident. This research nevertheless documents a mass of important findings, and it is one of the aims of the book to draw out the implications of these findings for a fuller understanding of both the meaning of ethnicity as a variable in health research, and the nature of ethnic patterns in the experience of health and health care.

2 General health status

Introduction

This chapter reviews current knowledge about the general health status of minority ethnic groups in Britain. It would be fair to say that researchers have devoted less attention to examining broad summary indicators of health among ethnic groups than to focusing on specific diseases where an 'ethnic effect' is apparent. As a result, the evidence remains rather fragmentary. Moreover, the quality of the ethnic variables employed both in general and disease specific research is questionable. In the light of the discussion in the previous chapter, which underlined the extraordinary social complexity of ethnicity, the use – though sometimes unavoidable – of highly aggregated country of birth data and often equally broad and ill-defined notions of ethnicity leaves much to be desired. In addition, as Stubbs (1993) has argued, understanding ethnic patterns in health must presumably involve examining majority as well as minority ethnic health experiences. In fact, in the context of research, 'ethnic' generally means 'minority ethnic'. In spite of these deficiencies, a considerable body of work exists which provides a useful baseline from which to evaluate ethnic patterns in general health status.

The chapter begins by examining patterns of mortality, outlining the findings of two large national studies. Although they suffer from shortcomings in scope, these remain the most comprehensive analyses relating to the health of minority ethnic populations. The section also examines patterns of infant mortality and – in anticipation of later chapters – considers some of the factors which have been suggested to account for them.

The second section examines ethnic patterns in general morbidity. It reviews evidence about the prevalence of chronic illness and disability among ethnic groups and examines some important recent studies of self-reported health. Age and gender dimensions in general morbidity are also considered. Finally, a third section summarises the evidence on ethnic patterns in lifestyle and behavioural factors which have a direct bearing upon health status, such as smoking, diet and alcohol use. Arguably, research on psychological wellbeing properly fits into a discussion of general morbidity. However, this question is examined in Chapter 3 in the section on mental illness, since its particular focus on South Asian women has substantially shaped research concerns in this area (Black Health Workers and Patients' Group, 1983; Littlewood, 1992).

Before proceeding, an important methodological issue needs to be addressed. Epidemiologists employ two distinct methods to examine the health of any defined subpopulations, including particular ethnic groups. The first focuses upon the frequency of disease *within* each ethnic group, whereas the second concerns itself with differences *between* groups. The former approach uses measures of disease frequency such as prevalence or incidence, which quantify the occurrence of disease within a particular group; the latter typically uses measures such as relative risk or standardised mortality ratios (SMRs) to indicate the degree of difference between groups. These terms are explained further in Box 2.1.

Relative measures do not indicate the overall burden of disease for the populations concerned. For example, women living in England and Wales who were born in the Indian subcontinent are over

Box 2.1   Measuring disease frequency

Epidemiologists have devised several important methods for quantifying disease within populations. Some of the epidemiological terms which are used frequently in this book are defined below.

The *prevalence* (or, strictly, *prevalence rate*) of a disease is the number of individuals from a given population who have a disease at a particular time, divided by the total number of people from that population at risk of having the disease at the same time. For example, if 10 people out of an 'at-risk' population of 100 suffered from diabetes, this disease would be said to have a prevalence of 10 per cent.

The *incidence* (strictly, *incidence rate*) of a disease is the total number of new cases of the disease in a given time period, divided by the population at risk of developing the disease in the same time period. For example, if one person developed diabetes out of a population of 100 people at risk of developing it over a year, the annual incidence would be 1 per cent. For researchers concerned with *aetiology* (disease causation) incidence measures are more useful than prevalence measures, since they better enable the identification of antecedent causal factors. However, it requires considerably more effort to collect incidence data.

A special type of incidence measure which sometimes provides useful information is the *case-fatality rate*. This expresses the number of people who die from a particular disease as a proportion of the total number of cases of that disease.

Often the incidence of disease will be compared between two populations, yielding a figure for the *relative risk* of developing the disease within the relevant populations. For example, if the annual incidence of diabetes in a given ethnic group was 2 per cent and the incidence in a second group was 1 per cent, the relative risk in the first group in comparison to the second would be 2. Measures of relative risk can help aetiological enquiry, since it may be possible to identify levels of risk which are associated with different levels of exposure to potential causal factors between the two populations. However, such apparent relationships between particular exposures and outcomes may be *confounded* by other factor(s), which are independently associated with both the exposure and the outcome. For example, the apparent relationship between smoking and cervical cancer may arise because both smoking and cervical cancer are independently associated with factors such as early loss of virginity and a higher number of sexual partners (Davey Smith and Phillips,1992).

A common problem which arises in comparing the disease burden between populations is that the rates are confounded by differences in demographic (age, sex) structures, which are associated with the outcomes of interest. In such circumstances, it is important to *control* or *adjust* for confounding. A frequently used measure for doing so is the *standardised mortality* (or *morbidity*) *ratio* (SMR). This expresses the ratio of the number of deaths (or cases) in a given population to the number that would be expected if that population had the same age- and gender-specific death (or disease) rates as some standard or reference population. In routine data this standard population is typically taken to be the whole national population. The national rate is set, by definition, at 100. Thus, if a particular population has an SMR greater than 100 it has a higher than expected rate, and vice versa for an SMR lower than 100. Since random variation in rates always exists, *confidence intervals* are often calculated around SMR values which indicate the range within which the true value falls with a specified degree of probability (typically 95 per cent). The confidence interval is, in effect, an indicator of *statistical significance* which helps to determine whether the finding is likely to reflect a stable underlying pattern of difference between populations.

Calculating SMRs involves *stratifying* the sample into specific categories of the confounding variable. Although this is a useful approach for a small number of variables, it quickly becomes unwieldy. Researchers often want to control for a wide range of demographic, social and clinical variables. In such circumstances, multivariate statistical techniques must be used (see Box 5.1).

For more detailed discussion, see Hennekens and Buring (1987); Last (1988).

ten times more likely to die of tuberculosis than the general female population of England and Wales, yet only 96 deaths were recorded from this cause among Indian-born women in the four-year period 1979-83 (Balarajan and Bulusu, 1990). By contrast, nearly 4,000 women born in the Indian subcontinent died of circulatory disease in the same period, even though the relative risk of death from this cause among them was much smaller than that for tuberculosis.

Which is the appropriate measure to use? For an epidemiologist interested in the cause of disease, measures of relative risk can provide important clues to disease mechanisms, since they may indicate different levels of exposure to causal agents in different populations. For a planner interested in improving public health, absolute measures are the relevant ones since they are the best indicators of a population's health needs. Bhopal (undated; 1988) has pointed out that the literature on minority ethnic health is dominated by studies of relative rather than absolute risk. This has a number of consequences. In Bhopal's view, it has led to an over-emphasis on diseases with high relative risk among minority ethnic populations at the expense of those which most contribute to the burden of ill health. Also, comparing the majority with the minority population can lead to the mistaken inference that the experience of the majority is somehow the 'normal' one. This in turn leads to an emphasis on diseases where the minority experience is poorer than the majority one, rather than better.

Due to the balance of the literature, both this chapter and the following one inevitably devote greater attention to analyses of relative rather than absolute risk. Nevertheless, an attempt is made to assess the overall implications of disease for minority ethnic populations. As Bhopal has pointed out, these do not differ fundamentally from those faced by the majority population. This is a point to which the book returns.

Mortality

The most comprehensive evidence about the health of minority ethnic populations comes from two studies using nationally collected mortality data. These are:

- The OPCS Immigrant Mortality Study, focusing on mortality among foreign-born residents of England and Wales, principally in the years 1970-72 (Marmot et al., 1984).

- An analysis of immigrant mortality as part of the OPCS study *Mortality and Geography* (Britton, 1990), focusing on deaths among foreign-born residents of England and Wales in the years 1979-83 (Balarajan and Bulusu, 1990).

This section first outlines the major findings of these studies with regard to mortality from all causes, and then turns to an examination of infant mortality which, as well as being of crucial importance in its own right, is widely thought to be a sensitive indicator of social and environmental conditions and is therefore particularly germane to the study of ethnic patterns in health.

All-cause mortality

The two OPCS studies described above have provided an important basis for understanding minority ethnic health experiences, although they suffer from a number of deficiencies in scope. For example, they focus on mortality to the exclusion of morbidity; they aggregate migrant groups – particularly South Asian ones – rather crudely; they relate only to England and Wales; they examine data which

Table 2.1   **Mortality from all causes by selected place of birth, England and Wales, 1979-83**

Place of Birth		Age 20-49			Age 20-69			Age 70+		
		SMR	95% CI*	N†	SMR	95% CI*	N†	SMR	95% CI*	N†
All Ireland	M	147	142-152	2,914	128	126-130	18,961	116	114-118	13,768
	F	123	117-129	1,632	120	118-122	10,403	115	113-117	15,828
Indian subcontinent	M	111	106-116	2,134	106	104-108	7,566	90	87-93	4,067
	F	94	88-100	879	105	102-109	3,427	107	104-110	4,518
Caribbean Commonwealth	M	90	84- 96	908	79	76- 82	3,190	78	72-84	673
	F	114	106-122	746	105	100-110	1,944	84	78-90	784
African Commonwealth	M	115	107-123	793	109	103-115	1,394	76	66-87	220
	F	127	115-140	421	114	105-123	652	71	61-82	173

* Approximate 95 per cent confidence interval   † Number of deaths

Source: Balarajan and Bulusu (1990)

is at best nearly a decade old; and, crucially, they refer only to people born abroad. Not only does this latter point exclude British-born people of minority ethnic origin, it also considerably complicates interpretation, since differences in the health of migrants may result from various selection factors acting upon the migrating population as well as from the process of migration itself (see Chapter 4). Nevertheless, these studies provide an impressive array of information as a baseline for examining the health of ethnic groups.

Balarajan and Bulusu (1990) provide the most recent evidence on differences between migrant groups in mortality rates. Table 2.1 summarises their key findings for all-cause mortality, providing a break-down into the 20-49 age group, the broader 20-69 age group, and the 70+ age group. Data are not available for Chinese migrants, and are available only in aggregate form for Indians, Pakistanis and Bangladeshis.

The table shows that mortality is raised with respect to the general population for two-thirds of the age-sex categories in the four migrant groups, and is particularly high among the Irish. The only group which has consistently lower mortality is Caribbean men, although older migrants and younger women from the Indian subcontinent also tend to have lower mortality relative to the whole population of England and Wales.

The figures in the table are standardised to national values within each gender category, so it is not possible to determine the relative mortality between genders within each ethnic group. Nevertheless, the table does show there to be marked differences in mortality between genders within some groups relative to national gender-specific rates. Differences also exist between age groups. For example, men from the African and Caribbean Commonwealth tend to be relatively healthier than women from these areas, whereas there are more complex relative differences between genders at different ages in the other two groups. Also, it would in general appear that the greatest differences in mortality occur for younger migrants between the ages of 20 and 49, while migrants over the age of 70 differ less from the overall population, and indeed often appear somewhat healthier. For all but two of the values shown in the table it is 95 per cent certain that the figure represents a genuine underlying difference from the national value and not just random variation.

The general pattern of raised mortality is broadly similar to the findings of the earlier OPCS Immigrant Mortality Study (Marmot *et al.*, 1984). Balarajan and Bulusu (1990) have calculated changes in age- and gender-standardised mortality by migrant group between 1970-72 and 1979-83 for the 20-69 year old age group. They found an absolute decline in mortality for all groups. However, the size of this decline varied between groups, from around 30 per cent in African and Caribbean men and women to just 7 per cent in Irish men and women, and Indian men. The mortality decline for the entire population of England and Wales was 13 per cent for men, and 9 per cent for women. These differences in the size of the decline resulted in changes in relative mortality between migrant groups over the decade in question.

Clearly, these figures provide only a fairly crude indicator of health status. The earlier OPCS study helps to provide a slightly broader context within which to consider them. For example, in the earlier study the effects on mortality of both home country experience and social class were examined. Marmot *et al.* (1984) showed that the overall mortality experience in England and Wales was better than that of most of the countries from which migrants had come, albeit that data were missing from two crucial areas, namely the African Commonwealth and the Indian subcontinent. The investigators found that, with the exception of the Irish, migrants tended to be more healthy than the populations in their home countries. However, raised mortality with respect to England and Wales led them to infer the persistence of home country influences. This intermediate health experience of the first generation is a common finding of migrant studies; subsequent generations increasingly take on the patterns of the rest of the population (Marmot, 1989; Syme *et al.*, 1975).

An important confounding variable in examining ethnic differences in health is socioeconomic status, which is powerfully and inversely associated with health experience, including mortality (Townsend and Davidson, 1992). Marmot *et al.* (1984) attempted to take this into account by computing social class-specific mortality ratios for men from each migrant group. Social class is defined on the basis of the Registrar General's classification of occupations. The investigators found that the class 'gradient' which is typically seen in the general population was apparent only in the case of the Irish group. The trends in the other migrant groups were far less clear. In fact, among Caribbean men the gradient appeared almost to be reversed, although the results require cautious interpretation since they were based on small numbers of deaths in some cases, increasing the chance of random effects. Nevertheless, Marmot *et al.* concluded that:

> *differences in social class distribution are not the explanation of the overall different mortality of immigrants; and ... the relation of social class (as usually defined) to mortality is different among most immigrant groups from the England and Wales pattern*

(1984, p.21).

Chapter 4 looks critically at such claims. However, the important empirical point to come out of the immigrant mortality studies is that mortality appears to be generally lower than in the home country but higher than England and Wales, and there are complex age, class and gender effects.

A major exception to the trend of intermediate mortality is among Irish migrants. Raised mortality with respect to both Ireland and Britain led Marmot *et al.* (1984) to postulate negative health selection in contrast to positive selection among migrants from other countries. In other words, they suggested that Irish people choosing to migrate tended to be less healthy than the Irish population as a whole, whereas the opposite was the case for other migrant groups. However, an important analysis conducted by Raftery *et al.* (1990) using OPCS Longitudinal Survey data showed the persistence of a poorer mortality experience among residents of England and Wales with one or both parents born in Ireland, even when controlling for other relevant characteristics, as well as effects associated with the year of migration and gender. These findings cast some doubt on the validity of a unitary selection hypothesis. Whether such patterns are also a feature of other second generation populations is not currently known. Selection effects are discussed in further detail in Chapter 4.

Infant mortality

Infant mortality in certain minority ethnic groups has been a prominent concern among both researchers and policy-makers. Most detailed research has been confined to South Asian populations, and is subject to a number of methodological caveats (Little and Nicoll, 1988). Nevertheless, there is a considerable body of evidence which points to the existence of major ethnic differences in infant health and mortality.

This part of the chapter begins by reviewing the empirical evidence on ethnic patterns in infant mortality and its underlying components. It then examines some of the 'proximal' factors which may underlie these patterns, such as the incidence of congenital abnormalities and sudden infant death. Finally, it describes research which has attempted to explain these patterns in terms of broader underlying causes.

The infant mortality rate is defined as deaths of children under one year of age per 1,000 live births. It is commonly sub-divided as follows:

- *Neonatal mortality,* comprising deaths in the first 28 days of life per 1,000 live births.

- *Postneonatal mortality,* comprising deaths at ages between 28 days and one year per 1,000 live births.

Another important definition is that of *perinatal mortality*, which comprises stillbirths and deaths in the first week of life per 1,000 live and stillbirths.

Table 2.2, based on the work of Balarajan and Raleigh (1990), shows each of these rates by mother's country of birth in 1982–85 for a number of different populations. It indicates that the infant mortality rate is raised with respect to the UK value for most migrant groups, and is particularly high for the infants of Pakistani-born mothers – at about 70 per cent above the UK value – and Caribbean-born mothers, at 33 per cent. Conversely, for Bangladeshi- and East African-born mothers the rate is some 4 per cent below the UK value. These figures conceal considerable variations between the other rates. For example, perinatal and neonatal mortality is raised with respect to the UK value for all of the groups, varying from just 3 per cent above the UK perinatal rate for mothers born in the Irish Republic, to over 80 per cent in excess of both perinatal and neonatal rates for mothers born in Pakistan. However, most groups – with the major exceptions of the Pakistani- and Caribbean-born – have lower postneonatal mortality. For Bangladeshi- and East African-born mothers this influences

Table 2.2   Infant mortality by mother's place of birth, England and Wales, 1982-85

Mother's Place of Birth	Infant Mortality		Perinatal Mortality		Neonatal Mortality		Postneonatal Mortality	
	Rate	N*	Rate	N†	Rate	N*	Rate	N*
UK	9.7	21,515	10.1	22,503	5.6	12,438	4.1	9,077
Eire	10.1	269	10.4	279	5.9	158	4.1	111
India	10.1	459	12.5	576	6.1	278	3.9	181
Bangladesh	9.3	145	14.3	225	6.5	101	2.8	44
Pakistan	16.6	892	18.8	1,022	10.2	549	6.4	343
Caribbean	12.9	274	13.4	288	8.4	179	4.5	95
East Africa	9.3	255	12.8	351	6.3	172	3.0	83
West Africa	11.0	128	12.7	149	8.0	93	3.0	35

* Number of deaths   †Number of deaths and stillbirths

Source: Balarajan and Raleigh (1990)

the overall position of the infant mortality rate. In 1981-85, sudden infant death was the major cause of postneonatal mortality among infants of UK-born mothers (Balarajan et al., 1989a). However, rates of sudden infant death were lower for all the main minority ethnic groups, with the exception of the Irish, and among Bangladeshis were nearly six times less.

These findings, based on national mortality data, are broadly consistent with the results of local studies (Chitty and Winter, 1989; Clarke et al., 1988; Gillies et al., 1984; Griffiths et al., 1989; Jivani, 1986; Terry et al., 1985). Two specific points worth noting from these studies are, first, the finding by Griffiths et al. of a greatly elevated postneonatal mortality rate among Caribbean infants (defined by ethnicity rather than country of birth), and Jivani's finding that South Asian babies within each birthweight category required less intensive care (such as assisted ventilation) than 'non-Asian' babies. Balarajan and Botting (1989) have also shown there to be considerable regional variations in perinatal mortality rates among mothers born in the New Commonwealth and Pakistan, although the extent to which this can be explained by local differences in the 'ethnic' sub-components of these rates is unclear.

Infant mortality rates have declined for all ethnic groups between the mid-1970s and 1980s (Balarajan and Raleigh, 1990). In fact, they have declined more rapidly for most minority ethnic groups than the UK rate, thus reducing the mortality excess among the infants of Indian-, Bangladeshi- and African-born mothers which was extant in the mid-1970s. However, for infants of Pakistani- and Caribbean-born mothers, the mortality decline has merely matched the overall trend so that disparities have remained.

Congenital abnormalities are a major cause of perinatal and postneonatal mortality. Balarajan et al. (1989b) have computed SMRs for death and stillbirth in infants from all congenital abnormalities in 1981-85 by mother's country of birth, standardising for the age and social class of the mother. They found there to be significantly higher rates among mothers born in Pakistan, India and East Africa (mainly of Indian origin). The Pakistani rate was greatly raised, being more than double that of the general population. Bangladeshi rates were also raised. Conversely, rates were lower among mothers born in the Caribbean and West Africa. Since the number of deaths in the last three groups was fairly small, it is not possible to be certain that these rates reflect genuine 'ethnic' differences. More generally, it has not been clearly established whether these patterns of mortality reflect a higher prevalence of abnormalities at birth, or a higher case-fatality rate (Little and Nicoll, 1988).

Balarajan *et al.* (1989b) provide a somewhat crude breakdown, essentially by 'manual' or 'non-manual' class, showing that infant mortality from congenital abnormalities standardised for mother's age against the general population has a relatively higher incidence in manual classes, although among Caribbean- and West African-born mothers the opposite is the case. Pakistanis are the only group with a significant excess mortality over the general population in the non-manual classes. In general, then, the Pakistani population stands out as having particularly high mortality from congenital abnormalities, although a hospital-based study in Birmingham found that the major lethal and non-lethal congenital abnormality rate was higher in the Indian population than in the Pakistani one (Terry *et al.*, 1985).

There is also some evidence of ethnic differences in the nature of specific abnormalities. For example, the infants of most migrant groups have lower mortality from spina bifida than the general population (Balarajan *et al.*, 1989b), although (mainly Punjabi) Indians have higher mortality from neural tube defects more generally (Little and Nicoll, 1988). Broadly speaking, research suggests that these patterns of general and cause-specific mortality from congenital abnormalities are in keeping with home country experiences.

Another important cause of infant mortality is neonatal and postneonatal infection. Evidence exists for possible differences in the incidence of gastroenteritis, rubella, hepatitis B and genital herpes (Nicoll and Logan, 1989). The potential impact of this on infant mortality remains little investigated.

Overall, then, striking patterns exist in infant mortality and its components, with disadvantage concentrated within the Pakistani and, to a lesser extent, Caribbean populations. But how can these patterns be explained? The aetiology of infant mortality is complex and not fully understood. Most attention has focused upon perinatal mortality, for which a major risk factor is low birthweight. This in turn is associated with:

- mother's age and parity

- the length of time between pregnancies

- parental socioeconomic status

- smoking during pregnancy.

Most minority ethnic groups display a greater level of risk according to some, though not all, of these characteristics than UK-born mothers. However, it has been shown that, broadly speaking, even when the rates for particular populations are stratified within given levels of risk by maternal age, parity or social class, those with higher rates of perinatal mortality also tend to exhibit higher category-specific rates (Balarajan and Raleigh, 1990; Balarajan and Botting, 1989). In other words, perinatal mortality appears to be higher even after controlling for specific risk factors. On the other hand, birthweight-specific perinatal mortality rates are lower than the UK value in the low-birthweight categories for all groups except the Pakistanis. However, this is more than compensated for in these groups by the overall distribution of birthweight, which tends towards lower levels. Balarajan and Raleigh (1990) conclude that the distribution of birthweight can explain some, but not all, of the differences in perinatal mortality rates.

Most studies have examined the distribution of risk factors within the relevant populations only at a bivariate level. That is, they have examined whether particular risk factors can explain differences between ethnic groups in mortality, but have not considered whether the additive or interactive effects of multiple risk factors can explain the mortality differentials. For example, it appears that a combination of high maternal age *and* high parity is associated with a greater risk of congenital abnormalities in the infant than the additive effect of maternal age and parity alone (Little and Nicoll, 1988). It could be that factors such as these in combination may explain much of the excess. However, if, as most commentators conclude, conventional risk factors alone cannot explain the difference, what else may be involved? Researchers have made a number of suggestions, including the possibility that observed patterns are:

- artefacts of measurement
- accounted for by socioeconomic factors not captured by social class
- associated with the practice of consanguinity (ie. marriage between relatives)
- associated with ethnic differences in access to or use of health services.

Some brief comments on each of these are given below.

Artefact explanations suggest that apparently genuine differences in infant health may arise through biases introduced in the design of studies or through ethnic differences in autopsy or termination rates. Alternatively, they may point to the problems inherent in attempts to filter out the effect of factors such as socioeconomic status or access to services, since it is not possible to do this adequately using readily available measures such as social class. Thus, it could be that higher class-specific infant mortality rates in migrant groups are simply an artefact of the inadequate nature of social class as a proxy for socioeconomic status.

Most existing studies are subject to biases which preclude the elimination of artefactual explanations. This is particularly the case where research attempts to move beyond the recording of simple death rates to examine more detailed underlying factors. However, in view of the extent and consistency of the findings described above, it would be a bold step to argue that no genuine underlying differences exist in infant mortality.

Turning more directly to socioeconomic factors, the problems with social class as an indicator of socioeconomic status are widely acknowledged (see Chapter 4). However, a number of British and US studies have examined the impact on infant mortality of more direct socioeconomic factors. Some of their main findings are as follows:

- Maternal unemployment is associated with poorer birth outcomes even when controlling for other relevant confounders (Poerksen and Petitti, 1991).

- Employment of the mother in manual work during pregnancy is associated with higher perinatal mortality (Clarke *et al.*, 1988).

- Poor birth outcomes are better predicted by a combination of maternal, paternal and household characteristics, including educational status, but ethnic differences in infant mortality may remain, even after controlling for these factors (Schoendorf *et al.*, 1992).

- The geographical segregation of minority ethnic populations and the degree of community integration are associated with infant mortality rates (LaVeist, 1993).

The overall implications of these studies are not entirely clear. As Andrews and Jewson (1993) have pointed out, 'materialist' explanations of ethnic differences in infant mortality couched solely in socioeconomic terms have difficulty in accounting for some of the observed patterns, such as the difference in mortality rates between the Pakistani and Bangladeshi populations, which are both highly deprived. On the other hand, more discerning indicators of socioeconomic status may provide a better clue to the aetiology of infant mortality.

One possible explanation of the extremely high infant mortality rate in the Pakistani population is the practice of consanguinity, or marriage between relatives. This typically takes the form of marriage between second or first cousins, and is quite widely practised in a number of Muslim populations. It has been suggested that if consanguineous marriages are highly prevalent within a population, the distribution and incidence of genetic abnormalities in the offspring is altered, and this can cause lethal perinatal malformations (Balarajan *et al.*, 1989a; Lancet, 1991).

Certainly, Pakistani populations in Britain display greater degrees of consanguinity than any other ethnic group. A study in Birmingham found that nearly 70 per cent of Pakistani mothers were in consanguineous marriages, compared to 13 per cent of Bangladeshis, 5 per cent of Indians and less than 1 per cent of European and Caribbean mothers (Bundey *et al.*, 1990). However, evidence for the impact of consanguinity on infant mortality is equivocal. Some commentators suggest that it explains the increased incidence of congenital abnormalities among Pakistani babies, but only part of the excess mortality (Bundey *et al.*, 1991; Chitty and Winter, 1989).

At the same time, the attribution of excess mortality to consanguinity has been criticised (Ahmad, 1994; Parsons *et al.*, 1993). Ahmad argues that a re-evaluation is occurring among geneticists and that the harmful consequences of consanguinity may have been overstated. He also emphasises both inconsistencies in the literature, such as Terry *et al.*'s (1985) finding of a higher prevalence of congenital abnormalities in populations with low consanguinity, and the problems inherent in ascertaining ethnic differences in the overall prevalence of congenital abnormalities. For Ahmad, the research focus on consanguinity reflects dubious assumptions about the supposed superiority of 'normal' British family patterns. These may deflect attention from the positive aspects of consanguinity in promoting the integration of families and communities, and from other possible causes of mortality such as poor socioeconomic status or poor services.

Utilisation of health care and the nature of the services provided are other possible agents underlying ethnic differences in infant mortality, although these have received comparatively little attention. Clarke *et al.* (1988) found that attendance for antenatal care late in pregnancy was associated with higher perinatal mortality in 'European' mothers, but not in South Asian ones. The association between late booking and the incidence of congenital abnormality is more equivocal, but may be significant (Bundey *et al.*, 1991; Chitty and Winter, 1989). Studies by Clarke *et al.* (1988) and Clarke and Clayton (1983) found that registration with a GP who was not on the obstetric list (ie. with recognised expertise in providing maternity care) was associated with higher perinatal mortality in both the South Asian and the 'European' groups, particularly the former. In view of the concentration of such GPs in inner-city areas where the bulk of people from minority ethnic populations live, this 'inner-city effect' could be a significant factor, although, by the same token, it could be some other effect associated with inner-city residence that underlies the association with GP status. Clarke and Clayton also found there to be a slightly greater proportion of avoidable factors present among the South Asian deaths. Another study found the quality of antenatal care to be poorer for mothers from minority ethnic populations (Bowler, 1993), while Parsons et al. (1993) describe ethnic differences in rates for induced labour and Caesarean section with a possible impact on birth outcomes. In particular, they describe lower rates of induced labour among Bangladeshi women. A Birmingham study found there to be significantly lower rates of induced labour among South Asian women than white women (MacArthur et al., 1993). A study by Firdous and Bhopal (1989) shared a number of these results, and also found that South Asian women experienced greater communication problems about their reproductive health, and had less knowledge and made less use of services. They suggested that such factors may partially underlie poorer pregnancy outcomes. All of these studies highlight the need to consider the role of health care in mediating infant mortality.

In summary, there is strong evidence of ethnic differences in infant mortality, with Pakistani populations appearing particularly disadvantaged. However, the ethnic patterning of infant health is complex and the factors underlying it little understood. It is probably the case that conventional risk factors cannot explain all of the differences, and some of the evidence – such as ethnic differences in birthweight-specific mortality and the prevalence of different kinds of congenital abnormality – suggest that different aetiological agents may underlie the experience of different groups.

Morbidity

Although mortality is an important indicator of population health, it provides only limited information. Some of the most important health issues in developed industrial countries relate to chronic illness, disability and mental health, which do not significantly figure in mortality statistics. At the same time, as Ayaniyan (1994) points out, medical effectiveness measured in terms of mortality does not reflect possible differences in the changes in quality of life achieved, which are the main outcome of many clinical procedures.

It is therefore important to consider ethnic patterns in morbidity as well as mortality. Unfortunately, information on morbidity and disability among minority ethnic groups is scarce, particularly at a national level. This might change with the use of 1991 Census data and the introduction of ethnic monitoring in the NHS, but few results are available to date.

A number of studies have examined morbidity from specific causes. These are covered in Chapter 3; this section focuses upon more general evidence about ethnic patterns in morbidity. It first examines studies of chronic illness and self-reported morbidity before proceeding to consider research on the age and gender dimensions of morbidity among ethnic groups.

Chronic illness and self-reported morbidity

Dunnell (1993) provides some early analysis of the 1991 Census, which required respondents to indicate whether they suffered from a long-term illness that limited their activities. She shows that – after controlling for age – all ethnic groups with the exception of the Chinese reported higher levels of limiting long-term illness than the white group.

Bone *et al.* (1994) provide provisional estimates of ethnic differences in healthy active life expectancy, a measure which combines mortality and morbidity measures in calculating the average expected number of years of disability-free life remaining at different ages for different ethnic groups. Restricting their analysis to London, the investigators derived disability rates from the long-term illness question in the 1991 Census, and estimated ethnic group-specific mortality rates 'synthetically' from ward-level mortality data. They found that both men and women from 'black' and South Asian populations could expect shorter healthy lives than the corresponding gender among the 'white and other' population, varying from 2.5 years less for South Asian men to six years less for 'black' women. These findings are based on a number of methodological assumptions, so they should be interpreted with some caution. Nevertheless, they are at least suggestive of a poorer health experience among the main minority ethnic groups in London.

It is also appropriate to consider more qualitative research about ethnic patterns in the actual experience of chronic illness. Unfortunately, although medical sociology has historically paid great attention to this question in studying how people manage chronic illness in their everyday lives, little research of this sort has been undertaken in Britain specifically among minority ethnic populations (but see Doyle *et al.*, 1994). In Canada, Anderson *et al.* (1991) discuss ethnic differences between women in the management of diabetes, suggesting that the 'ideology of self-care' which is typically shared by health professionals and middle class white women is less appropriate to working class Chinese women, especially in view of the limitations imposed by the material realities of their lives. Turning to more acute forms of suffering, there is some evidence to suggest that ethnic differences may exist in Britain in the experience of pain (Thomas and Rose, 1991), and that this in turn is associated with antecedent factors such as parental attitudes to childhood injury.

Four recent studies have examined the prevalence of self-reported morbidity within ethnic groups more directly. These are:

- A health and lifestyle survey of the minority ethnic population of Bristol (Pilgrim *et al.*, 1993).

- A study of the Punjabi population of Glasgow, providing a comprehensive assessment of general physical, mental and self-reported health (Williams, 1993; Williams *et al.*, 1993).

- A Bradford study which examines the influence of South Asian ethnicity and unemployment on perceived health (Ahmad *et al.*, 1989b).

- A study employing secondary analysis of national and London-wide data to examine the factors associated with differences in self-reported health, including ethnicity (Benzeval *et al.*, 1992).

The Bristol study provides comprehensive data for 574 people concerning, *inter alia,* self-reported physical and psychosocial health. The study selected people of African, Caribbean, South Asian

(Bangladeshis and Urdu, Punjabi, Hindi and Gujarati speakers), Chinese and Vietnamese origin, both UK and foreign born, although most of its results are presented in an aggregate format. The survey methodology aimed at achieving a representative sample from each group and was conducted on the basis of FHSA and electoral registers, as well as contact via community organisations and 'snowball' sampling techniques. No comparator group from the majority population was selected. Instead, comparisons of prevalence were made, where the questions were comparable, on the basis of other local surveys and the national *Health and Lifestyle Survey* (Blaxter, 1990). Compared to the predominantly white respondents to these surveys, the investigators found that the Bristol respondents were less likely to report their overall health as 'excellent', and more likely to report suffering from a range of problems such as arthritis, 'bad back' and 'always feeling tired'. Conversely, they were less likely to report conditions such as bronchitis and varicose veins.

When comparing responses to the census question on limiting long-term illness with reported prevalence of specific chronic illness, the study found considerable discrepancies, with 50 per cent or more of respondents suffering from diabetes, asthma, cancer and epilepsy reporting no limiting long-term illness, although the last two findings are based on very small numbers. The investigators suggested that the minority ethnic populations of Bristol may have a greater tendency to view ill health in functional terms than whites (in other words, only complaints which hinder everyday activities are regarded as 'illness'). This finding is consistent with other research (Howlett *et al.*, 1992), but the Bristol study was unable to examine the extent to which this apparent misreporting also occurs in the white population. Clearly, any possible ethnic differences in the validity of long-term illness questions are relevant to analysis of the 1991 Census. If such differences do exist, Dunnell's (1993) results would suggest that 'true' levels of limiting long-term illness among minority ethnic populations are very high indeed, although any such speculation needs to be substantiated empirically.

Turning to the second study, Williams *et al.* (1993) investigated the health experience of the South Asian, predominantly Punjabi, population of Glasgow. They examined 159 South Asian people between the ages of 30 and 40, and a comparator group of 319 randomly selected white people aged 35. They recorded physical attributes (height, body mass index, blood pressure etc.), mental health, chronic conditions (including self-reported limiting long-term illness), and reporting of symptoms and sickness behaviour. Their aim was to assess the balance of positive and negative health differences between the South Asian and general populations.

The investigators found that there were significant differences between the populations in both directions for about half of the measures. The most striking differences were in physical development, South Asians of both sexes tending to be shorter and more overweight. The investigators argued that these characteristics were likely to be due in part to childhood environmental deprivation, with concomitantly greater risks of developing a number of illnesses, including cardiovascular disease, although this theory remains controversial (Baker *et al.*, 1993; Barker, 1991). Other differences included poorer mental health scores for South Asian women, but less reporting of long-term illness and days off work for South Asian men, although they reported a similar number of chronic symptoms. This may relate to their predominantly self-employed status. Certainly, further analysis taking closer account of socioeconomic status is warranted. Nevertheless, the investigators concluded that the balance of health differences between the two populations was roughly equal, although there appeared to be some concentration of disadvantage among South Asian women.

Williams (1993) used the same sample in an innovative way to investigate the impact of length of UK residence on the health of the South Asian population. In essence, he found that longer length of residence was associated with generally poorer health status, particularly in terms of higher body mass index and more clinical overweightness, greater respiratory illness and more reported heart problems. Since the study was restricted to adults between the ages of 30 and 40, these findings were not confounded by age.

In the third study, Ahmad *et al.* (1989b) compared the impact of unemployment on the perceived health of a sample of white and South Asian general practice attenders in Bradford using the Nottingham Health Profile, a well established instrument for the measurement of perceived health status. They found that unemployment was associated with poorer health status in all groups, with the exception of young South Asian women. However, employed South Asian men had better perceived health than their white counterparts, whereas health profiles were similar in the other categories, although older unemployed South Asian women reported generally poorer health. Since unemployment among the South Asian population was double that for the whites, the study usefully demonstrates how controlling for relevant socioeconomic confounders can alter judgments about ethnic differences in health.

In the final study, Benzeval *et al.* (1992) analysed the somewhat unsatisfactory ethnicity data – ascribed in broad categories by interviewer observation – from the *Health and Lifestyle Survey,* a national study conducted in 1984-85 on the health, attitudes and behaviour of some 9,000 adults (Blaxter, 1990). They showed that, after controlling for other relevant socioeconomic factors, being 'non-white' was associated with higher levels of self-reported psychosocial and overall 'subjective' ill health. They also used the smaller *Survey of Londoners' Living Standards* (Townsend and Gordon, 1989) to show that 'non-white' people were significantly *less* likely to report recent illness, but those who reported experience of racial harassment were *more* likely to do so, again after controlling for relevant confounding factors. In addition, they showed that people who experienced discrimination in employment were more likely to report poor 'subjective' health, recent illness and their health as a 'major problem', although the discrimination referred to was not solely confined to racism.

The latter finding is important in suggesting that there may be a direct link between experience of racism and perceived health status. This issue has received little attention, but US research on blood pressure confirms the possible impact of the experience of racism upon physical health. Two US studies which investigated the relationship between self-reported stressors and high blood pressure found there to be an inverse association (Krieger, 1990; Winkleby *et al.*, 1988). In other words, people who reported fewer symptoms of stress were more likely to experience high blood pressure, even after controlling for relevant confounding variables. Krieger's study specifically examined experience of race and gender discrimination among white and black women; she found that black women who said that they normally kept quiet about instances of unfair treatment were over four times more likely to report high blood pressure, and women who recounted no instances of discrimination – the inference being drawn that they repressed the reporting of such instances – were nearly three times more likely to do so.

To account for this inverse association Winkleby *et al.* (1988) postulate that either repression of the psychological symptoms occasioned by anger and stress can cause the physical symptoms of high blood pressure, or that high blood pressure alters perceptions of stress. They cite evidence in support of both hypotheses. Other US studies have shown that exposure to anger-provoking racist situations can increase blood pressure, whereas exposure to similar non-racist situations does not (Armstead *et al.*, 1989), and that patterns of social behaviour which correlate with high blood pressure and other physical symptoms vary between ethnic groups (Dressler, 1993).

Most of these studies are small scale and exploratory in nature. They are nevertheless suggestive of important social factors affecting physical health via ethnic differences in the experience of psychosocial stress.

Age and gender dimensions in general morbidity

A growing body of research literature highlights age and gender dimensions in the health experience of ethnic groups, focusing particularly on the health of the elderly and upon women's reproductive health. Much of this research examines interactions with health services and is therefore examined in Chapters 5 and 6. This section briefly outlines some of the main findings concerning health status.

Several studies have examined chronic illness, disability, self-assessed health or physical characteristics of South Asian and Caribbean elders (Blakemore, 1982; Donaldson, 1986; Ebrahim *et al.*, 1991; Fenton, 1985). Ebrahim *et al.* found chronic illness among Gujaratis aged 54 and over (average age 63) registered with a North London general practice to be generally higher than an age-matched sample of whites from the same practice, and broadly in keeping with known patterns of morbidity. However, they claim that the prevalence of 'common problems of old age' was the same or lower than in the white sample; this was particularly true of low life satisfaction, falls and urinary incontinence. On a number of physiological measures such as peak flow and grip strength, the Gujaratis scored more poorly than the whites, suggesting that the onset of difficulties in daily living may occur at an earlier age in this still relatively youthful population.

Donaldson (1986) identified high levels of disability, as measured by activities of daily living, in a sample of older (over 65) South Asians resident in Leicester. Blakemore (1982) found levels of 'common health problems' among South Asian, Caribbean and white populations in Birmingham to be similar, but the white group was, on average, older. Other researchers have identified problems with hypertensive disease and diabetes among elderly Caribbean populations (Fenton, 1985), femur fracture – possibly associated with vitamin D deficiency – and asthma in South Asian populations, and cataracts, probably associated with a raised prevalence of diabetes, in both South Asian and Caribbean populations (Blakemore and Bonham, 1994; Calder *et al.*, 1994). Fenton (1985) describes poor levels of general health among the Caribbean population of Bristol: more than two-thirds report a health cause for regular medical visits compared with only half in the white and South Asian groups.

These results need to be interpreted with caution since they may be subject to several sources of bias, particularly in areas such as life satisfaction. In general they are consistent with known patterns of morbidity, but they point to a situation of some complexity between different minority ethnic populations. Analysis of patterns in immigrant mortality shows that, if anything, the greatest burden of ill health falls in younger age groups. This pattern occurs more starkly in the USA, where a 'mortality crossover' exists in which black elders experience lower mortality than whites; Markides (1989) explains this in terms of a selective survival hypothesis, whereby high mortality rates at earlier ages remove 'less hardy' individuals so that the group which survives into old age is comprised of the most 'robust' people. In Britain, any such pattern is likely to be complicated by the possible selective effects of migration. In addition, levels of community support and changing social norms regarding intergenerational relationships – the so-called 'migrant transition' (Mays, 1983) – may also affect both the incidence and impact of disease on the elderly population. In contrast to a developing US literature (Rushing *et al.*, 1992; Worobey and Angel, 1990) little specific attention has so far been paid in Britain to the impact on health of social isolation and poor social support among minority ethnic elders (but see Blakemore and Bonham, 1994; Norman, 1985); further attention to these issues is certainly warranted.

At the other end of the age spectrum, even less attention has been paid to general issues of child health among minority ethnic populations. Black (1985a-g) provides an overview, but although discussing 'cultural' issues and the 'difficulties' of living in Britain, his analysis tends to focus upon specific 'exotic' diseases. Indeed, most relevant research has focused upon specific areas of concern. The most widely researched is infant mortality which was examined above. Some attention has also been paid to accidents (see page 75), respiratory illness (see page 76) and nutrition. Concern about nutritional deficiency in children was manifested particularly in efforts to tackle rickets in South Asian populations in the 1970s and early 1980s. This is described in more detail in Chapter 7. More recently, some attention has been paid to iron deficiency and infant feeding and weaning practices among South Asian populations (Kurtz, 1993). Bhopal and Donaldson (1988) provide a critical account of some of these concerns (see Chapter 7). More generally, interaction between minority ethnic status, inner-city residence and deprivation is clearly likely to have a major impact on the health of children from minority ethnic groups. This is supported by evidence on childhood growth, which is associated with subsequent health. Rona *et al.* (1988) have shown that children from all minority ethnic groups, with the exception of those from Caribbean populations, have a lower average height than the national figure, and that height is associated with factors such as parental socioeconomic status, household overcrowding and school meal provision. However, research of this kind on the general health of minority ethnic children remains relatively uncommon, which is perhaps rather surprising in view of the age structure of most minority ethnic populations.

Although greater attention has been paid to women's health, most research in this area has focused upon attitudes to health and health care and the uptake of specific services; this is summarised in Chapters 5 and 6. There is also a considerable body of research on the psychological wellbeing of South Asian women (see Chapter 3). Another focus of interest is, from a variety of perspectives, women's reproductive health and the interaction between women's and children's health (Firdous and Bhopal, 1989; MacArthur *et al.*, 1993; Mayall, 1991). These studies are not in general primarily concerned with the the broader implications for women's health. MacArthur *et al.* (1993) did, however, examine long-term health problems following childbirth among South Asian women attending a maternity unit in Birmingham, finding there to be a significantly greater prevalence of musculo-skeletal symptoms even after controlling for demographic and obstetric characteristics. The investigators speculated that greater levels of vitamin D deficiency may account for the finding, although conceding that it might also be a methodological artefact.

Despite the range of studies mentioned above, again there is a dearth of detailed analysis on the general health of women from minority ethnic populations. Writers such as Bryan *et al.* (1985) and Wilson (1978) provide eloquent impressionistic accounts of how women's dual role as both paid and domestic labourers interacts with experiences of material disadvantage and racism to damage their health. Formal research has been slower to examine gender as a specific dimension in the health experience of minority ethnic groups. Although the health experiences of men and women are typically analysed separately – for example, in calculating separate SMRs standardised to a gender-specific reference population (Balarajan and Bulusu, 1990) – comparison is rarely made between men's and women's health within given ethnic groups. As Krieger and Fee (1994) point out, gender-specific exposures to health-damaging agents often exist. Failure to examine such exposures may well conceal the broader importance of gender as a factor in the health experience of ethnic groups.

Health behaviours

This section examines the evidence on patterns of behaviour with a direct impact upon health. It focuses in particular upon alcohol and tobacco use, diet and exercise.

Balarajan and Yuen (1986) analysed responses to the *General Household Survey* of 1978 and 1980 to determine levels of alcohol and tobacco use by country of birth. Standardising for age, sex and socioeconomic group, they computed ratios for heavy drinking and smoking for each migrant group. They found raised levels of both behaviours for Irish men and raised smoking for Irish women compared to the 'all countries of birth' figure. Levels of both behaviours among people born in the Indian subcontinent and the Caribbean were very much lower. Standardising for socioeconomic group may, however, conceal the extent of the risk resulting from smoking among minority ethnic populations, since these populations are in general more heavily concentrated in the lower socioeconomic strata, which are typified in the majority population by greater levels of smoking. Further examination of drinking and smoking patterns in specific socioeconomic strata of minority ethnic groups is certainly warranted.

The *General Household Survey* findings are generally consistent with community-based studies (Ahmad *et al.*, 1988; Bhopal, 1986a; Pilgrim *et al.*, 1993) although these reveal considerable differences between age groups, religions and particularly gender. Among most South Asian populations, alcohol and tobacco use by women is negligible, but usage is increasing among certain groups of men, once again indicating the deficiencies of analysis at an aggregate level. An occupational study of South Asian factory workers by Jackson *et al.* (1981) found that over 40 per cent smoked. McKeigue *et al.* (1988) found still higher rates of smoking among Bangladeshi men in East London, and Balarajan and Raleigh (1993) report high levels of alcohol-related morbidity among Punjabi Sikhs in Southall. On the other hand, research in Glasgow indicates that traditional patterns of low usage among South Asians there have persisted among schoolchildren (Kohli, 1989). In Hull, Watt *et al.* (1993) and Fong and Watt (1994) found alcohol and tobacco use among Chinese people, particularly women, to be low.

Very little attention has been paid to the impact of other behavioural and lifestyle factors upon the health of different ethnic groups. Research on diet and nutritional status is summarised by Pacy (1989). Although considerable dietary variation exists between ethnic groups, and between religious groups among South Asian populations, all groups appear to be adequately nourished. Concerns have been raised about adult iron deficiency and deficiencies of vitamins B_{12} and D in certain South Asian populations, particularly those adhering to a vegetarian diet. Other behaviours in some South Asian populations which have been linked to health concerns include chewing betel, using ghee in cooking and the use of lead-based *surma* cosmetics. The prevalence of these behaviours, the extent to which they constitute a problem and the formulation of appropriate policy responses have all been the subject of considerable but inconclusive debate (Donovan, 1984; Jacobson, 1987; Pacy, 1989; Peach, 1984; Stop Rickets Campaign, 1983).

Patterns of exercise among ethnic groups have also been little investigated. In their Bristol study, Pilgrim *et al.* (1993) found that levels of exercise among men from the minority groups surveyed approximated to that of the general population, whereas women – particularly South Asian women – appeared to exercise rather less. By contrast, R. Williams *et al.* (1994) found both men and women of Punjabi origin in Glasgow to be less likely than the general population ever to take vigorous exercise, the difference for men being statistically significant.

In conclusion, relatively little attention has been paid to patterns of health behaviour among minority ethnic groups, or to the environmental circumstances which either constrain or enable them. Such patterns are clearly complex and dynamic, and it is therefore inappropriate to generalise between different populations in different areas. On the face of it, however, there are few striking differences between ethnic groups, with the possible exception of alcohol and tobacco use, where behaviours appear in general to be healthier than among the majority ethnic population.

3 Specific diseases

Introduction

This chapter reviews the evidence for ethnic patterns in the occurrence and nature of specific diseases. It is split into nine sections, each of which describes the ethnic patterning of a particular disease or group of diseases, and goes on to describe and evaluate research into the apparent causes of these patterns. The sections are divided as follows:

- Circulatory diseases

- Diabetes

- Cancer

- Mental illness

- HIV/AIDS and sexual health

- External causes

- Respiratory disease and tuberculosis

- Sickle cell disorders

- Rickets and osteomalacia.

These diseases have been chosen either because they are a major cause of mortality and/or morbidity among one or more ethnic groups, or because their incidence within particular groups has been a focus of special concern. They encompass but go beyond the five key areas of the National Health Strategy – coronary heart disease and stroke; cancer; mental illness; HIV/AIDS and sexual health; and accidents – which are set out in *The Health of the Nation* (Secretary of State for Health, 1992). A recent book, *Ethnicity and Health,* addresses more directly some of the ethnic issues which arise in these key areas (Balarajan and Raleigh, 1993).

Before proceeding to examine each area in detail, it is worth describing the impact of these diseases on the overall health experience of different ethnic groups. Table 3.1 indicates the number of deaths between 1979 and 1983 from all causes and from specific causes by selected place of birth, acting here as a proxy for ethnic group. The proportion of the total number of deaths accounted for by each cause within the relevant population is given in brackets. Data are not separately available for HIV/AIDS and sickle cell disorders, while mental illness and rickets cannot be represented by mortality figures.

The table indicates that the diseases described in this chapter account for the majority of deaths in each group. Despite some differences between groups, circulatory diseases, cancer and respiratory diseases appear consistently to be the major killers. The table provides some support for Bhopal's argument (undated; 1988) that research has often failed to focus upon diseases which contribute most to the burden of ill health among minority ethnic groups. For example, little attention has been

Table 3.1   **Number of deaths by place of birth, age 20+, England and Wales, 1979-83**

| Place of birth | All causes | Number of deaths (percentage of all deaths within group) | | | | | |
		Circulatory disease	Diabetes	Cancers	TB	Respiratory disease	External causes
All Ireland	58,960 (100)	27,434 (47)	283 (0)	14,971 (25)	220 (0)	8,672 (15)	2,777 (5)
Indian subcontinent	19,578 (100)	10,679 (55)	355 (2)	3,467 (18)	198 (1)	2,139 (11)	1,003 (5)
Caribbean Commonwealth	6,591 (100)	3,095 (47)	196 (3)	1,610 (24)	29 (0)	489 (7)	520 (8)
African Commonwealth	2,439 (100)	1,030 (42)	32 (1)	482 (20)	26 (1)	182 (7)	403 (17)

Source: Balarajan and Bulusu (1990)

devoted to cancer or respiratory diseases relative to their incidence in comparison with tuberculosis or sickle cell disorders. The table also underlines the fact that there are major commonalities, as well as important differences, between groups in their experience of ill health.

This point is also brought out in examining morbidity data. Table 3.2 lists the most common causes of hospital admission in Trent Region in the years 1977-78 for South Asian and 'non-South Asian' patients identified by name search. It is based on a re-analysis by Bhopal and Donaldson (1988) of data originally presented by Donaldson and Taylor (1983). It can be seen that the five most common causes of admission are identical in the two groups, albeit that there are some differences in the precise order,

Table 3.2   **Most common causes of hospital admission by ethnic group, Trent Region 1977-78**

| South Asians | | Non-South Asians | |
Diagnostic category		Diagnostic category	
1	Accidents/poisonings	1	Accidents/poisonings
2	Digestive system	2	Circulatory system
3	Respiratory system	3	Digestive system
4	Symptoms and signs	4	Symptoms and signs
5	Circulatory system	5	Respiratory system
6	Infectious diseases	6	Neoplasms
7	Nervous system	7	Nervous system
8	Genitourinary system	8	Genitourinary system
9	Perinatal	9	Musculoskeletal
10	Congenital anomalies	10	Congenital anomalies
11	Neoplasms	11	Infectious diseases

Source: Bhopal and Donaldson (1988)

and only one out of the top eleven causes of admission is not shared between the two groups. The ordering of causes is remarkably similar, with only infections appearing considerably more important among South Asians and neoplasms (cancer) among non-South Asians. Thus, from the point of view of the overall burden of clinically presented disease (which admittedly may differ from the actual incidence within the population), it would appear that there are substantial similarities between the two groups.

Although the sections that follow often emphasise differences rather than similarities, the picture painted by these two tables is worth bearing in mind.

Circulatory disease

Circulatory disease is a major cause of mortality and morbidity in Britain, accounting for about 40 per cent of all deaths. Table 3.3 displays deaths from all circulatory diseases and for coronary (ischaemic) heart disease (CHD) and cerebrovascular disease (CVD) – commonly known as stroke – for selected ethnic groups, as measured by place of birth. CHD and CVD together account for the bulk of mortality from circulatory disease in most ethnic groups.

Although circulatory diseases are a major cause of death for all ethnic groups, the table indicates that there are important ethnic differences in mortality both from circulatory diseases as a whole and from CHD as compared with CVD. Major gender differences also exist which are less clearly demonstrated in the table; in general, circulatory diseases account for a smaller proportion of overall mortality for women than for men, particularly in younger age groups. It should perhaps be pointed out that the table slightly overstates the extent of ethnic difference since – as it was suggested in the previous chapter – mortality at ages greater than 70 in minority ethnic groups tends more closely to resemble that of the majority ethnic population, a finding which is replicated in the case of circulatory disease.

Table 3.3 **Mortality from circulatory diseases by selected place of birth, age 20-69, England and Wales, 1979-83**

Place of Birth		All Circulatory Diseases		Coronary Heart Disease		Cerebrovascular Disease	
		SMR	N*	SMR	N*	SMR	N*
All Ireland	M	117	8,656	114	6,225	123	1,175
	F	118	3,685	120	2,023	117	922
Indian subcontinent	M	133	4,494	136	3,410	153	645
	F	136	1,431	146	798	125	347
Caribbean Commonwealth	M	77	1,514	45	669	176	419
	F	141	783	76	214	210	316
African Commonwealth	M	127	618	113	400	163	103
	F	136	191	97	62	139	58

* Number of deaths
Source: Balarajan and Bulusu (1990)

The paragraphs below subject the findings given in Table 3.3 to further scrutiny, describing patterns of mortality and – where available – morbidity for CHD and CVD in turn, and discussing research evidence concerning the factors underlying these differences.

Coronary heart disease

CHD is the single largest cause of death for both men and women from several ethnic groups, including the white population. Even among Caribbean-born women, for whom it contributes least to overall mortality out of the groups displayed in Table 3.3, it causes more than one in every ten deaths. As may be expected of a *Health of the Nation* key area, it therefore constitutes a major health problem in contemporary Britain.

The table also indicates that, after adjusting for age, CHD mortality is raised for men and women born in Ireland and the Indian subcontinent in comparison with gender-specific rates for the whole population of England and Wales. It is also raised for African-born men, but is low for men and women born in the Caribbean. As Cruickshank (1989a) has argued, it is probably lower still for people of African descent born in the Caribbean compared with people born there of South Asian descent. Excess mortality among Irish, African and South Asian men is greater in the younger age groups. For example, men aged 20-49 born in the Indian subcontinent have 65 per cent greater mortality than the national figure (Balarajan, 1991); as Table 3.3 shows, the corresponding value for men aged 20-69 born in the subcontinent is 36 per cent. Moreover, trends in mortality between 1970-72 and 1979-83 indicate that, unlike most other ethnic groups, the gap between the Irish and South Asian groups and the overall population is not narrowing (Balarajan, 1991).

The available evidence would suggest that raised mortality is likely to persist within UK-born Irish and South Asian populations, while CHD mortality may rise among Caribbean populations (Cruickshank, 1989a; Hughes and Cruickshank, 1989; McKeigue, *et al.*, 1989; Meade *et al.*, 1978; Raftery *et al.*, 1990). From a public health point of view, this has serious long-term implications. For example, Lowy *et al.* (1991) have estimated, on the basis of the demographic structure of the South Asian population of Leicester, that the number of deaths from CHD within this population will more than double between 1988 and 2008, even if it is at no higher risk of CHD than the general population. More realistic assumptions suggest a larger increase.

What are the causes of these mortality patterns? Unfortunately, relatively little attention has been paid to CHD incidence in the Irish and Caribbean populations, despite the fact that the considerable differences these groups exhibit from the general population might provide important clues about CHD aetiology. Neither group conforms entirely to the typical pattern of intermediate migrant mortality between old and new country rates outlined above (Marmot *et al.*, 1984). It is often pointed out that the high rates of both smoking and CHD in Irish migrants are consistent with one another (Balarajan and Yuen, 1986; Marmot *et al.*, 1984). Meade *et al.* (1978) found that the distribution of biochemical factors associated with CHD in a factory-based comparison of white and mainly Caribbean people was broadly consistent with CHD incidence. Differences were greater between men than between women. Fuller investigation of CHD patterns among these populations is certainly warranted.

More generally, most of the work on CHD suffers from the familiar problem of a focus on mortality. Little attention has been paid to differences in symptoms and morbidity, and also to the role of health care in mediating CHD events. However, McKeigue (1993) reports a greater prevalence of ischaemic ECG abnormalities among South Asian men, which was highly significant statistically and consistent with mortality data. The available evidence also appears to suggest that hospital admissions for coronary events among the Irish, Caribbean and South Asian populations are consistent with known patterns of mortality (Cruickshank *et al.*, 1980; Fox and Shapiro, 1988; Pedoe *et al.*, 1975). Shaukat *et al.* (1993) have shown that South Asian men referred to a regional cardiothoracic centre with suspected angina experienced greater referral delay than white men. Research in the USA has shown that black people experience a greater incidence of out-of-hospital CHD events and a higher case-fatality rate, even after adjusting for a variety of risk factors (Becker *et al.*, 1993; Lee *et al.*, 1990). Evidence also exists for underdiagnosis of CHD, less surgical intervention and poorer coding of death records for blacks than for whites, although the impact of this on overall incidence and mortality is not clear (Ayaniyan, 1993; Lee *et al.*, 1990; Peterson *et al.*, 1994). Greater understanding of these kinds of issues in Britain would clearly be useful.

Despite these deficiencies, a good deal of research effort has been devoted to examining CHD in the South Asian population. This stems in part from international evidence of raised CHD rates in expatriate South Asian populations throughout the world (McKeigue *et al.*, 1989). CHD rates in the subcontinent itself are difficult to determine, but the available evidence points to relatively low rates, at least in rural areas (McKeigue *et al.*, 1989). In addition, the evidence from expatriate populations suggests that high incidence may persist beyond the first generation.

These findings constitute something of an epidemiological puzzle. Why should South Asian populations living in countries as diverse as Britain, Fiji and Trinidad, and with widely varying geographical origins, social backgrounds and lifestyles, all experience excess CHD mortality? As McKeigue (1992) points out, the consistency of the pattern implies a common underlying disease mechanism, yet the distribution of most common CHD risk factors such as smoking, blood pressure, obesity, haemostasis and serum and plasma cholesterol varies widely between these populations (McKeigue *et al.*, 1989). Moreover, the consensus of community-based studies in Britain is that these risk factors are generally less prevalent in the South Asian than in the majority population (Knight *et al.*, 1993; McKeigue, 1992; McKeigue *et al.*, 1985). The latter finding is not universal, however. A study by R. Williams *et al.* (1994) of non-biochemical CHD risk factors among Punjabis in Glasgow shows that only in smoking rates does the Punjabi population experience a lower prevalence of risk factors.

Perhaps the two most promising unifying explanations for the phenomenon identified by recent research are socioeconomic factors and the insulin resistance hypothesis. These are examined further below. Other explanations include fetal and infant environmental stress (Barker, 1991; Williams *et al.*, 1993) and the use of ghee in cooking (Jacobson, 1987). These may explain some of the excess in particular populations, but are unlikely fully to account for the phenomenon.

Most studies of the prevalence of CHD risk factors among South Asian populations in Britain have principally examined biochemical or physiological rather than socially determined risk factors (Knight *et al.*, 1993; McKeigue *et al.*, 1989; 1985). Indeed, McKeigue *et al.* (1989) are rather dismissive of possible social factors such as low socioeconomic status, lack of social support, stress, lifestyle change and the effect of racism. Nevertheless, the study by R. Williams *et al.* (1994), based on the same sample as described for Williams *et al.* (1993) on page 45, and a major review by the Coronary Prevention Group (1986) devote considerable attention to these factors, and are suggestive of a significant role.

The link between social stress and CHD is unproven, but remains a plausible and powerful hypothesis (Coronary Prevention Group, 1986; Fox and Shapiro, 1988). Systematic differences in stress between populations are conventionally thought of as arising through structural inequalities (eg. poverty), which can in certain circumstances lead to stressors (either particular negative life events or chronic strains); these in turn can lead to poor stress outcomes (distress, depression), particularly in the absence of mediators such as networks of social support (Aneshensel, 1992; R. Williams *et al.*, 1994).

Certainly, structural inequalities exist in many South Asian populations in Britain. The R. Williams *et al.* study (1994) found Punjabi respondents in Glasgow to experience structural inequalities in several dimensions. Contrary to popular stereotypes, they also found that the Punjabis had less social support than the white sample. However, self-reported stress outcomes were equivocal, and the investigators raised the possibility that stress arises directly from poor work and home environments regardless of self-reported stressors. In order to account in these terms for the pattern of CHD incidence in Britain, however, it is necessary to explain why this does not lead to high CHD in the Punjab. Williams *et al.* suggest that it may relate to urban factors associated with coping resources, or to incongruities between lifestyle and economic position. These have been observed in other minority ethnic or 'Westernising' populations (Aneshensel, 1992; Dressler, 1988; R. Williams *et al.*, 1994). Thus, lack of social support and stress arising as a consequence of lifestyle change and racism may underlie part of the excess in CHD mortality.

Such an explanation may account for the lack of a socioeconomic gradient in CHD mortality among South Asian populations similar to that observed for the majority ethnic population (Marmot *et al.*, 1978; Whitehead, 1992). Alternatively, the lack of such a gradient may be more apparent than real, reflecting the problems of measuring socioeconomic status among the South Asian population (see Chapter 4). But any explanation of CHD among ethnic groups on the basis of socioeconomic status or migratory stress would have to account for the lower incidence in the Caribbean population. More research on the cultural and behavioural mediation of stress across ethnic groups may help to clarify the nature of such differences (Dressler, 1993; Shaukat and Cruickshank, 1993).

The second unifying explanation for the incidence of CHD among South Asian populations focuses upon insulin resistance. It has often been noted that diabetes – a major risk factor for CHD – is highly prevalent in expatriate South Asian populations and may explain the excess of CHD (Balarajan, 1991). However, McKeigue (1992) argues that most South Asian people with CHD do not have diabetes and that this explanation alone can only account for a fraction of the excess. Instead, he suggests that:

> the high prevalence of diabetes is but one manifestation of a pattern of physiological disturbances related to insulin resistance in this group

(1992, p.341).

In essence, the insulin resistance hypothesis suggests that South Asian populations share a tendency to metabolise the hormone insulin in such a way that several features of coronary and diabetes risk are manifested. These include glucose intolerance, hyperinsulinaemia, low plasma concentrations of high-density lipoprotein cholesterol, and possibly hypertension (McKeigue, 1992; B.Williams, 1994). Insulin resistance is associated with a pattern of abdominal fat deposition, or 'central obesity', which characterises South Asian populations. Thus, although these populations may not be more obese than others, as defined by measures such as body mass index, the nature of their fat deposition may nevertheless underlie excess coronary risk.

It has been suggested that abdominal fat deposition is biologically advantageous in situations of food scarcity, and that South Asian populations may share a 'thrifty genotype' for this characteristic (McKeigue, 1992). It is also the case that lack of exercise and obesity lead to insulin resistance (B.Williams, 1994). Thus, greater coronary risk in expatriate South Asian populations may arise through the interaction of a genetic proclivity with exposure to novel environmental factors. The precise mechanisms of association between central obesity and insulin resistance remain unclear (McKeigue *et al.*, 1991). Nevertheless, the results of several community studies in Britain among different South Asian populations are consistent with the existence of an insulin resistance syndrome (McKeigue *et al.*, 1991; 1988; R.Williams *et al.*, 1994).

McKeigue (1993) has argued that the insulin resistance hypothesis may explain up to two-thirds of the excess coronary risk among South Asian men, after adjusting for smoking and cholesterol. Nevertheless, it should perhaps be emphasised that insulin resistance is also relatively common among the majority ethnic population. Moreover, the extent to which the metabolic correlates of insulin resistance fit neatly into a defined syndrome remains unclear (Godsland, 1994), indicative perhaps of a more complex underlying reality. At the same time, as the discussion above suggested, smoking, diet and stress may also play a significant role in some populations. R.Williams *et al.* suggest:

> *The vexed question of why South Asian migrant communities throughout the world should have a raised level of [CHD] is unlikely to have a simple answer and the powerful hypothesis concerning insulin resistance is unlikely to be the full explanation*

(1994, p.36).

It is worth noting in passing that the prevalence of diabetes among Caribbean populations in Britain is also high relative to whites, but these populations do not exhibit raised insulin resistance (McKeigue *et al.*, 1991). Clearly, the aetiology of diabetes and CHD in these populations is different from the South Asian case. One theory is that the incidence of diabetes among Caribbean populations is associated with early insulin deficiency and other environmental effects rather than insulin resistance. This may lead to differences in insulin composition from South Asian populations, and it may be that the CHD-causing agent within insulin is confined to a particular subcomponent of the hormone which is less marked among Caribbean populations (Shaukat and Cruickshank, 1993).

To conclude, it may be stated that:

- CHD is a major cause of death for all ethnic groups in Britain, but its incidence varies widely between groups and is particularly high among South Asian populations. Its incidence is likely to increase over time in these populations due to changes in age structure.

- Ethnic patterns in CHD incidence are not well understood, although among South Asian populations social factors and a syndrome of insulin resistance are implicated.

- Education about smoking and diet is an important means of tackling CHD in all ethnic groups (Secretary of State for Health, 1992; Bhopal, 1993). In addition, control of obesity and increased physical activity are likely to be effective strategies among South Asian populations (McKeigue, 1992).

- More research is required into CHD incidence among British-born people from minority ethnic groups, and among the Caribbean and Irish populations, and South Asian subpopulations. The role of health services in mediating the impact of CHD events also needs to be examined.

Cerebrovascular disease

Much less attention has been paid to CVD than to CHD among minority ethnic populations. It is nevertheless a major cause of death in all ethnic groups, ranking second after CHD among white, South Asian and Caribbean populations in Britain, and accounting for up to 40 per cent of all deaths from circulatory disease in some groups (Balarajan, 1991; Marmot et al., 1984). Between 1970-72 and 1979-83 CVD mortality in the whole population of England and Wales fell by 28 per cent, a decline which was shared by most ethnic groups, and exceeded by Caribbean and African Commonwealth populations (Balarajan, 1991). However, the mortality decline among men born in the Indian subcontinent in this period was just 3 per cent.

As Table 3.3 shows (page 53), CVD mortality is very substantially raised for a number of migrant groups, particularly people from the African and Caribbean Commonwealth. CVD is the leading cause of death in Jamaica, from where most Caribbean migrants in Britain originate, so high rates among this population in Britain may not be entirely unexpected (Cruickshank, 1989b). Nevertheless, relatively little attention has been paid to the possible causes of the phenomenon.

CVD shares a number of common risk factors with CHD, of which hypertension is particularly important (Cruickshank, 1989b). It is well known that black people in the USA experience, on average, higher blood pressure than whites (Lancet, 1992), although the reasons for this are not well understood. There is little evidence of raised blood pressure with respect to whites among black populations of African descent in the Caribbean, West Africa or Britain (Cruickshank, 1989c). Two factory-based studies in Britain found slightly higher blood pressure among black women, although this could be accounted for by greater obesity (Cruickshank et al., 1983; Meade et al., 1978). The latter study also found significantly raised blood pressure among one occupational grouping of black men. Kaplan (1994) cites other evidence for raised blood pressure among UK black populations, but the evidence overall is equivocal. Certainly, patterns of CVD mortality do not appear to be explicable in terms of blood pressure alone. Moreover, there is no evidence of any ethnic difference in the risk of mortality for a given level of blood pressure (Lancet, 1992).

Cruickshank (1993) has proposed a 'competing cause' hypothesis for high rates of CVD in the Caribbean population. In other words, since there is a low incidence of CHD more people are 'available' to die of CVD at a later age. Another possible cause of high CVD in Caribbean and African populations is as a consequence of sickle cell disorders (Brozovic et al., 1989; Diggs, 1992), but this is unlikely to account for a major part of the difference.

More work is required to elucidate the mechanisms underlying ethnic patterns in the incidence of CVD. As with CHD, existing research has been over-reliant upon mortality data, and has scarcely examined the role of health services in mediating CVD events. In contrast to CHD, research has tended to focus on the Caribbean and African populations rather than South Asian ones, even though CVD mortality remains high among the South Asian population. It may be that a greater prevalence of hypertension due to insulin resistance among South Asian populations explains some of the excess CVD mortality. For all ethnic groups, optimum preventive strategies must encompass both 'population' and 'high risk' approaches to blood pressure and obesity reduction, attempting to lower the distribution of blood pressure in the whole population, while also controlling hypertension through clinical management (Cruickshank, 1993; Rose, 1992).

Diabetes

Diabetes is a chronic disease which, as the discussion above indicated, can lead to lethal secondary complications such as CHD and end-stage renal disease (ESRD). It occurs in a number of forms. Insulin-dependent diabetes mellitus (IDDM) is a more severe form of the disease which tends to manifest itself relatively early in life. The available evidence, though somewhat sketchy, suggests that the prevalence of IDDM in both South Asian and Caribbean populations may be less than in the white population. Studies of clinically presented diabetes suggest that around 4 per cent of all South Asian and Caribbean diabetics have IDDM, as compared with some 20 per cent of the white diabetic population (Nikolaides *et al.*, 1981; Odugbesan *et al.*, 1989; Odugbesan and Barnett, 1985). Although the community prevalence of IDDM among different ethnic groups cannot be calculated from these figures, they are at least suggestive of lower prevalence among the relevant minority ethnic populations. The authors cited above suggest that their findings can be accounted for by both genetic factors and environmental ones, such as lack of exposure to particular viral infections. It is therefore possible that the incidence of IDDM will increase within South Asian and Caribbean populations.

By contrast, non-insulin dependent diabetes mellitus (NIDDM) – which is of later onset than IDDM and requires less rigorous management – appears to be more highly prevalent among most minority ethnic populations. As the figures cited above show, it also occurs more frequently than IDDM in all ethnic groups, thus contributing more to the overall burden of disease. Table 3.4 indicates

Table 3.4   **Mortality from diabetes by selected place of birth, England and Wales, 1979-83**

Place of Birth		Age 20-69		Age 70+	
		SMR	N*	SMR	N*
All Ireland	M	92	93	66	56
	F	55	47	68	87
Indian subcontinent	M	297	148	165	53
	F	103	93	153	61
Caribbean Commonwealth	M	292	82	242	15
	F	424	71	320	28
African Commonwealth	M	219	20	150	3
	F	161	8	43	1

*Number of deaths
Source: Balarajan and Bulusu (1990)

that there are large ethnic differences – as measured by place of birth – in mortality from diabetes. Mortality is raised in all the major ethnic groups, with the exception of the Irish. Considerable gender differences also exist within ethnic groups relative to the mortality experience of the corresponding gender in the general population. Caribbean-born women suffer a particularly large excess.

Mortality data reveal only part of the impact of diabetes. Evidence suggests that death certificates under-report the extent of diabetes-related death in Britain (Cruickshank, 1989d). Moreover, since diabetes is a chronic disease with which a number of secondary diseases are associated, its prevalence within particular populations is as important an indicator as the deaths it causes directly. Several community studies have provided prevalence estimates for diabetes within minority ethnic populations (Mather and Keen, 1985; McKeigue *et al.*, 1991; 1988; Simmons *et al.*, 1989). Some of their main findings are displayed in Table 3.5.

In general, the prevalence estimates shown in the table are in keeping with the mortality patterns described above, although no data on prevalence among Caribbean women are presented. McKeigue's figure for Caribbean men is rather higher than findings in Wolverhampton among known Caribbean diabetics (both men and women), although the discrepancy might be accentuated by methodological

Table 3.5 **Estimated community prevalence of diabetes**

Study	Location	Age	Ethnic Group*	Males Age-adjusted prevalence (%)	N†	Females Age-adjusted prevalence (%)	N†
McKeigue *et al.* (1991)	W. London	40-64	(European	4.8	1,515	2.3	246
			(S Asian	19.6	1,421	16.1	291
			(Afro-Caribbean	14.6	209	–	–
McKeigue *et al.* (1988)	E.London	35-64	(Bangladeshi	22.0	74	23.0	41
			(Non-Asian	10.0	88	4.0	41
Simmons *et al.* (1989)	Coventry	20-79	(White	2.8	831	4.3	879
			(Asian	11.2	1,087	8.9	1,196

Study	Location	Age	Ethnic Group*	Males and Females prevalence (%)	N†
Mather & Keen (1985)	W.London	25-29	(European	0.3	1,685
			(Asian	0.2	3,735
		35-39	(European	0.5	1,470
			(Asian	1.7	1,920
		45-49	(European	0.9	1,575
			(Asian	6.0	1,705
		55-59	(European	1.7	1,905
			(Asian	9.0	975

* As described in respective studies   †Number in total sample

differences (Odugbesan *et al.*, 1989). The studies by Simmons *et al.* and Mather and Keen indicate that, among South Asians, there is a rather different age and gender profile from that of the white population, with relatively greater prevalence among men and among the younger adults within the 30-64 age bracket. None of the studies found body mass index – a major risk factor – to differ significantly between ethnic groups.

Research in an affluent suburb of Delhi associated with the Southall study found a similar age profile for diabetes prevalence, apparently confirming the existence of an 'ethnic susceptibility' to NIDDM, although the Delhi and Southall populations – comprising mainly Hindus and Punjabi Sikhs respectively – cannot necessarily be regarded as concordant (Verma *et al.*, 1986). Certainly, however, these findings underscore the case for the existence of an additional aetiological factor underlying NIDDM prevalence among South Asians. As the discussion of CHD indicated, the most plausible current hypothesis is the existence of an insulin resistance syndrome associated with central fat deposition. The hypothesis conforms to broader theories of NIDDM pathogenesis, which suggest that highly varying prevalence rates among different populations can be explained through the interaction between environmental (particularly dietary) factors and genetic propensity (B.Williams, 1994).

Such an explanation does not appear to account for high NIDDM prevalence among Caribbean populations, and further aetiological research is required in this case. The explanation offered by Shaukat and Cruickshank (1993) of early insulin deficiency may prove a fruitful line of enquiry. Parenthetically, it is worth noting that a particular form of diabetes among young, non-obese Jamaicans has been identified, although current thinking is that this is simply a manifestation of NIDDM (Cruickshank, 1989d). Such a form has not been identified among Caribbean populations in Britain.

Evidence from Britain and the USA also suggests that, even controlling for differences in diabetes prevalence, some minority ethnic groups – including both South Asian and 'black' populations in Britain – have a greater incidence and poorer outcomes from diabetes related complications, particularly ESRD (Brancati *et al.*, 1992; Clark *et al.*, 1993; Feehally *et al.*, 1993; Roderick *et al.*, 1994). Clark *et al.* (1993) found statistically significant differences in the relative risk of ESRD among admissions to a Birmingham hospital, with both South Asian and 'black' populations experiencing nearly double the white rates. Surprisingly perhaps, diabetes appeared to be a more common cause of ESRD among 'blacks' than among whites or South Asians. Similarly, Roderick *et al.* (1994) found the crude prevalence of ESRD in a sample of patients attending renal units to be nearly three times higher among both "black" (Caribbean and African) and South Asian patients.

Clearly, further research is required into the interaction between genetic, environmental and lifestyle factors in accounting for ethnic differences in the prevalence of diabetes and its secondary complications. In doing so, aetiological investigation may be improved by greater discrimination within the broad national and regional groupings between which patterns of disease are generally mapped. For example, although there appears to be a common experience of raised NIDDM prevalence within disparate South Asian populations, significant differences in prevalence may exist between groups of different religion and social status (Ramaiya *et al.*, 1991), which would yield clues as to the precise role of social and environmental factors. There is also a need to address the issue of undiagnosed diabetes, which may be more prevalent among certain ethnic groups (Simmons *et al.*, 1989).

In order to reduce the prevalence of NIDDM, as with CHD, preventive efforts need to be focused on the control of obesity and advice on diet and exercise among all ethnic groups. Attention should also be devoted to addressing ethnic differences in the progress of secondary complications.

Cancer

Relatively little attention has been devoted to the occurrence of cancer in minority ethnic groups. Even after controlling for age – which is positively associated with the incidence of cancer – mortality from cancer is lower among the main migrant populations, with the exception of the Irish, for both men and women than in the general population of England and Wales (Balarajan and Bulusu, 1990; Marmot *et al.*, 1984). Nevertheless, cancer remains a major killing disease, accounting for around 20 per cent of all deaths in each group (Balarajan and Bulusu, 1990).

Table 3.6 displays SMRs by place of birth for all cancers and for selected cancer sites. These figures have to be interpreted with some caution since many are based on small numbers of deaths. Nevertheless, as well as demonstrating lower overall cancer mortality in comparison to the general population among all minority ethnic groups with the exception of the Irish, the data also point to considerable ethnic differences in mortality from different cancer sites. For example, cancer of the oral cavity and pharynx is higher among those born in the Indian subcontinent and African Commonwealth, whereas cancer of the cervix (and also of the stomach and lymphatic tissue, not shown in the table) appears to be high for populations born in the Caribbean Commonwealth. For most minority groups, cancer of the liver and intrahepatic bile ducts is also raised. The primary cause of this in 'New Commonwealth' migrants is prior infection with the hepatitis B virus, although it may also be

Table 3.6 **Mortality from cancer by selected place of birth and cancer site, age 20-69, England and Wales, 1979-83**

Place of Birth		All Cancers		Breast		Cervix		Skin (Melanoma)		Lung		Lip, Oral Cavity & Pharynx		Liver & Intrahepatic Bile Ducts	
		SMR	N*	SMR	N*	SMR	N*	SMR	N*	SMR	N*	SMR	N*	SMR	N*
All Ireland	M	123	5,323	–	–	–	–	106	40	126	2,195	206	154	152	67
	F	113	4,071	100	934	115	201	90	36	139	798	144	52	82	18
Indian	M	59	1,183	–	–	–	–	29	7	47	346	108	40	170	36
subcontinent	F	68	939	71	267	66	52	31	6	38	74	202	27	104	9
Caribbean	M	65	744	–	–	–	–	22	3	35	151	78	17	317	39
Commonwealth	F	71	590	78	191	112	55	49	6	32	36	102	8	98	5
African	M	71	219	–	–	–	–	32	2	39	37	150	9	552	19
Commonwealth	F	83	195	77	52	38	7	20	1	75	19	409	9	118	2

*Number of deaths
Source: Balarajan and Bulusu (1990)

associated with alcohol consumption in some populations (Marmot *et al.*, 1984). The overall incidence of this cancer is, however, very low.

Despite these variations, mortality from most cancer sites in most minority ethnic groups is lower than for the general population. Indeed, with the exception of cervical cancer in Caribbean-born women, mortality is lower among Caribbean, African and South Asian populations for the four cancers (breast, cervix, skin and lung) for which targets have been set in the National Health Strategy (Secretary of State for Health, 1992). Balarajan *et al.* (1984) found that, in general, low cancer mortality was common to South Asian subpopulations, which they defined as 'Punjabis, Gujaratis and Muslims'.

Information on cancer incidence rather than mortality is scarce, since ethnic group is not routinely recorded in cancer registrations. Studies in Leicester (Donaldson and Clayton, 1984) and Bradford (Barker and Baker, 1990) analysed registration data among South Asians by attributing ethnicity on the basis of name. Again, the small number of cases for some sites precludes definitive conclusions, but their results were broadly consistent both with each other and with the mortality data presented above. The most noteworthy difference is in cancer of the oesophagus, which was found by Donaldson and Clayton to be high relative to the general population.

The Bradford study also compared cancer registrations in the South Asian population with 'home country' registrations using data from the Bombay cancer registry as a proxy for the latter (Barker and Baker, 1990). It was found that age-standardised registration ratios were about 50 per cent lower than the local 'non-Asian' values for South Asian men and women, but slightly higher than those from Bombay. For younger (presumably UK-born) South Asians, however, registrations approximated to the local value.

The methodology of this study and the size of its sample are such as to preclude firm conclusions. Nevertheless, at face value it would seem to point to the familiar 'migrant effect' of intermediate incidence between the old and the new country, with a subsequent trend towards the patterns of the new country. This implies that cancer incidence in the South Asian population will probably increase over time.

Few studies have directly examined exposure to cancer risk factors in minority ethnic groups, although work on smoking behaviour summarised earlier suggests that currently this is less prevalent in most South Asian populations. It has been suggested that the practice of betel-chewing in some South Asian populations may underlie the higher incidence of oral cancer, either through the carcinogenic effect of the betel nut itself or through additives such as tobacco leaves, with which it is frequently combined (Donaldson and Clayton, 1984). However, such an association has not been directly proven, and not all South Asian populations chew betel.

Although most minority ethnic populations enjoy a relatively low incidence of most cancers, specific causal factors underlying this finding have rarely been identified. However, cancer is still a major cause of death among these populations and its incidence is probably likely to increase. Thus, similar strategies of prevention and treatment to those employed in the majority ethnic population are required.

Mental illness

The existence and aetiology of mental illness in minority ethnic populations has become a particularly controversial arena of debate. Indeed, Sashidharan and Francis refer to a "major crisis within British psychiatry around the issue of race" (1993, p.98). This crisis has been played out largely with regard to the observation of apparently high rates of schizophrenia among Caribbean populations in Britain. Another focus of attention has been high rates of suicide and parasuicide (ie. attempted suicide and self-poisoning) among South Asian women. Despite the predominance of these concerns, a much broader literature also exists on the psychological wellbeing of minority groups, although in Britain research has been largely confined to South Asian populations.

This section briefly examines the overall evidence on ethnic patterns in psychiatric illness, before considering in some detail the important debate about the apparent ethnic differences in the incidence of schizophrenia, particularly among the Caribbean population. It goes on to discuss suicide and parasuicide, before examining more general evidence about psychological wellbeing among minority ethnic populations.

Table 3.7 displays age-standardised rates for psychiatric hospital admission in 1981 by place of birth, based on the work of Cochrane and Bal (1989; 1987). Psychiatric admission rates are commonly used as an indicator of the underlying prevalence of psychiatric morbidity, although as it is argued below, the assumption is not always a sound one. Cochrane and Bal were specifically concerned with the mental health of migrants, but for present purposes it is worth noting once again the deficiency of place of birth as a proxy for ethnicity.

Table 3.7 **Age-standardised rates of admission to mental hospitals by selected place of birth, age 16+, 1981**

Place of Birth	Standardised admission rate for all diagnoses per 100,000 population*			Standardised admission rate for schizophrenia & paranoia per 100,000 population+	
	Male	Female	All	Male	Female
England	418	583	504	81	74
Northern Ireland	793	880	838	–	–
Eire	1,054	1,102	1,080	–	–
All Ireland	–	–	–	191	162
Caribbean	565	532	548	278	181
India	317	326	321	77	82
Pakistan/Bangladesh#	259	233	245	105	31

* Refers to admissions in England and Wales
+ Refers to admissions in England
# All diagnoses figures refer to Pakistanis only

Source: Cochrane and Bal (1989; 1987).

Notwithstanding this problem, the table indicates that South Asian migrants have, on average, low admission rates relative to the majority population. In contrast to common conceptions, rates among the Caribbean-born population, although slightly higher, are fairly comparable. They are very much higher among Irish migrants. These patterns have been a characteristic feature of most research findings, although some local studies have found rates among Caribbean populations to be greatly elevated, as well as finding higher rates in South Asian populations (Carpenter and Brockington, 1980; Harrison, 1993; Ineichen, 1987; Rack, 1990). The table also indicates that considerable gender disparities exist in the English and Irish populations, with higher admission rates among women. Among the Caribbean and South Asian populations, however, the pattern is if anything reversed.

Table 3.7 also indicates admission rates for schizophrenia and paranoia; these are severe psychotic disorders involving delusions, hallucinations and a range of other symptoms. Among South Asian populations admission rates are in general low, strikingly so in the case of Pakistani and Bangladeshi women. Rates for Irish-born people are, in keeping with the 'all admissions' rate, more than double the England value. Most striking of all is the schizophrenia and paranoia admission rate for Caribbean-born people. The 'all admissions' rate for this population is only some 9 per cent greater than the England value, but admissions for schizophrenia and paranoia display more than a threefold excess for men and a twofold excess for women.

A number of explanations have been advanced for these findings. Cochrane and Bal (1987) cite evidence to suggest that the low rate for Pakistani women is apparent rather than real, probably reflecting 'exit' from the health care system subsequent to schizophrenia diagnosis. The high rates among the Irish-born mirror the situation in Ireland itself where, according to Williams, the problem:

> is one, not of pathogenic conditions, but of the much greater tendency for psychiatric disorders, once established, to get beyond the care resources of the local family and community. This collapse of community care is common in the areas of Ireland where there is a high proportion of elderly ... and a high rate of celibacy ... These features of rural Ireland are closely connected, but they are in no sense 'traditional'... On the contrary, this pattern was an anguished, costly, but in the end effective demographic response to the trauma of the Great Famine
>
> (1992, p.96).

Drawing upon Cochrane's work in order to explain broad patterns of mental health among the Irish in both countries, Williams infers the existence of a 'twin selection' process in migration, whereby the majority of Irish migrants are positively selected for mental health but a second negatively selected migrant population also exists which has typically high levels of mental illness and little community support. The significance of selection is examined further in Chapter 4.

By far the greatest amount of attention has been paid to schizophrenia in Caribbean populations. Elevated hospitalisation rates for schizophrenic disorder among Caribbean populations has been a consistent research finding in Britain over the past three decades (Bagley, 1971; Cochrane, 1977; Harrison, 1993; Littlewood, 1992; McGovern, 1989; McGovern and Cope, 1987). Recent studies have also shown that rates are, if anything, higher among British-born people of Caribbean origin (Harrison et al., 1988; McGovern and Cope, 1987). However, most studies have involved retrospective analysis of hospital admissions data; this introduces several potential sorts of bias which prevent any inferences being made about the underlying incidence of schizophrenia in the population. Two exceptions are, first, a study in Nottingham by Harrison *et al.* (1988) which – though still hospital based – adopted a more rigorous prospective design, using face-to-face interviews and standard assessment instruments in place of crude admission rate data. This study apparently confirmed the findings of other research, yielding at least a tenfold excess incidence in both the younger (16-29) and the older (30-44) Caribbean populations. A recent study in London by King *et al.* (1994) also used standardised diagnostic criteria prospectively to identify psychotic illness in patients presenting to both hospital and – unusually – community-based services. Compared to the Harrison *et al.* study more accurate denominator data from the 1991 Census was available to calculate community incidence (see Chapter 4 for a discussion of denominator bias). The researchers also found an excess incidence of schizophrenia in the Caribbean population, although it was not as marked as that in the Harrison *et al* study.

These broad findings have been supplemented by important research detailing differences between ethnic groups in the pathways to care and the type of care received. For example, it has been shown that Caribbean patients are:

- Less likely to have been in prior contact with a GP and more likely to have been referred by the police or detained by them in a 'place of safety' under the 1983 Mental Health Act (Cope, 1989; Moodley and Thornicroft, 1988).

- Up to three times more likely to be admitted or detained compulsorily under the 1983 Mental Health Act (Cope, 1989; Littlewood, 1986).

- More likely to be diagnosed as violent and to be detained in locked wards, secure units and special hospitals (Cope, 1989; Moodley and Thornicroft, 1988).

- More likely to receive more 'physical' treatments – such as major tranquillisers and electro-convulsive therapy in cases where it does not appear to be indicated – at a more intensive level and without earlier recourse to less radical therapy (Littlewood and Cross, 1980).

- More likely to be seen by junior staff (Littlewood and Cross, 1980).

Moreover, these findings conceal even greater differences at a more detailed level. For example, Cope (1989) reports compulsory detention rates for male Caribbean migrants aged 16-29 in Birmingham under Part II of the 1983 Mental Health Act (ie. civil commitment instigated by a social worker or relative) to be seventeen times in excess of the admission rate for whites of the same age. Admissions under Part III (for patients involved in criminal proceedings or under sentence) for male migrants in this age group display a twenty-fivefold excess. Although less dramatic, these patterns repeat themselves for men from other age-groups, women, British-born individuals and when first admissions only are considered. Elevated rates of psychiatric admission and psychotic diagnosis among Caribbean populations were insufficient to explain the excess.

It is important to emphasise that these findings have not been replicated by all research studies, and the small numbers of individuals typically involved in any one study make it difficult to discern whether they constitute an overestimate or an underestimate of the true picture. Nevertheless, taken together they indicate clear ethnic differences, with Caribbean patients experiencing less voluntary contact with mental health services, less control over their treatment and perhaps harsher treatment regimens.

How can these patterns of admission and treatment be explained? At the broadest level, analysts are divided between those who regard the data as faulty and misleading, and therefore remain unconvinced that any real differences in incidence exist, and those who think that the data genuinely reflect the existence of a schizophrenia epidemic among the Caribbean population, and seek explanations accordingly.

Commentators of the former school have provided powerful methodological critiques of much of the empirical research cited above. For example, Sashidharan and Francis (1993) emphasise the deficiencies of hospital admissions data, since they may reflect as much the attitudes and policies of health professionals as any underlying incidence of disease. Also, in view of the differences in pathways to care outlined above, these authors suggest that the 'filters' by which Caribbean people come to the attention of acute psychiatric services are different from and probably weaker than those experienced by whites, thus increasing admissions. They point to the uncertainties that exist in defining a case of schizophrenia, and argue that these may lead to differential overdiagnosis in Caribbean patients. They emphasise the difficulties in obtaining accurate data on the at-risk population, showing how small errors in both case identification and population counting can lead to widely differing results. They also point out that most studies have been undertaken in large inner-city hospitals, where the possibility of differential ethnic 'drift' of mentally ill patients into the inner-city cannot be excluded. Finally, they make the criticism, familiar from research in other areas, that most studies fail to control for other relevant differences between ethnic groups, particularly socioeconomic status, which is also associated with the incidence of schizophrenia. As Francis (1993) argues, the aetiology of schizophrenia is conventionally particularised in individual pathology, rather than sought in the broader fabric of social and environmental conditions.

The latter point is well taken, but it may be possible to overstate the extent to which socioeconomic status underlies ethnic differences. Although a strong association exists, British evidence suggests that it may arise largely through social selection. In other words, it may be factors associated with the disease itself which lead schizophrenics to experience lower socioeconomic status, rather than *vice versa* (Cochrane and Bal, 1987). On the other hand, US research employing more sophisticated loglinear techniques to examine the relationship between schizophrenia and social mobility suggests that earlier research based on other methods may overestimate the significance of social selection (Fox, 1990). Clearly there is a need for prospective research which carefully disentangles the relationship between ethnicity, mental health and social circumstances. Such research may also usefully consider whether community resources and attitudes to mental illness and mental health services interact to produce distinctive patterns of service use and illness presentation among the Caribbean population.

Many commentators suspicious of the 'schizophrenia epidemic' hypothesis suggest that the findings summarised above reflect the racism or ethnocentrism of British psychiatry. This criticism can be separated into three broad strands:

- Psychiatrists are racist or prone to invoking racial stereotypes which inform their diagnoses.

- Ethnic or cultural differences in the presentation of disease are such that psychiatrists mistake minor symptoms or delusions for schizophrenia.

- Psychiatry is an instrument of social control which identifies people from minority ethnic groups with 'madness' and, in association with other instruments such as the systems of education and criminal justice, conspires to marginalise and pathologise them.

It would be rash to argue that racist psychiatrists do not exist. Moreover, evidence for the mobilisation of racial stereotypes exists in attitudes to the differential encounters with mental health services between South Asian and Caribbean populations (Beliappa, 1991; Moodley and Thornicroft, 1988) and in data from the 1980s on the hugely elevated rates of the now largely discredited diagnosis 'cannabis psychosis' among Caribbean patients (Littlewood, 1992). More direct attempts to investigate racial stereotyping have involved eliciting responses from psychiatrists to clinical vignettes which differ only in the ethnicity of the patient described. They have yielded equivocal results. Littlewood (1992) found no evidence of differential diagnosis, whereas Lewis *et al.* (1990) showed some racial stereotyping to exist, but found that psychiatrists were significantly *less* likely to diagnose schizophrenia among 'Afro-Caribbeans', and were no more likely to recommend compulsory detention. Since direct racism on a massive scale would have to be invoked to explain the patterns demonstrated above, it would appear unlikely that this factor alone constitutes sufficient explanation.

Nevertheless, it could be that psychiatric practice is effectively racist in misapplying case definition criteria for illnesses abstracted from the experience of the majority ethnic population. For example, Carpenter and Brockington (1980) found that although rates of schizophrenia diagnosis among migrants admitted to hospitals in Manchester were elevated with respect to the 'British' population, a number of the psychotic syndromes typically associated with schizophrenia were no more common. Thus, they suggested that much of the excess incidence of schizophrenia may arise through non-schizophrenic delusions and paranoia being diagnosed as true schizophrenia. Similarly, it has been argued that the experience of stress among Caribbean populations may manifest itself in brief psychotic episodes, in contrast to depression and neurosis among the majority ethnic population (Cochrane and Bal, 1987; Rack, 1982). Such differences could conceivably lead to misdiagnosis by predominantly white psychiatrists. More recent studies employing standardised case definition criteria such as DSM-III have produced no evidence of misdiagnosis (Harrison *et al.*, 1988; Harvey *et al.*, 1990; McGovern and Cope, 1991), but US research has shown that even the use of such standardised criteria does not necessarily prevent 'race' and gender stereotypes from affecting diagnosis, most notably in disproportionately allocating black men to the most serious and most violent categories of illness (Loring and Powell, 1988). Significantly, however, other US research which used DSM-III to reclassify records of 1,023 patients originally diagnosed under an earlier and less stringent nosological system found that 64 per cent of black patients who had been diagnosed schizophrenic failed to meet DSM-III criteria for the condition, compared to only 21 per cent of white patients (Craig *et al.*, 1982). Thus, while the use of criteria such as DSM-III may not preclude the possibility of misdiagnosis, earlier diagnostic systems – upon which much of the evidence about ethnic patterns of schizophrenia incidence depend – may be still more seriously flawed.

Aside from these doubts about the possibility of constructing diagnostic instruments that can be applied in a truly standard manner, interpretation of the divergent findings outlined above on schizophrenia symptomatology depends to some extent on broader judgments about the cultural specificity of mental illness. For example, Kleinman (1987) argues that the rigid application of diagnostic criteria based on models of mental illness in one population to another for whom it lacks any coherence constitutes a 'category fallacy' which obscures ethnic differences in the experience of illness. He criticises cross-cultural research on the incidence of schizophrenia for arbitrarily choosing to emphasise cultural similarities, rather than manifest cultural differences. Similarly, Littlewood and Lipsedge (1989) have shown that misdiagnosis may occur in the absence of a dynamic understanding among psychiatrists of the cultural and religious iconography of different ethnic groups.

Following the logic of these arguments, it could be that ethnocentric assumptions are implicit even in the standardised diagnostic instruments employed in recent studies. However, the fact of migration and the apparent epidemic in the second generation undermines any hypothesis of simple and persistent cultural difference. Indeed, Harvey *et al.* (1990) suggest that some convergence of symptomatology has occurred over the last two decades. Moreover, such a position has been attacked, both by psychiatrists who point out that its proponents have failed to define alternative culturally-specific criteria (Cope, 1989) and by activists who argue that essentially multicultural propositions of this sort constitute a new form of racism which reifies black culture and deflects attention from structures of continued oppression (Black Health Workers and Patients Group, 1983).

The third strand of criticism, that psychiatry – along with a range of other social institutions – applies a medicalised 'technology' of social control to disempowered social groups, including minority ethnic populations, thereby pathologising them and reproducing their disadvantage, owes much to the pioneering analyses of the social historian Michel Foucault (1979; 1967), and is widely made by commentators on the mental health of minority ethnic populations in Britain (Black Health Workers and Patients Group, 1983; Fernando, 1991; Francis, 1993; Knowles, 1991; Mercer, 1986; Sashidharan and Francis, 1993). In view of the dubious history of psychiatry and its antecedents in legitimating racism and slavery (Fernando, 1992; Littlewood and Lipsedge, 1989), and the persistence of other forms of oppression, the argument is a plausible one. One need look no further than the evidence cited above on police referral, compulsory detention and treatment regimens to discern a pattern of systematic social control over the Caribbean population. Discussing psychiatry's 'medicalisation of racism', Francis suggests:

> *In a context when black people are criminalized and overrepresented in the criminal justice system, we are being decanted from the penal justice system to psychiatry in disproportionately high numbers compared to other groups*

(1993, p.200).

In consequence, Francis emphasises the need to examine the processes by which Caribbean people are admitted to hospital rather than a reductive focus on the nature of their apparent disease. But despite this clear empirical agenda, and the observation that "there is overwhelming evidence that psychiatry generates racist effects" (Knowles, 1991, p.178), writers in this tradition have failed significantly to extend their work into empirical analysis of how such a system of social control operates. As Littlewood has suggested:

> *It has proved easier to discuss the history of post-colonial psychiatric theory using a Foucauldian perspective of power and knowledge than to use empirical studies in teasing out the logic of current decision-making, medical education and perception, and patterns of psychiatric services*

(1992, p.143).

Moreover, echoing Gilroy's (1990) critique of anti-racist theory, Littlewood (1992; 1986) suggests that the social control perspective has failed to provide a convincing theoretical discussion of the potentially complex ways in which psychiatry interacts with other social institutions, tending to lapse into unitary conspiratorial theories, which, incidentally, are very much at odds with the subtlety of Foucault's notion of power. Nevertheless, the social control perspective is important in refusing to particularise minority ethnic mental health issues, linking them instead to a broader analysis of the social significance of 'race'. As Littlewood puts it:

> *if psychiatry no longer seems to contain any specific theories linking black people to insanity, neither does it diminish the increased number of blacks in custodial institutions…if there is a general bias in society which places blacks in these situations, white psychiatry merely reaffirms it*

(1992, p.147).

Although the evidence for the artefactual nature of excess schizophrenia incidence is equivocal, proponents of the 'schizophrenia epidemic' position have fared no better in marshalling convincing empirical support for their hypotheses. Three explanations for genuine ethnic differences in the incidence of schizophrenia could be offered. First, there is the possibility of an underlying genetic vulnerability. The biological basis of schizophrenia remains a controversial topic (Rose *et al.*, 1984). However, although it may be the case that individuals *within* a given population have varying genetic predilections for the disease, few researchers have been prepared to argue that systematic differences exist *between* populations.

Second, the explanation could lie in some factor or factors associated with the process of migration. Possibilities include greater environmental exposure to psychogenic influences in the country of origin, negative health selection whereby people who are most likely to suffer from mental illness are also most likely to migrate, or some 'maladaptive' response to the experience of migration. There is little evidence to support any of these hypotheses in the case of Caribbean migrants. The incidence of schizophrenia in Jamaica, the home country for the majority of Caribbean migrants to Britain, is not consistent with elevated rates in Britain (Hickling, 1991). There is some general international evidence to suggest that negative selection and 'maladaptation' occur among immigrants (Furnham and Bochner, 1986; Hull, 1979), but this has not been shown to be the case for Caribbean migrants to Britain, and is not consistent with other evidence concerning their health status and social profile. Nor are migration-based hypotheses supported by apparently high rates in the second generation.

Finally, it could be that the experience of racism and disadvantage in Britain has caused a genuine epidemic of schizophrenia in Caribbean populations. Glover (1989) suggests this possibility on the indirect basis of an observed 'unhealthy cohort effect' among young men. Direct evidence for the impact of racism upon mental health is scarce. US research indicates that 'race' may be independently associated with poorer psychological wellbeing after controlling for socioeconomic factors, suggesting a role for racism in the experience of mental health (Kessler and Neighbors, 1986), although this is contested (Cockerham, 1990), and there is a considerable gulf between the experience of poor psychological wellbeing and a severe illness such as schizophrenia.

In Britain, Bagley (1971) examined the attitudes of Caribbean and white schizophrenics and a non-schizophrenic Caribbean comparator group, finding that the Caribbean schizophrenics had significantly higher 'goal-striving' scores than the other two groups. In other words, they displayed a greater desire for economic advancement and a belief in an open opportunity structure. For Bagley, following earlier US work, this suggested a social cause for schizophrenia, based upon "goal striving in a climate of limited opportunity" (1971, p.295). Unfortunately, work of this sort has not been repeated more recently but, as Cochrane and Bal (1987) suggest, it would seem unlikely that many people of Caribbean origin in Britain today still believe in the existence of an open opportunity structure, and would therefore internalise any lack of economic success. Nor does such a hypothesis appear consistent with generally low rates for other mental disorders among Caribbean populations. The role of racism and other social factors in producing mental disorder certainly warrants further prospective investigation, but it seems doubtful that the experience of racism alone can explain the apparent excess of so severe a condition as schizophrenia among Caribbean populations.

A related argument is that schizophrenia and psychopathology in Caribbean people is an act of cultural resistance to the dominant 'symbolic system' by which pathology is determined (Littlewood, 1992). Clearly, such a hypothesis is difficult to prove and is open to the charge of romanticism, or even, in the view of Francis (1993), racism. Nevertheless, as Littlewood points out, the attribution of mental pathology is in some measure a cultural artifice, and an extensive anthropological literature attests to how subordinate groups appropriate cultural symbols to articulate their own identity (Comaroff, 1985). Again, however, the extent to which this alone could explain such a severe disorder as schizophrenia may be open to question.

In summary, the existence of a genuinely elevated incidence of schizophrenia among the Caribbean population in Britain must be regarded as unproven. It seems probable that at least some of the excess is a methodological artefact, but this does not preclude the possibility of genuine differences. As Sashidharan and Francis (1993) point out, the onus here is upon psychiatric epidemiologists to show that the high rates apparently demonstrated in earlier research accurately reflect underlying patterns of the disease, and there is a need for further carefully designed studies, particularly ones which are community rather than hospital based. At the same time, the issue is nested within broader questions about the definition and aetiology of schizophrenia and about the relationship between racism and mental health. Here, opinions are rather polarised between those who would 'blame the victim' and those who would 'blame the psychiatrist' (Littlewood, 1992). An easy resolution of the debate appears unlikely.

The incidence of suicide and parasuicide among minority ethnic groups has been another issue of concern in the mental health field. Clearly, any potential cause of death raises public health issues, and suicide is no exception. But perhaps more importantly, ever since Durkheim's (1952) classic study of the social patterning of suicide rates, first published in 1897, researchers have attempted to address questions about the impact of migration, new social environments and, more controversially, 'culture conflict' upon patterns of suicide in ethnic and migrant populations.

Table 3.8 displays mortality figures for suicide by place of birth. It indicates that, with the exception of Caribbean-born people and men born in the Indian subcontinent, suicide rates are higher for the main migrant groups than for the general population. Relative to the general population, it also appears that suicide rates among migrants are particularly elevated in younger age groups. Comparisons of suicide between home and new country are complicated by definitional differences, but more

Table 3.8   Mortality from suicide by selected place of birth, England and Wales, 1979-83

Place of Birth	Age 20-49*		Age 20-69				
	M	F	M		F	
	SMR	SMR	SMR	N†	SMR	N†
All Ireland	143	165	126	331	130	197
Indian subcontinent	74	121	71	149	103	84
Caribbean Commonwealth	80	67	80	84	59	30
African Commonwealth	125	132	122	94	126	32

* Number of deaths not available

† Number of deaths

Source: Raleigh and Balarajan (1992)

detailed research appears to suggest that these rates are broadly in keeping with home country levels, even, for example, among long-established Polish migrants with very high suicide rates (Marmot *et al.*, 1984; Raleigh and Balarajan, 1992).

Suicide and parasuicide among young South Asian women have been a particular focus of attention. Table 3.8 indicates that suicide in women aged 20-49 born in the Indian subcontinent is 21 per cent higher than the general female population; in the 15-24 age group there is nearly a threefold difference (Balarajan and Raleigh, 1993). A study by Merrill (1989) found that the incidence of deliberate self-poisoning by South Asian-born men aged 16-34 was up to three times less than that for English-born men; corresponding figures for women showed about a 10 per cent excess for the South Asian born.

These figures are interesting in that they do not appear to be consistent with rates in the subcontinent. Merrill documents two common scenarios among young South Asian women of 'culture conflict' around the issue of traditional or Western-style marriage, and marital problems among women who have recently come to Britain to join their husbands. Although many writers are suspicious of apparent cultural stereotypes such as these (see Chapter 4), Merrill avoids some major pitfalls in suggesting that parasuicide – which must be distinguished aetiologically from suicide – is a Western 'culture-bound syndrome' which young South Asian women have appropriated from their European counterparts, and which constitutes a form of ritual whereby non-dominant members of a social group are able to resolve inevitable intergenerational conflicts. Although further empirical research is needed to clarify the issue, Merrill's argument may help to explain observed patterns of disease without recourse to static or particularly negative stereotypes of minority culture. Some further comments on culture-bound syndromes are made below.

Rather less attention has been paid in the research literature to broader aspects of mental health among minorities, particularly Caribbean populations. Studies of primary care attendance for mental disorder suggest that age- and sex-standardised rates for Caribbean attenders are in general lower than those for whites (Balarajan and Raleigh, 1993; Gillam *et al.*, 1989), although one study found rates for men to be significantly higher (McCormick and Rosenbaum, 1990), and Burke's (1984) community study in Birmingham found a higher prevalence of depression and psychosomatic illness in the Caribbean population.

Similarly, most studies of South Asian populations have found there to be lower or equivalent rates of GP consultation for mental disorders (Gillam et al., 1989; McCormick and Rosenbaum, 1990). Community studies of psychological symptoms using standard assessment instruments have also generally found South Asian – particularly Indian – populations to report fewer psychological symptoms (Cochrane and Stopes-Roe, 1981a,b; Williams et al., 1993). The first of these studies examined psychological symptoms among South Asian populations by place of birth and social class, showing that the gradient from high to low levels of symptoms with increasing social status which obtains in the majority ethnic population was reversed among Indians, a finding that was accounted for by the high level of symptoms among Indian women of high status. Cochrane and Stopes-Roe (1981b) also found differences to exist according to degree of 'acculturation' (see Chapter 4) and spouses' employment status.

In attempting to account for such patterns, Cochrane and Stopes-Roe (1981a) emphasise the possibilities of either social causation or health selection among migrants. Since psychological wellbeing appears to be better in the Indian population despite poorer social circumstances, the researchers favour an explanation couched in terms of a complex process of differential selection between social classes and subsequent post-migration experiences. This is a plausible argument, but it may be premature to rule out the possibility of social causation. First, social class may not be an adequate discriminator of social status among the Indian population (see Chapter 4). Moreover, it could be that a process of cultural 'buffering' exists which protects the psychological wellbeing of the minority population. Halpern (1993) cites international evidence in support of an 'ethnic density effect' whereby minorities which are clustered residentially enjoy better mental health. Research by Ecob and Williams (1991), which found a gradient towards more psychological symptoms from high- to low-density areas of South Asian residence in Glasgow, underscores the need for closer examination in Britain of possible area effects on mental health.

Another important international literature examines the role of social consistency on mental health (Dressler, 1988). This research emphasises that social mobility in both directions can have problematic consequences for mental health, particularly among people from minority populations who are unable to achieve goals or rewards commensurate with their status. As Cochrane and Stopes-Roe (1981a) point out, the fact that high status Indian women share similar backgrounds to those of lower status may indicate that their poorer psychological wellbeing arises precisely because of their social mobility.

In addition to the kinds of research outlined above, there is a considerable body of literature which adopts a more qualitative approach in investigating the psychological wellbeing of minority ethnic populations, particularly South Asian women (Beliappa, 1991; Currer, 1986; Fenton and Sadiq, 1993; Krause, 1989; Pilgrim et al., 1993; Wilson, 1978). These analyses are useful in providing rich detail on the social contexts in which individuals experience poor mental health, and the meanings which such experiences have for them. They also testify to the complexity of interpreting cultural patterns in mental health. For example, some studies speak of the isolation experienced by many migrant South Asian women who find themselves separated from familiar sources of social support, living in poor conditions, suffering racist abuse and unable to develop new forms of social interaction because of peer and male attitudes, and institutions such as *purdah* (Fenton and Sadiq, 1993; Wilson, 1978). On the other hand, extensive networks of social support clearly do exist among minority ethnic populations in Britain, and allegiance to religious and cultural norms can be seen as health-promoting (Currer, 1986; Levin, 1994). As Currer points out, it may be too simplistic to contend that apparent social isolation leads to poorer mental health among South Asian women. Moreover, as research such as Currer's and Krause's (1989) indicates, attitudes to the causes and meanings of mental illness or psychological distress may differ considerably from those of the majority population.

This returns the argument to the work of Kleinman (1987), which was discussed earlier. Is it sufficient to regard culture as merely a mediating factor in the experience of mental illness, or should mental illness be regarded fundamentally within its cultural context? Such a question is germane to the issue of 'somatisation' whereby, it is sometimes suggested, South Asian patients present psychological distress in terms of physical symptoms (Rack, 1982), and to culture-bound syndromes such as 'sinking heart' among Punjabis (Krause, 1989). There is a tendency to regard these phenomena as particular cultural expressions of stable underlying disease processes. Yet, as Kleinman argues, invoking the sociological distinction between 'illness' as experienced by the patient and 'disease' as attributed by clinical models:

> *Depression experienced entirely as low back-pain and depression experienced entirely as guilt-ridden existential despair are such substantially different forms of illness behaviour…that though the disease in each case may be the same, the illness rather than the disease is the determinant factor*

> (1987, p.450).

Such sensibilities underlie Fernando's (1992; 1991) implicit criticism of psychiatry's ethnocentric attitude to culture-bound syndromes. Although it may be conceded that culture produces distinctive health experiences, in 'racialised' societies such as Britain particular majority cultural expressions may often come to be regarded as definitive or paramount. Clearly, the development of a more dynamic understanding of culture and illness is required by researchers and practitioners in mental health (Helman, 1990; Littlewood, 1986), especially in view of the new cultural circumstances occasioned by settlement in Britain.

Fernando states bluntly that "black people in Britain do not trust psychiatry" (1992, p.11), while others criticise the 'racist categories' of violent Caribbean male youths and hysterical South Asian girls which they discern underlying research interests in schizophrenia and parasuicide (Black Health Workers and Patients Group, 1983). From a policy point of view, serious questions must be asked about the extent to which mental health services interact with other areas of public and welfare policy to produce patterns of excessive and involuntary contact which undoubtedly contribute to such mistrust. From the point of view of research, important questions remain about the incidence of schizophrenia in particular, but broader analyses of the mental wellbeing of different ethnic groups are also required.

HIV/AIDS and sexual health

Very little is known about the prevalence and incidence of HIV/AIDS among Britain's minority ethnic populations. At the end of 1992 there were 5,591 reported AIDS cases among white people,

521 among 'black' people and 119 among South Asian people, but reliable prevalence estimates cannot be made (Balarajan and Raleigh, 1993).

On the basis of information reported to the Communicable Disease Surveillance Centre, Balarajan and Raleigh (1993) suggest there may be some ethnic differences in exposure categories. A greater proportion of notified cases among white people have arisen from sexual intercourse between men and from injecting drug use, whereas the main mode of transmission among 'black' people appears to be intercourse between men and women. There is also a higher proportion of mother-to-infant infection. Chrystie et al. (1992) reported that some 2 per cent of women of African origin attending their hospital antenatal clinic were HIV positive, compared with just 0.2 per cent of women of other ethnic origins. They did not specify the meaning of the term 'origin' and, notoriously, the research was linked to press reports of infection from abroad (Haour-Knipe and Dubois-Arber, 1993). Patterns of exposure type among South Asian people appear to be intermediate between the other groups. However, since neither HIV nor AIDS are statutorily notifiable, great potential exists for bias in reporting. Hart and Durante (1991) cite US evidence for ethnic differences in sexual behaviour and condom use which are relevant both to pathways of transmission and preventive strategies. It is unclear whether such differences exist in Britain.

The National Health Strategy has set targets for the reduction of infections from HIV and other sexually transmitted disease, and for the reduction of unwanted pregnancies and conception rates in girls under the age of 16. There is little available information on these areas among minority ethnic groups, although Nicoll and Logan (1989) report ethnic differences in rates of past infection with genital herpes.

External causes

'External causes' refers to mortality or morbidity occasioned by injuries, poisonings and violence (including suicide: see page 71). Very little is known about their occurrence in minority ethnic groups. As Table 3.9 shows, in 1979-83 SMRs for these causes were considerably raised for most migrant populations, particularly the Irish. However, these are not major causes of death and some of the results should be interpreted cautiously since they are based on small numbers. Nevertheless, taken at face value the figures indicate that all groups have higher homicide rates than the general population, and all but women born in the Indian subcontinent and men born in the African Commonwealth have higher rates for accidental poisoning and fire.

Alcohol consumption and low socioeconomic status are major risk factors for injuries. Certainly on the latter count, one may expect raised mortality among minority ethnic groups. In fact, a study based in a London hospital of accident and emergency admissions for child injuries in the home showed that there were no significant differences by ethnic group, but a strong socioeconomic gradient in all groups (Alwash and McCarthy, 1988), particularly as measured by housing tenure, overcrowding and mother's employment status. Other local research, summarised by Balarajan and Raleigh (1993), broadly confirms the finding that socioeconomic and home circumstances are more significant predictors of injuries than ethnicity. However, a study by Williams et al. (1993) of a sample of Glasgow Punjabis aged 30-40 found that a significantly smaller proportion had experienced injuries either at work or at all than an age-matched sample of whites, although this study did not control for socioeconomic status.

Table 3.9 **Mortality from external causes by selected place of birth, age 20-69, England and Wales, 1979-83**

Place of Birth		All External Causes*		Accidental Poisoning		Fire		Homicide	
		SMR	N†	SMR	N†	SMR	N†	SMR	N†
All Ireland	M	190	1,556	272	96	410	74	366	51
	F	159	670	303	78	188	25	215	25
Indian subcontinent	M	85	581	128	42	121	15	261	34
	F	113	266	79	12	214	15	279	24
Caribbean Commonwealth	M	105	352	157	24	248	16	242	15
	F	100	143	160	15	191	8	511	26
African Commonwealth	M	99	279	130	19	98	4	105	6
	F	136	110	132	7	313	7	185	7

* includes suicide   † number of deaths

Source: Balarajan and Bulusu (1990)

Respiratory disease and tuberculosis

Table 3.10 displays mortality figures for diseases of the respiratory system. Overall, the minority ethnic groups – with the exception of the Irish – have about the same or lower mortality than the general population. The two major contributors to respiratory mortality are pneumonia and chronic obstructive lung diseases such as bronchitis, emphysema and asthma. It is the incidence of these chronic obstructive diseases that are particularly low among minority ethnic groups, so much so that Marmot *et al.* (1984) term them the 'British' disease. The major risk factors are smoking, pollution and respiratory infection; Marmot *et al.* ascribe incidence in the majority population mostly to smoking, and among South Asian populations mostly to respiratory infection. They also suggest that risk of death from respiratory disease is largely determined by factors operating early in life, so that migrants from countries with a lower incidence retain their advantage in Britain. Clearly, these patterns may change in subsequent generations.

A study of hospital admissions in Birmingham between 1974 and 1979 (Jackson *et al.*, 1981) produced findings which are slightly at odds with mortality patterns in that bronchitis admissions for South Asians were somewhat higher than for whites, although admissions among Caribbean people were lower; unusually, data collected from a local factory showed that smoking prevalence was quite high among the South Asians, but could not account for excess admissions. Admissions for asthma were also significantly higher for both minority groups. A study of schoolchildren in twenty inner-city areas in 1983 found, after adjusting for age, family size and mother's education, that Caribbean and white children had similar prevalences of respiratory illness, whereas South Asian children had significantly lower prevalences except for asthma (Melia *et al.*, 1988). The main factors associated with respiratory illness among Caribbean and white children were lone-parent families and use of paraffin heaters in the home.

Table 3.10   **Mortality from respiratory diseases and tuberculosis by selected place of birth, age 20-69, England and Wales, 1979-83**

Place of Birth		All Respiratory Diseases*		Bronchitis, Emphysema and Asthma		Pneumonia		Tuberculosis	
		SMR	N†	SMR	N†	SMR	N†	SMR	N†
All Ireland	M	157	1,911	150	783	171	742	330	123
	F	140	918	149	332	122	363	164	30
Indian Subcontinent	M	88	455	74	161	107	201	400	75
	F	104	242	88	70	115	119	1,009	74
Caribbean Commonwealth	M	61	173	48	58	82	84	175	19
	F	101	127	99	44	116	63	112	5
African Commonwealth	M	105	80	73	22	145	43	516	17
	F	106	39	94	12	118	19	557	8

* Does not include tuberculosis

†Number of deaths

Source: Balarajan and Bulusu (1990)

Clearly, patterns of respiratory illness can be quite complex. Closer attention may need to be paid to asthma among minority ethnic populations, and childhood environmental conditions are also an appropriate focus of concern. Nevertheless, there is little evidence of major ethnic differences in this area.

As Table 3.10 indicates, the same cannot be said of tuberculosis (TB). Among women from the Indian subcontinent mortality from the disease in 1979–83 was ten times higher than the general female population, and TB mortality is very considerably raised in all the major migrant groups.

A study of national TB notification rates, in which ethnicity was allocated by physician observation, confirmed the general pattern of the mortality data (MRC Tuberculosis and Chest Diseases Unit, 1985). In 1983 rates among Caribbean people were about four times higher than the white value, and rates among South Asians were about 25 times higher. Among the South Asians the highest rates were for people who had arrived in the country in the previous five years, but even those who had come to Britain more than 20 years ago had a fifteenfold excess incidence. However, South Asians tended to experience the illness in a less acute form than whites.

The issue of TB in the South Asian population has been a controversial one. In view of the very high relative risk it has rightly been the focus of concern among health professionals, but it is sometimes forgotten that TB is not necessarily a major health problem overall: even in women born in the Indian subcontinent, it accounts for only 2 per cent of deaths. Moreover, concern about TB is often negatively associated with fears of infection from abroad and a restrictive view of minority ethnic health issues associated with 'port health' thinking (Bhopal, 1988; Donovan, 1984; see also Chapter 7).

Certainly, TB is highly endemic in the Indian subcontinent and the higher prevalence of the disease among recently arrived migrants may lend support to this line of argument, although an alternative hypothesis for which there is some international evidence might be that migration itself and contact with new populations increases susceptibility (Hull, 1979). It has also been argued that frequent trips to the home country may contribute to a higher incidence in the South Asian population. Other commentators have suggested that poor social and environmental conditions in Britain are largely responsible for raised incidence among minority ethnic populations (Donovan, 1984). The fact that rates are raised for migrant populations from areas such as Ireland and the Caribbean, where TB incidence is low, lends some support to this hypothesis. Whatever the case, the proven association between poor environmental conditions and TB incidence indicates the need for targeted preventive measures to be taken.

Sickle cell disorders

Sickle cell disorders (SCDs) are inherited diseases which affect the haemoglobin in red blood cells. SCDs include sickle cell anaemia, the milder haemoglobin SC disease and sickle beta thalassaemia. Complications include 'painful crises', stroke, infection, and damage to the bone, eyes and other organs, and life expectancy in sufferers is considerably reduced.

The prevalence of SCDs varies between ethnic groups. Since the genetic trait for the diseases – as opposed to the diseases themselves – may help to protect the carrier from malaria, they are most commonly found in populations whose origins lie in areas where malaria is endemic (Anionwu, 1993). Thus, sickle cell anaemia and haemoglobin SC disease are most prevalent in African and Caribbean populations, while sickle beta thalassaemia also affects people originating from South Asia, Southern Europe and the Middle East. It may be worth pointing out that other inherited diseases, such as cystic fibrosis, are more highly prevalent among North European populations. Clearly, such patterns change over time.

Brozovic et al. (1989) cite an estimate of five sickle cell disorder cases per 1,000 African and Caribbean population in London in 1984. This leads to a minimum estimate of 6,000 cases nationally by the year 2000. Research suggests that the nature of the symptoms in Britain may be different from that in the areas of origin, with a greater incidence of 'painful crises', but relatively little is known about geographical variations in the symptomatology of the disease. Although sickle cell anaemia is very rare in the population as a whole, some studies have suggested that in certain areas it accounts for up to 40 per cent of hospital admissions in the haematology specialty (Brozovic et al., 1989).

Rickets and Osteomalacia

Rickets and osteomalacia are diseases which cause softening and deformity of the bones. They are caused by inadequate intake of vitamin D, which is obtained either in the diet or through exposure to sunshine. Rickets affects children, whilst osteomalacia is an adult disease which has particularly serious consequences for pregnant women.

In the 1970s and early 1980s a number of studies suggested that the prevalence of rickets and osteomalacia was high in South Asian populations in Britain, particularly among children and young women (Donovan, 1984). Both lack of sunshine and a vitamin D-impoverished diet were implicated, and the Department of Health established the 'Stop Rickets' health education campaign among South Asian populations. The identification of the diseases with unhealthy behaviours in these populations and the resulting policy emphasis on individual behavioural change have been the subject of keen debate (see Chapter 7). Certainly, some commentators have stressed the role of the poor environmental conditions with which many people of South Asian origin have to contend in raising the prevalence of rickets and osteomalacia (Donovan, 1984), and some have even questioned whether such a raised prevalence existed, criticising the methodologies of the relevant studies on a number of grounds (Peach, 1984). Whatever the case, these diseases no longer appear to be of major significance among South Asian populations in Britain. More recently Calder et al. (1994) have suggested that hip fracture among elderly South Asians may be exacerbated by vitamin D deficiency. Although there is no evidence that vitamin D deficiency causes a higher incidence of hip fracture, the ageing of the South Asian population is such that the incidence of such fractures is likely to increase in future years.

4 Explaining patterns of health status

Introduction

In previous chapters ethnic patterns in health status were examined and explanations sought largely in terms of the distribution of known risk factors for specific diseases within the relevant populations. However, such approaches rarely explain all of the observed difference, and sometimes account for very little. Often, broader explanatory frameworks have to be invoked in order to account for observed patterns. In fact, specific proximal causes of particular diseases can usefully be thought of as falling into these broader explanatory categories. This chapter devotes specific attention to some of these broader categories, focusing in particular upon:

- artefact explanations

- material explanations

- cultural explanations

- social selection

- the effects of migration

- the effects of racism

- genetic explanations.

These factors are examined with particular reference to explaining differences in health status, but some of the issues are also relevant to the questions of access and utilisation covered in Chapters 5 and 6.

It is important to emphasise that these categories of explanation are not always mutually exclusive. For example, a plausible explanation for the apparently high prevalence of schizophrenia in Caribbean populations might encompass artefact, material and racism-based theories; the insulin resistance hypothesis for CHD incidence in South Asian populations implicates genetic and material factors; the notion that consanguinity in Pakistani populations underlies high rates of congenital malformations combines genetic with cultural factors. Having isolated 'ethnicity' as a category of interest – somewhat arbitrarily, as Chapter 1 showed – researchers must analyse the factors underlying any revealed differences in as sophisticated a manner as possible.

A key task for future research is to examine how interaction between the multiple dimensions of social position may explain ethnic patterns of health status, and how ethnicity itself shapes these interactions. In doing so, it becomes possible to avoid some of the determinism of 'incremental burden' perspectives to disadvantage, which regard individual social experience as fixed by gender, class and ethnic relations (Mayall, 1991), while enabling the particular health experiences of minority ethnic populations to be related to a broader understanding of the nature of ethnic relations in contemporary British society. However, the aim of this chapter is rather more modest. In considering in turn the role of each of the categories of explanation identified above, it seeks simply to illuminate the major analytical contexts within which the health of minority ethnic populations can be framed.

Artefact explanations

In accounting for observed ethnic differences in health, the first question which any careful investigator should ask before seeking other explanations is whether the finding is valid. An artefact explanation would suggest that it is not, and that the results are a product of some aspect of the study itself, such as the manner in which ethnicity or health status are defined or measured.

Certainly, as Chapter 1 indicated, considerable problems exist in finding acceptable methods to operationalise concepts such as ethnicity. Perhaps more significantly, many of the major studies which have examined ethnic patterns in health status fall short of methodological ideals. A key aim of carefully designed epidemiological research is to minimise the possibility of introducing *biases* – systematic errors in the data – so that artefact explanations for any observed effects can be largely ruled out. Unfortunately, it is rarely possible to achieve the ideal, and it could be argued that much of the evidence about ethnic patterns of health experience may be compromised by:

- biases in sampling

- biases in outcome measurement

- biases in adjusting for confounders.

To illustrate briefly some of the relevant issues, many studies produce prevalence estimates for diseases by dividing cases presented in a health care setting (numerator) with overall population figures (denominator), often derived from routine sources such as census data. If there are systematic ethnic differences in utilisation independently of morbidity, then the results will be compromised by numerator biases. Moreover, there is some evidence to suggest that census data may differentially underenumerate minority ethnic populations (OPCS, 1994), thus potentially introducing denominator biases which would overestimate the prevalence of disease relative to the majority population. For these reasons community-based studies are preferable, but here there is evidence to suggest that non-responders among minority ethnic groups tend to have a poorer health experience than responders, so prevalence may be underestimated, and considerable problems remain in finding representative community samples of minority ethnic populations (Chaturvedi and McKeigue, 1994; Ecob and Williams, 1991).

Moving on to outcome measurement, possible biases exist in both mortality data (Lee *et al.*, 1990), and particularly morbidity data. The use of professional assessments of health is particularly prone to bias, but standard health status instruments may also be inadequate if they are not rigorously applied or if they have not been validated across ethnic groups, although it is not always easy to determine what 'validation' might mean in this context.

Finally, apparent ethnic differences may stem from the fact that adjustment for relevant confounding factors can be achieved less successfully for some ethnic groups than others. This is a particularly important point in the measurement of socioeconomic status, and is discussed in the following section.

If for no other reason, the preponderance of retrospective, hospital-based and cross-sectional studies in the literature on ethnic patterns in health is such that artefact explanations must always be given serious consideration. Unfortunately, little systematic empirical attention has been given to their overall significance (Macintyre, 1986). Certainly, methodological shortcomings weaken several specific findings, such as the apparently high rates of schizophrenia among Caribbean populations and the association between consanguineous marriage and congenital abnormalities among Pakistanis (Ahmad, 1994; Sashidharan and Francis, 1993). However, given the consistency of the research evidence in many areas it would be a bold step to assert that no true ethnic differences in health exist. Indeed, the nature of bias is such that it is often difficult to determine whether underestimates or overestimates of the true effect are produced. Nevertheless, artefact explanations are useful in introducing a note of caution into the interpretation of study findings which, as Bhopal (1989) argues, has not always been apparent. It can only be hoped that existing research evidence will be supplemented in the future by more rigorously designed prospective studies.

Material explanations

Material explanations encompass a variety of positions, but all of them emphasise the more or less direct role of economic and environmental circumstances in producing health. Such explanations typically point to the persistence of structural inequalities in society which substantially allocate social position and, it is argued, underlie the social patterning of health.

Certainly, low socioeconomic status and poor health are powerfully correlated. The negative impact upon health of a weak command over material resources – in terms of poverty, unemployment, poor housing and poor occupational and recreational environments – has been extensively documented (Macintyre, 1986; Townsend and Davidson, 1992). In Chapter 1 it was shown that an association existed between minority ethnic status and disadvantage of this sort. Thus, a plausible explanation for poor health in minority ethnic populations is their material disadvantage.

Remarkably, in view of these strong associations, the direct impact of material disadvantage upon the health experience of minority ethnic groups has been little investigated. Many studies, but by no means all, attempt to control for socioeconomic status in examining ethnic patterns of health status, often by using proxy measures such as social class, thus eliminating it as a confounding variable in the relationship between ethnicity and health. Yet few studies have attempted directly to address the importance of socioeconomic factors in *producing* ethnic patterns of health experience. Perhaps this reflects the relative neglect of the ethnic dimension in broader studies of social inequalities in health, as Stubbs (1993) has argued, along with the predominance of a narrower concern for specific diseases in 'ethnic health' research. Whatever the reason, it is clearly important for researchers to pay closer attention to the material determinants of health among minority ethnic populations, and in particular to examine the extent to which they may differ from those of the majority population.

On the latter point, at least two issues are worthy of further consideration. First, as was noted in Chapter 1, the geographical distribution of minority ethnic populations is very different from that of the majority, with concentrations typically in inner-city and major urban environments. If, as some researchers suggest, area of residence is itself an important determinant of health status (Macintyre *et al.*, 1993), it could be that national comparisons of ethnic patterns in health are failing to compare like with like, and obscuring the extent to which common determinants of health status exist across ethnic groups at the local level. It is noteworthy that the OPCS publication *Mortality and Geography* (Britton, 1990), the most authoritative source of information in this regard, provides analysis of area differences in general mortality and national differences in migrant ('ethnic') mortality, but does not examine area differences in mortality by ethnicity. As D. Williams *et al.* (1994) have shown in the USA, some apparent 'ethnic' differences in disease prevalence can in fact be explained geographically, the ethnic effect merely representing differences in patterns of residence.

Second, US research has also shown the importance of distinguishing between income, social status and wealth. In the USA, at every level of income black people have less wealth than whites, with a consequently poorer call on material resources. The possible significance of this phenomenon for the health of minority ethnic populations in Britain has not been investigated. Moreover, potential ethnic differences in the *distribution* of resources, regardless of their absolute level, may also be important. If ethnic differences exist in the nature of intergenerational, intrafamilial and community transfers of material or human resources or support, this again may have a significant impact upon ethnic patterns in health status.

Much more work needs to be done on these issues but, although few commentators would deny that material factors have a major bearing on ethnic patterns of health experience, purely material explanations do not always appear to fit the empirical record particularly well. An obvious example discussed earlier is the large difference in postneonatal mortality rates between the infants of Pakistani- and Bangladeshi-born mothers. Another example cited by Marmot *et al.* (1984) is that of greater mortality among Caribbean-born men of higher social class compared to those of lower class. Indeed, Marmot *et al.* argue more generally that, for many diseases, social class is a poorer predictor of mortality among minority ethnic groups than for the majority population. They take this to be evidence that material factors alone are insufficient to explain ethnic differences in health status, and suggest alternative cultural and selection hypotheses.

While this may well be the case, it is also possible that conventional measures of socioeconomic status or material disadvantage are inadequate to capture the experience of minority ethnic groups. For example, the Coronary Prevention Group (1986) argued that many self-employed South Asian people who would be occupationally classified into higher classes have a lifestyle more akin to that of lower classes. Moreover, the routine classification of women according to their husband's social class – though problematic for all populations (Benzeval *et al.*, in press) – may introduce even more serious distortions among minority ethnic populations, where gender differences in social and occupational status are often starker still (Ahmad, 1994).

More direct measures may also fail to take minority ethnic experience fully into account. For example, housing tenure is often used as a direct indicator of socioeconomic status, but although the proportion of home owner-occupiers is higher in most South Asian groups than among whites, evidence suggests that the quality of this accommodation tends to be poorer (Jones, 1993). On the other hand, the work of Ahmad *et al.* (1989b), discussed in Chapter 2, showed how consideration of unemployment levels could substantially modify apparent ethnic differences in health status. This underlines the case for multiple adjustment of socioeconomic factors in examining ethnic dimensions of health. Centerwall's (1984) US study of domestic homicide provides a good example. Even after controlling for education level, blacks suffered higher levels of homicide than whites. However, successive adjustment for income, purchasing power and residential overcrowding removed the excess. Thus, any single adjustment for socioeconomic status preserved a 'racial' difference – which may have led investigators to postulate a black 'culture of violence' – but multiple adjustment showed the excess to be essentially a socioeconomic effect.

The effects of migration may also undermine the utility of conventional measures of socioeconomic status. As Andrews and Jewson (1993) have argued, the experience of material conditions in Britain for migrants will – in contrast to British-born residents – be mediated by a pre-existing store of experiences and expectations of conditions in the new country. Regardless of whether these render experiences in Britain more positive or more negative, the effect may be to change the impact of material circumstances, as conventionally measured, on the health experience of migrants. Moreover, the impact of fetal or childhood material circumstances abroad may have longer-term health effects which confound cross-sectional measures of socioeconomic status.

Another relevant argument, put most forcefully by Navarro (1990; 1989) is that, as a result of the 'racialisation' of disadvantage, people of minority ethnic status within any particular socioeconomic stratum will be disadvantaged relative to their white counterparts, a point which was made earlier with regard to income and wealth. Certainly, there is much documentary evidence of poorer conditions among minority ethnic groups across social strata, from more nightshift work in unskilled 'black' as compared with white workers (Amin and Oppenheim, 1992) to a concentration of South Asian doctors in junior grades and unpopular specialties (British Medical Journal, 1992).

From a methodological point of view, the 'racialisation' of disadvantage suggests that it may be inadequate simply to control for socioeconomic status when examining ethnic patterns in health, on the assumption that the 'effects' of socioeconomic status and ethnicity upon health are additive. As Kessler and Neighbors (1986) have suggested in investigating 'racial' differences in psychological distress in the USA, research which fails to consider possible higher-level interactions between ethnicity and socioeconomic status will, in these circumstances, tend to overestimate the significance of the latter at the expense of the former. Investigation of this point in other settings would clearly be worthwhile.

The US literature appears to be divided as to whether socioeconomic status alone can account for 'racial' disparities in health, with empirical evidence which both supports the proposition (Logue and Jarjoura, 1990; Rogers, 1992) and contradicts it (Otten et al., 1990; Sorlie et al., 1992). From a public health or planning viewpoint perhaps it does not much matter, since the important thing is simply to know what the absolute level of 'need' is. But in order to develop a better understanding of the determinants of health status among different ethnic groups so that improved policy interventions can be devised, it is important to seek to understand the extent to which material circumstances underlie ethnic patterns in health status and the way in which they do so. Material factors are almost certainly a major determinant. Arguably, however, rather little progress has so far been made in Britain in pursuing such questions, and – as the discussion above demonstrates – fundamental issues remain to be resolved about how best to do so.

Cultural explanations

It is commonly suggested that differences between ethnic groups in cultural values, beliefs and lifestyles may explain patterns of health status and utilisation. In the preceding pages, health issues such as consanguinity and smoking behaviour were discussed which clearly implicate such factors. However, 'culture' is often invoked much more broadly as a convenient category of explanation to account for ethnic diversity in patterns of health experience, particularly where other explanations appear to fail. Unfortunately, such arguments are rarely developed, and culture is typically invoked in a residual and undifferentiated way as an independent variable, with little effort expended in postulating which particular aspects of culture may be injurious or protective of health (see, for example, Marmot *et al.*, 1984). Where hypotheses have been advanced, there has been an unfortunate proliferation of stereotyped assumptions about behaviour and beliefs, communication and family structure which is little supported by empirical research, reflecting broader historic positions in social science (see, for example, summaries by Ahmad, 1993b; Donovan, 1984; Lawrence, 1982b; Pearson, 1983).

As these and other writers have argued, in 'racialised' societies cultural practices and values among minority ethnic populations which differ from the majority 'norm' are all too easily regarded as deviant or pathological, and there is but a small step from 'cultural' to clinical pathology. Littlewood has argued that:

> *'Pathology' is always a measure of difference, and medical understanding of 'culture' was simply one of cultural difference, easily accessible as a checklist of discrete items such as religious belief, family pattern, goals and expectations in Britain, each of which could be argued to associate statistically with pathology one way or the other*
>
> (1992, p.142).

Such ethnocentrism is compounded by the very decision to compare minority experiences with the supposed norm of the majority. Indeed, as was remarked in Chapter 2, there has been a striking failure to analyse the health experiences of white populations in 'ethnic health' research. In her discussion of ethnic patterns in the delivery of maternity care, Bowler points out that:

> *the construction of 'normal' motherhood is based on white middle class behaviours … studies have omitted black and working class mothers from studies of normal processes, but included them in studies of deviance*
>
> (1993, p.169).

Arguments of this sort underpin the powerful critiques of unitary cultural explanations for ethnic patterns in health which a number of writers have produced (see, for example, Ahmad, 1993b; Donovan, 1984; Francis, 1993; Knowles, 1991; Littlewood and Lipsedge, 1989; Pearson, 1983; Stubbs, 1993). In emphasising the role of a unitary or stereotypical and unchanging 'cultural difference', these writers argue that such explanations mislocate the source of ethnic differences in health within minority culture itself, thus 'blaming the victim' and, wittingly or not, diverting attention from more pressing social factors such as material deprivation and racism. Indeed, Francis goes so far as to identify cultural explanations with racism itself:

> *To cite 'culture' … is merely to divert attention from the real objects of concern. Culture, in fact, is a problem of racism rather than the means of its analysis*
>
> (1993, p.193).

Despite such arguments, if culture is to be understood not as Littlewood's 'checklist' but dynamically, as an active social process linked to broader socioeconomic patterns, then presumably it must be legitimate to consider how it may affect health. Indeed, a developing North American literature has begun to demonstrate the salience of culture for an understanding of health experience, pointing to the multifaceted and culturally-determined nature of the expression and experience of illness, the resources mobilised to address it and the role of community and religious processes in promoting health (Anderson et al., 1989; Brown et al., 1992; Dressler, 1993; Kleinman, 1987; LaVeist, 1993; Levin, 1994; Rushing et al., 1992; D.Williams et al., 1994; Williams et al., 1992; Worobey and Angel, 1990).

For example, Williams et al. (1992) have shown that ethnic differences exist in the consequences for mental health of divorce or a spouse's death, suggesting that marriage may have different social meanings or engender different social relationships within different ethnic groups. Perhaps more pertinently, a considerable body of work exists, both in the health field (Worobey and Angel, 1990) and more generally (Henry, 1992; Stack, 1974) which argues that cultural patterns can be understood to a considerable degree as a response to environmental and material constraints. For example, Thorogood (1989) suggests – albeit speculatively – that the attitudinal differences she discerned towards health care between Caribbean women in Britain and the general population arises as a consequence of their historical–political experience of oppression. Thus, it should not necessarily be a surprise that cultural patterns affecting health vary between ethnic groups. However, attempts to map this variability and its consequences for health are complex and not always consistent with the 'adaptive' model of cultural patterns outlined above (see, for example, Brown et al., 1992). To the extent that culture must entertain some degree of autonomy from material circumstances if the 'adaptive' model is to represent anything other than an unconvincingly deterministic materialism, such inconsistencies are perhaps inevitable. Clearly, although the 'adaptive' model of culture is an appealing one, it requires further elaboration of both a theoretical and empirical nature.

In Britain, with a few noteworthy exceptions (Currer, 1986; Donovan, 1986; Fenton, 1985), attempts to examine the beliefs, values and behaviours of individuals and groups within particular ethnic populations in a proper context for developing an understanding of their health experience have been rare. It is possible that this deficiency has arisen as a consequence of the very success of the critiques described above in problematising the use of culture to explain ethnic patterns in health experience, with the legitimate role for a properly conceived concept of culture rejected along with the manifest deficiencies of unitary cultural explanations. This rather mirrors the broader debate mentioned in Chapter 1 between anti-racism and multiculturalism. Clearly, approaches which fail to look beyond 'cultural difference' are severely limited, but an a priori choice of material and racism-based theories to the exclusion of any role for cultural explanations may not be much more satisfactory.

US researchers, with fewer inhibitions about invoking a notion of culture, have attempted to examine the direct impact of 'acculturation' – ie. adjustment to the cultural norms of the host country – on the health of Mexican migrants. Hazuda et al. (1988) found acculturation, as measured by a multidimensional index based on linguistic preferences, social interaction and attitudes, to be associated with a lessening in the prevalence of obesity and diabetes independently of socioeconomic status. By contrast, Scribner and Dwyer (1989) found acculturation to be independently associated with poorer birth outcomes. In Britain, Cochrane and Stopes-Roe (1981b) found acculturation to be associated with lower levels of psychological disturbance among Indian migrants.

It is difficult in studies such as these to disentangle acculturation from other possible material or selection effects. However, assuming that a genuine relationship exists, it begs the question as to whether acculturation represents nothing more than increased exposure to host country risk factors – the familiar 'migrant effect' – or to psychosocial processes associated with the dynamics of culture (Dressler, 1988; Nickens, 1990). In neither case is it necessarily implied that the 'native' culture is health-damaging. Further clarification, both theoretical and empirical, is required in order to understand the role of acculturation.

In summary, there is probably a legitimate role for invoking cultural factors in explaining part of the observed ethnic patterns in health experience in Britain. At present, however, such explanations remain little developed. Earlier unitary explanations which tended to isolate culture from society and blame the former for the ills of the latter have been widely and convincingly criticised. What is now needed are more refined approaches to the dynamic interactions between culture, socioeconomic status and health experience, for which recent North American research can provide some useful pointers.

Social selection

Theories of social selection reverse the intuitive causal pathway from social position to health, suggesting that it is health itself which allocates social position. For example, if people become ill and unable to work their social and economic status is likely to decline, thus producing an association between poor health and low socioeconomic status. The role of selection in accounting for socioeconomic differences in health has been much debated (Blane et al., 1993). Clearly, with reference to ethnicity, an individual's ethnic group is entirely independent of their health status. Nevertheless, social selection is of some relevance in considering migrant health. It is possible that migrants will, in comparison to their peers, be either positively selected for health – as with ambitious young people looking to improve their prospects by travelling abroad – or negatively selected, as with socially marginal, perhaps mentally ill, people moving on from communities which cannot support them.

It has been suggested that both types of selection may operate among migrants to Britain. For example, Marmot et al. (1984) postulate the existence of positive health selection for several migrant groups on the basis of a better mortality experience than that which prevails in the country of origin, an effect which appears to 'wear off' over time. Certainly, positive health selection may explain the low SMR for men born in the Caribbean Commonwealth, in spite of their generally poorer socioeconomic status. On the other hand, Marmot et al. postulate negative health selection among Irish migrants to explain their high SMR, although the study by Raftery et al. (1990) summarised on page 38 casts some doubt upon this hypothesis. The work of, inter alia, Cochrane and Stopes-Roe (1981b) and Williams (1992) indicates the potential complexity of such issues, suggesting the existence of simultaneous positive and negative health selection in distinctive subpopulations.

Although selection is often invoked to explain patterns of migrant health, the empirical evidence for it is rather scarce, apart from the somewhat indirect results of Marmot et al. (1984). Almost by definition, migration involves a process of social selection, but it does not necessarily follow that health selection also occurs. Indeed, in some forms of migration, such as the enforced departure of South Asians from East Africa, there is no particular reason to suppose that health selection should occur.

One of the few studies to examine the case for health selection in any depth is Williams' (1993) account of the impact of length of UK residence on an age-controlled sample of Glaswegian Punjabis, which was discussed in Chapter 2. In examining the possibility that the more recent migrants – who appeared healthier – were positively selected for health, he assessed current evidence that their height, body mass index, blood pressure, lung function and mental health were superior to that of the Punjabi population from which they originated. He concluded that this was not the case.

To corroborate a hypothesis of health selection, detailed research is required which examines the circumstances of particular groups of migrants in both their old and new countries of residence. Such studies are few and far between, and it would be difficult indeed to extrapolate from them to speculate as to the overall significance of health selection in mediating ethnic differences in health status in Britain. Not only might there be major cohort effects, ie. selective differences between populations migrating from the same region at different times or from different sub-areas (see, for example, Mays, 1983), but interaction with subsequent social and economic experiences in Britain may further complicate interpretation. However, the logic of selection is such that, whatever the extent of its original impact, as length of residence in Britain and the proportion of British-born people of minority ethnic origins increase, its effects are likely to diminish.

The effects of migration

In addition to social selection and cohort effects, the experience of migration itself may have a direct impact on health. Despite major methodological difficulties, international evidence cited by Hull (1979) suggests that migration often leads to poorer health outcomes among the migrants, especially where the new country is 'culturally dissimilar' from the home country (although she does not explain how this is defined). In contrast to the positive health selection hypothesis outlined above, Hull also cites research into the psychodynamics of the decision to migrate, suggesting that migrants are often more marginal individuals with a greater propensity to poor health outcomes. An extensive psychological literature also exists on migration stress and 'culture shock'; international evidence generally suggests that this leads to greater social stress and mental illness among people who migrate (Furnham and Bochner, 1986).

Again, the type of migration is likely to be significant. Enforced migration, lack of economic and social resources upon migration, the move from Third World rural settings to Western urban ones, and long-term separation from families can all plausibly be regarded as stressors. The fact that many of the older South Asian migrants to Britain are doubly displaced, having been refugees during Partition, may also be significant, as is the so-called 'myth of return', that is, the persistent but often impractical thought of returning to the country of birth (Anwar, 1979).

Although her work has been criticised by Lawrence (1982a) among others, Khan (1979b) provides interesting ethnographic evidence of the social stress occasioned by migration among Mirpuri Pakistanis in Bradford. She argues that complex social realignments typically occur which can both alleviate traditional sources of stress and create new ones. The process of migration can alter the balance of gender relationships, the nature of social support and the migrants' views of their possible future, either in Kashmir or in Bradford. Clearly, all of these may affect both health status and the utilisation of services. In addition, the persistence of gender imbalances in the migrant population and economic commitments to the home country may be significant. Another relevant factor which is sometimes invoked is intergenerational conflict between migrants and their British-born offspring. Although James (1993) is probably correct in arguing that this phenomenon has been overemphasised in writings on 'race' in Britain, it nevertheless appears to be the case that such conflict may in some circumstances be relevant to the health experience of both young and older people from minority ethnic populations in Britain (Larbie, 1985; Mays, 1983; Merrill, 1989).

As with several other categories of explanation for ethnic patterns in health experience, it is difficult and perhaps inappropriate entirely to isolate migration effects. Again, however, the direct impact of migration upon the health of minority ethnic populations in Britain will clearly diminish over time with the demise of large-scale primary immigration. Nevertheless, the broader significance of recent migration in material, environmental and cultural terms does not necessarily disappear immediately, even in subsequent British-born generations.

The effects of racism

It is clearly impossible to provide a sensible account of the health experience of minority ethnic groups in Britain without making reference to racism. However, the appropriate status of racism as an explanatory category is less easy to specify. The 'racialisation' of society substantially allocates social and economic positions to people, with consequences for their health and access to health services. This point is often made by those seeking to emphasise social continuities in the health experience of minority ethnic populations (Ahmad, 1992b; Bryan et al., 1985). Clearly, it is vital to recognise that, ultimately, racism largely underlies the allocation of social position, but in order to develop an understanding of ethnic patterns in health experience it may be of more use to identify directly the material factors bearing upon the health of minority ethnic populations rather than identifying a primary aetiological role for racism itself. As Andrews and Jewson have argued:

> rather than being a discrete alternative explanation, racism is better regarded as integral to whatever analysis is developed … The question is not whether racism operates but when, where and how. The need, once again, is to disentangle the various and divergent experiences of different populations
>
> (1993, p.149).

Nevertheless, racism may also have a direct impact upon health status. For example, evidence was presented in Chapter 2 which linked racial stressors to health outcomes such as psychological wellbeing and raised blood pressure, although these findings are far from conclusive. Clearly, many people who have experienced racism do not necessarily experience these outcomes, but it remains possible that some differences in health between populations can be explained – at least in part – directly by racism. Thus, it may be useful to think of racism as an important *underlying* cause of ethnic differences in overall health experience and a potentially significant *immediate* cause of certain specific outcomes.

Genetic explanations

In view of the troubled history surrounding genetic explanations of 'racial' difference (Gould, 1981; Rose et al., 1984), social scientists are generally wary of invoking genetic factors to explain ethnic differences in health. The lay appeal of genetic explanations lies perhaps in their attempt to seek uniformity within the complex experiences of human populations, as well as in shifting attention from less convenient political realities. Yet, as Kleinman points out, "biology is the source of diversity, not just uniformity" (1987, p.449). Indeed, as Chapter 1 suggested, socially–identified ethnic groups are characterised by enormous within-group genetic heterogeneity and substantial between-group similarities. Moreover, phenotype is powerfully mediated by environmental circumstances as well as by genotype. Unitary genetic explanations for differences in health experience between ethnic groups are therefore generally unconvincing.

Despite the absence of a genetic basis to ethnic difference, genetic factors are germane to certain health issues. For example, the hereditary nature of sickle cell disorders is uncontroversial. As it was suggested in Chapter 3, there is also some evidence for the existence of an insulin resistance syndrome among South Asian populations which is genetically based. Another relevant issue, although controversial, is the possibility that congenital abnormalities among Pakistani infants arise in part as a genetic consequence of the practice of consanguinity. These issues underline the point that the significance of genetic factors lies in their interaction with environmental or cultural processes. Indeed, as D.Williams *et al.* (1994) point out, the essence of genetics is in describing how biological development proceeds through interaction with the environment. Since human populations manipulate their own environments to an unprecedented degree, there is certainly scope for longer-range biological explanations for the development of human differences. Moreover, socially identified ethnic groups often share common geographical-environmental origins, such that genetic explanations for ethnic differences in health may in some cases be relevant, as with sickle cell disorders. However, it is doubtful that such explanations could be of much help in accounting for a significant part of the overall differences in the health experience of contemporary ethnic groups.

5 Health care access and utilisation

Introduction

This chapter examines ethnic patterns in the access to and utilisation of health services. In doing so, a major question is the extent to which minority ethnic populations enjoy equality of access to appropriate health services. However, actual use of services depends upon the desire or ability to use them as well as their availability. Thus, ethnic differences in utilisation may reflect differences in the demand for services as well as inequities in supply.

Many commentators argue that the most appropriate equity goal in the delivery of health services is equal access for equal need (Donaldson and Gerard, 1993). On the other hand, from a public health point of view, differences in the demand for services may lead to undesirable consequences in resultant health outcomes. This normative question is here left to one side. However, a more practical problem must be confronted. Most of the major studies which describe the encounter of people from minority ethnic populations with health services are based upon utilisation data, since this proves an easier research strategy than operationalising a concept of access. But utilisation data alone usually reveal little about the underlying determinants of care-seeking behaviour, or, indeed, about the nature of the care experienced. This requires more detailed, often qualitative, studies about particular aspects of the health care experiences of people from minority ethnic populations.

The approach adopted here is to set out the empirical findings from major studies concerning patterns of health care utilisation among minority ethnic populations. The next chapter then attempts to place them in a broader context by describing research which has addressed the multiplicity of factors, on both the demand side and the supply side, that affect the way people from these populations think about and use health services.

Evidence on ethnic patterns in the utilisation of services is based on a relatively small body of research. Only two major studies have examined the utilisation of acute in-patient and out-patient services (Balarajan et al., 1991; Benzeval and Judge, 1993). Information on the utilisation of GP services is also provided by Benzeval and Judge, and in another study by Balarajan et al. (1989c), as well as the *GP Morbidity Survey* (McCormick and Rosenbaum, 1990). A number of local studies have produced useful additional information on the use of GP and primary services, and of 'alternative' practitioners (Ahmad, 1992c; Gillam et al., 1989; Johnson et al., 1983; McNaught, 1990; Pilgrim et al., 1993).

Researchers have also examined the uptake of preventive services – particularly cervical cytology and childhood immunisation – among different ethnic groups (Baker et al., 1984; Bhopal and Samim, 1988; Bradley and Friedman, 1993; Doyle, 1991; Feder et al., 1993; Hoare, 1993; Johnson et al., 1983), although little has been written about the utilisation of community health services more generally.

A number of the studies discussed below employ multivariate statistical techniques to analyse the factors underlying patterns of utilisation. Box 5.1 explains how such techniques are used.

Box 5.1 **Multivariate analysis**

When two or more factors are thought to be associated with an outcome of interest – such as health care utilisation – multivariate statistical techniques can be used to examine the simultaneous associations between utilisation (the **dependent variable**) and the other hypothesised explanatory factors (the **independent variables**). These techniques are useful where a particular association of interest, such as that between ethnicity and utilisation, is confounded by other factors, such as age and socioeconomic status, since it can be estimated independently of the confounding factors.

In studies of health care utilisation the technique of **logistic regression** is often used, since this can be applied in situations where the dependent variable is only able to take two values, eg. where an individual either used health services or did not use them. Logistic regression analysis yields **odds ratios** for the independent variables included in the statistical model. In essence, these express the probability of the event described by the dependent variable occurring for an individual or case taking a particular value for the independent variable with respect to some reference category, holding all other variables in the model constant.

For example, a model of utilisation including age, gender, illness and ethnicity as independent variables might yield an odds ratio of 2 for the variable 'Pakistani' with respect to a 'white' reference category. This would indicate that people classified as Pakistani are twice as likely to use health services as white people, even after controlling for possible difference in patterns of age, gender and illness between the two categories. Thus, odds ratios greater than 1 indicate a higher probability of utilisation occurring than is the case for the reference category, whereas odds ratios less than 1 indicate a lower probability.

As with other similar measures, **confidence intervals** can be calculated around odds ratios to estimate the range over which the true value for the population from which the study sample is drawn must lie with a specified degree of probability.

Acute services

Balarajan *et al.* (1991) examined ethnic patterns in the self-reported utilisation of acute in-patient and out-patient services using data from the OPCS *General Household Survey* (GHS) aggregated over the years 1983-87. The GHS asks whether the respondent has been an in-patient in the previous year or an out-patient in the previous three months. Balarajan *et al.* analysed a GHS sample comprising some 110,000 individuals below the age of 65, of whom about 3,500 were from minority ethnic groups, which the investigators subdivided into 'Indian', 'Pakistani' and 'West Indian' on the basis of self-reported ethnicity.

The investigators found there to be a U-shaped distribution of acute in-patient utilisation by age for males, with no significant differences between ethnic groups after adjusting for age and socioeconomic status, the latter being measured by socioeconomic group (an occupationally defined classification akin to social class). In other words, utilisation among all ethnic groups was higher in the younger age groups, but then declined with increasing age until rising again in the older age groups. For females there was an inverse U-shaped distribution, consistent with raised utilisation by women of child-bearing age. Pakistani women had significantly higher levels of utilisation than white women in the 16-44 age-group, being more than twice as likely to have used acute in-patient services, even after adjusting for differences in age and socioeconomic status. Older Pakistani women also had higher levels of utilisation, but these differences were not statistically significant. The investigators suggested that the higher levels among younger Pakistani women probably reflected a greater use of maternity services due to higher fertility.

Out-patient attendance was lower than among whites for both males and females in the 0-44 age range for all minority ethnic groups, again after adjusting for age and socioeconomic status. However, these differences were only significant in the case of Indian males and Indian and Pakistani females in the 0-15 age range. In the 45-64 age range, out-patient attendance was higher for all minority ethnic groups, but only significantly so for Indian males and females.

The investigators did not control for ethnic differences in morbidity, arguing that little is known about the ethnic patterns of disease most commonly accounting for hospital attendance, such as breast and genital diseases in women of childbearing age and injuries and poisoning in men under the age of 44. They suggested that one might expect greater out-patient attendance among people from South Asian and Caribbean populations on the basis of their higher incidence of a number of chronic complaints, although they conceded that these groups also experienced a lower incidence of other chronic illnesses.

The inferences which can be drawn from this study are somewhat unclear in the absence of adjustment for morbidity. A more sophisticated model was provided by Benzeval and Judge (1993) in a study of the factors associated with health care utilisation. Using data from some 13,000 individual responses to a national household survey, the investigators adjusted utilisation simultaneously for morbidity (on the basis of self-reported limiting long-term illness and permanent sickness), supply side factors (the local availability of hospital and GP resources), and a range of sociodemographic factors. They found no significant ethnic differences in the utilisation of hospital care.

Little research has been undertaken on the use of hospital services by minority ethnic elders. A study by Blakemore (1982) in Birmingham found that a higher proportion of Caribbean elders had visited hospital in the previous year than either whites or South Asians, for whom rates were comparable. This excess was accounted for by higher utilisation among women. The white sample in this study was, on average, somewhat older than the two minority ethnic groups, which would suggest these findings may underestimate the extent of ethnic difference. In North London, Ebrahim *et al.* (1991) found in-patient utilisation among Gujarati general practice attenders to be up to four times higher than in an age-matched sample of whites.

A US study by Wolinsky *et al.* (1989) examined the determinants of health care utilisation (physician visits and hospital care) among elderly people within five ethnic groups using survey data from 31 metropolitan areas. The investigators adopted the 'behavioural model' of utilisation, which postulates that utilisation is a function of individual willingness to seek treatment on the basis of social positioning ('predisposing' characteristics), the ability to do so on the basis of income and both individual and community – ie. supply side – resources ('enabling' characteristics), and of the need to do so on the basis of individually or professionally assessed illness ('need' characteristics). They estimated for each ethnic group the extent to which utilisation could be explained by each of these three classes of characteristics, as measured by variables such as education (predisposing), income (enabling) and perceived health status (need). Significant ethnic differences were found. In essence, utilisation – particularly physician visits – was more closely related to 'need' among minority ethnic groups. By contrast, among 'Anglo-Americans' it appeared to be less constrained by need and more random. The researchers took this to indicate that treatment-seeking behaviour among minority ethnic groups occurred only when need was relatively greater, thus providing evidence of the existence of inequalities in access to the health care system which, they concluded, are "nested within the larger pattern of inequalities that permeate all social institutions" (1989, p.444). Some of the details of this approach may not be relevant to the British situation. Nevertheless, there is much to be said for this kind of careful modelling of the determinants of utilisation among ethnic groups.

Data on acute mental hospital admissions were presented in Chapter 3 (Table 3.7), since these are typically used as a proxy for the incidence of mental illness. It was shown that, compared to those born in England, utilisation was greatly raised for people born in Ireland, slightly raised for Caribbean-born people and lowered for people born in India or Pakistan.

GP and primary health care services

Balarajan *et al.* (1989c) employed a similar methodology to their acute study in examining ethnic patterns in GP consultations for people under the age of 65, using a GHS sample of about 64,000 people from the years 1983-85 which included some 2,200 people of self-ascribed minority ethnic status. The GHS asks respondents if they have consulted a GP within the previous two weeks. The investigators found that both males and females from all minority ethnic groups consulted most frequently in the 45+ age range, whereas among whites the age group which consulted most frequently was the 0-15 one in the case of males and the 16-44 one in the case of females. The only substantial gender difference within a particular ethnic group was among Pakistanis aged 0-15, where the male consultation rate was 60 per cent higher than the female one.

The investigators computed odds ratios to indicate the probability that people from each minority ethnic group consulted a GP in the previous two weeks relative to the probability of white people consulting (see Box 5.1). These were adjusted for differences in age structure and socioeconomic status between groups. Table 5.1 displays their results, along with 95 per cent confidence intervals. Among the 0-15 age group the confidence intervals for each ethnic group span the value for whites, so no statistically significant differences exist from the white consultation rate in any group in this age range, although utilisation by Pakistani males is substantially raised. In the 16-64 age group, utilisation is raised for males and females of all minority ethnic groups and these values differ significantly for males from all minority ethnic groups and for Pakistani females. Thus, for example, the table shows that Pakistani men are nearly three times as likely to have consulted a GP in the previous two weeks as white men, even after adjusting for age and socioeconomic differences.

Again, since the study did not control for morbidity, interpretation of the results is complex. The investigators suggested that low consultation rates among children from minority ethnic populations were surprising in view of their typically higher infant mortality, which might be expected to have broader implications for child health. They also pointed to the high consultation rate among Pakistani women, in view of their supposed poor antenatal attendance. Of course, high GP consultation does not necessarily imply good antenatal attendance and, as Chapter 2 showed, ethnic patterns in infant mortality and antenatal attendance are complex and unlikely to relate to GP consultation in a simple way.

McCormick and Rosenbaum (1990) describe ethnic patterns of GP consultation from the third national *GP Morbidity Survey*, which is based upon data from twenty-five general practices in England and Wales in 1981-82, and uses country of birth (or parents' country of birth in the case of children)

Table 5.1   **Adjusted odds ratios for GP consultation by ethnic group,** *General Household Survey 1983-85*

Ethnic Group	Age Group	Males		Females	
		Odds Ratio*	95% Confidence Interval	Odds Ratio*	95% Confidence Interval
White	0-15	1.00		1.00	
	16-64	1.00		1.00	
Indian	0-15	0.91	0.60-1.40	0.94	0.60-1.47
	16-64	1.53	1.12-2.09	1.23	0.94-1.61
Pakistani	0-15	1.44	0.88-2.34	0.78	0.43-1.41
	16-64	2.82	1.86-4.28	1.85	1.22-2.81
West Indian	0-15	1.00	0.55-1.81	0.97	0.53-1.77
	16-64	1.65	1.16-2.34	1.17	0.85-1.60

* Adjusted for age and socioeconomic group

Source: Balarajan et al. (1989c)

to allot ethnicity. Again, the study does not control for population morbidity. Consultations were found to be significantly raised for men from the Indian subcontinent, being some 13 per cent higher than the general population after adjusting for differences in age structure, but they were 9 per cent lower for men of 'other' ethnic origin (ie. other than UK, Irish, Caribbean or Indian subcontinent, including 'not known'). No other significant differences existed for either males or females.

Table 5.2 displays age-standardised consultation ratios (calculated in a similar way to SMRs) from the *GP Morbidity Survey* for conditions described as 'serious'. It can be seen that consultations were significantly higher for Caribbean women and for both men and women from the Indian subcontinent. They were also substantially raised for men from the Irish Republic and the Caribbean. Again, men of 'other' ethnic origin consulted significantly less. In view of the similarities between ethnic groups in overall consultation rates, these raised rates for 'serious' conditions may suggest that the populations concerned are generally more likely to seek GP attention only for more serious conditions.

The *GP Morbidity Survey* also breaks down consultations according to diagnostic category. Some of its key findings are as follows:

• After adjusting for age, significantly higher consultation rates exist among Caribbean-born men and women for endocrine, nutritional and metabolic disorders, diseases of the nervous and circulatory systems and for 'symptoms, signs and ill-defined conditions'. In addition, Caribbean-born women have significantly higher consultation rates for neoplasms and skin diseases, whereas Caribbean-born men consult more often with mental disorders.

• Men and women from the Indian subcontinent have higher consultation rates for endocrine, nutritional and metabolic disorders, respiratory diseases, skin diseases, diseases of the digestive and

Table 5.2 **Standardised GP consulting ratios for 'serious' conditions, by ethnic group, all ages, 1981-82**

Ethnic Group		Standardised Consulting Ratio	N*	95% Confidence Interval
Irish Republic	M	117	210	101-134
	F	104	213	90-118
Caribbean	M	120	125	100-143
	F	142	167	122-166
Indian subcontinent	M	141	157	119-164
	F	154	148	130-181
Other	M	82	187	71- 95
	F	92	266	82-104
United Kingdom	M	99	8,318	97-101
	F	99	10,403	97-101
All Groups	M	100	8,997	98-102
	F	100	11,197	98-102

*Number of consultations
Source: McCormick and Rosenbaum (1990)

musculoskeletal systems, and for symptoms, signs and ill-defined conditions. Women from the Indian subcontinent have significantly lower consultations for mental disorders.

• Men and women from the Irish Republic have significantly higher consultation rates for mental disorders and for symptoms, signs and ill-defined conditions.

These findings are broadly consistent with the ethnic patterns in morbidity which were outlined in the previous chapter, the high rates for endocrine disorders probably reflecting a greater prevalence of diabetes. However, the higher consultation rates in all three groups for symptoms, signs and ill-defined conditions certainly warrants further investigation.

The study by Benzeval and Judge (1993) cited earlier examined the factors associated with GP as well as hospital utilisation, on the basis of survey responses to the same question employed in the GHS about GP use within the previous two weeks. Again, the investigators tested a comprehensive model of GP utilisation which included age, gender, socioeconomic status, morbidity and the availability and quality of GP services. After adjusting for these factors, they found that South Asian people were significantly more likely to have had contact with a GP, consulting 1.5 times more often than whites. No other significant ethnic differences were found.

Similar patterns were found in two local studies of the utilisation of GP services. In a household survey of some 2,000 individuals from selected wards in Birmingham, Coventry and Wolverhampton (including a total of about 1,200 'Asian' and 'Afro-Caribbean' people, of unspecified country of birth), Johnson *et al.* (1983) found similar and very high rates of registration with a GP among all ethnic groups. South Asians made the most consultations, with Caribbean people displaying only a small excess over whites, although those who did attend appeared to do so more frequently. On the other hand, whites made more direct use of hospital services, whereas South Asian and Caribbean people always went through their GP. The researchers claimed that higher South Asian consultation rates could be explained simply in terms of differences in socioeconomic status, although they did not demonstrate that this was the case. In contrast to the *GP Morbidity Survey*, they found that South Asians did not present more frequently with 'vague and ill-defined' symptoms. The fact that the West Midlands study, in contrast to the *GP Morbidity Survey*, was based on self-reported presentation of symptoms may be significant in this regard.

Gillam *et al.* (1989) studied ethnic differences in consultation rates among attenders at a single large practice in Brent, northwest London, between 1979 and 1981. As with the *GP Morbidity Survey*, they computed cause-specific consultation rates, adjusted for differences in age structure. They also calculated 'patient consultation ratios' which take account of possible ethnic differences in the number of consultations per episode of illness, thus giving a better picture of underlying morbidity. Their results were broadly similar to those of the *GP Morbidity Survey*, including the finding of higher consultation rates among South Asians – especially men – for symptoms and ill-defined conditions. In some cases, differences existed within particular ethnic groups between standardised consultation and patient consultation rates, indicating differences in the relative frequency of consultation for a particular condition. However, more detailed analysis would be required to determine the causes of these differences.

In Bristol, Pilgrim *et al.* (1993) report similar GP consultation rates among the minority ethnic populations they surveyed to those found nationally in the GHS for all age-sex groups, except for men in the 45-64 age group, where the rate was over twice the national value. Employment status did not appear to account for this finding; the investigators speculated that it might have arisen through sampling bias.

A number of studies have examined the use of GP services by minority ethnic elders (Blakemore, 1982; Donaldson, 1986; Ebrahim *et al.*, 1991; Pilgrim *et al.*, 1993). They have consistently found higher utilisation than appears to be the case among white elders. Most of these studies refer to South Asian populations, but the work of Blakemore and Pilgrim *et al.* is suggestive of similar rates in other minority ethnic populations. Gender-specific patterns of utilisation among elders vary between studies, with higher rates found for both men (Pilgrim *et al.*, 1993) and women (Ebrahim *et al.*, 1991).

Little attention has been paid to the utilisation of community health services by minority ethnic populations. Research in Bristol by Hek (1991) found that fewer Caribbean and South Asian elderly people received care from district nurses than would be expected on the basis of population estimates, a finding which she attributed to lack of information and knowledge about the service among minority ethnic elders and the attitudes of the nurses themselves. Norman (1985) provides some corroborative impressionistic evidence on the basis of discussion with community nurses in Leeds. Ebrahim *et al.* (1991) found use of dental and chiropody services to be lower in a sample of Gujarati elders in North London. On the other hand, in a study among young South Asian women in Glasgow, Bowes and Domokos (1993) found the use of GP, health visitor, school health and dental services to be widespread, a finding which would perhaps be expected since all but one of the respondents had children.

It is sometimes suggested that people from minority ethnic groups make greater use of 'traditional' or 'alternative' medicine. Most attention has focused upon *hikmat* therapies, practised by *hakims* among Indian and Pakistani populations, but few studies have examined the extent of recourse to *hikmat*. Summarising the research evidence, Ahmad (1992c) suggests that it appears to be relatively uncommon in this country, although true rates of utilisation may be higher than that revealed in research. There is also some evidence of the use of alternative therapies among Caribbean populations (Donovan, 1986; Morgan and Watkins, 1988; Thorogood, 1993). In general, however, the weight of the evidence does not suggest that use of alternative therapies significantly affects the utilisation of mainstream services.

Preventive services

Research in this area has focused principally upon ethnic patterns in the uptake of childhood immunisations and cervical cytology. In the West Midlands study described above, Johnson *et al.* (1983) found that uptake of childhood immunisation was higher among both the Caribbean and South Asian populations than the white group. Baker *et al.* (1984) examined differences in the uptake of childhood immunisations in Bradford among children born in 1980. Unusually, they distinguished 'half-Asian' and 'half-negro' groups in addition to the usual Caribbean, Indian, Pakistani and Bangladeshi populations. In essence, they found immunisation uptake to be significantly better in the Indian group, in terms of both the proportion of children immunised and age at immunisation. Pakistanis also had higher levels of uptake, while the 'half-negro' group had a lower level. Other groups did not differ significantly from the 'British' value. A study of the predominantly Punjabi South Asian population in Glasgow produced similar findings (Bhopal and Samim, 1988), demonstrating similar or higher rates for all childhood immunisations among each of the main South Asian religious groups (Muslim, Sikh and Hindu), even after controlling for socioeconomic status and access to care (on the basis of residence) and health visitor contact.

The apparently consistent finding that the uptake of childhood immunisations is generally higher among minority ethnic groups – particularly South Asian ones – than is the case for the majority population is perhaps surprising in view of the fact that well-recognised barriers to access such as socioeconomic status and communication difficulties are likely to be greater among these populations. Bhopal and Samim (1988) speculate that high immunisation rates may reflect a traditional emphasis on prevention, child health and infectious disease in South Asian health beliefs. Moreover, they suggest, barriers to communication may have had the paradoxical effect of keeping levels of pertussis immunisation high, despite fears about its safety which dissuaded parents from other ethnic groups from having their children immunised.

In a rare study focusing on Traveller Gypsies, Feder *et al.* (1993) found completion of childhood immunisation to be low, when compared with an age- and gender-matched non-Gypsy comparator group. They suggested that this may relate not only to the mobility of the Gypsies, with a consequent deleterious effect on access to care, but also to health beliefs which regarded infectious childhood illnesses as 'normal', and a suspicion of immunisation as a violation of the social space which defines their ethnic separateness, although Taylor (1991) suggests that this is less problematic among children, for whom adult ideas of contamination do not apply.

Turning to the uptake of cervical smears, the same barriers to care as those that are thought to exist in the case of childhood immunisations may be postulated. Indeed, research on South Asian women's knowledge about cervical smears has generally shown it to be poor and past utilisation low (Doyle, 1991; Firdous and Bhopal, 1989; McAvoy and Raza, 1988). However, evidence on actual current uptake is equivocal. In a general practice-based study in Oldham, Bradley and Friedman (1993) found uptake of cervical smears among older South Asian women (predominantly Pakistani migrants in the 50-64 age group) to be very similar to rates in the 'non-Asian' population. The investigators conceded that this may have arisen through bias in the sample or the effect of an extensive health education campaign conducted locally. By contrast, Pilgrim et al. (1993) found that the proportion of 'African/Caribbean' women reporting they had had a smear in the last five years – at 77 per cent – was only slightly less than the overall figure locally, whereas only 34 per cent of South Asian women reported having a cervical smear in the same time period. Research in West London by Doyle (1991) also appears to suggest that uptake may be lower among South Asian women. Doyle found that, in addition to poorer knowledge, greater population mobility among the South Asian sample accounted for part of the poor uptake, an interesting finding which warrants further investigation (see also Hoare et al., 1992).

Finally, Hoare (1993) has examined the available evidence on the uptake of breast cancer screening by women from minority ethnic populations. The relevant data are generally poor, and are confounded by socioeconomic status, but they would appear to suggest lower uptake – particularly among South Asian women – than among white women, although regional variations exist, with 'black' women (not defined) in London appearing to have a high uptake. Uptake also appears to be associated with length of residence in Britain for all minority ethnic groups, perhaps explaining to some extent the lower uptake among South Asian women. Hoare also contends that South Asian women tend not to understand the value of receiving health care when they are not ill, a suggestion rather at odds with Bhopal and Samim's comment on the traditional emphasis on prevention in South Asian health beliefs.

Conclusion

Ethnic patterns in health care utilisation are clearly complex. On the face of it, there is no compelling evidence that people from minority ethnic populations do not *in general* receive adequate levels of care. However, as Farooqi (1993) cautions, it cannot be assumed from crude utilisation rates alone that appropriate access exists. Differences in utilisation would be expected on the basis of the age and gender structures of the populations of interest, as well as their socioeconomic structure and patterns of morbidity. Most of the studies described above were able to adjust for the effects of the first two factors, but dealt less successfully with the last two, a point which needs to be borne in mind when considering their implications. Patterns of utilisation appear to be generally consistent with known patterns of morbidity, but both under- or over-utilisation relative to need may be indicative of poorer services (eg. lack of information or lack of appropriate care necessitating further consultation) or of demand side differences. Without rigorous analysis of these possibilities within particular studies, it is difficult to assess the implications of some of the findings presented above. However, as it was suggested above, other kinds of analysis exist which help to place such findings in context. These are the subject of the next chapter.

6 Explaining patterns of utilisation

Introduction

It was suggested in Chapter 5 that there are a range of factors underlying the utilisation of health services, related both to the 'need' for them (demand side) and their provision (supply side). Many of the major factors which are conventionally thought to underlie patterns of utilisation, such as age, socioeconomic status and 'objective' morbidity will, broadly speaking, be common determinants across ethnic groups, although it is clearly possible that they may be experienced in different ways, with a consequently differential impact upon patterns of service use. Other factors are likely to vary still more between groups. However, many of the same comments about the difficulties of controlling for morbidity and socioeconomic status made in Chapter 4 apply to studies of utilisation. Thus, it should not be assumed that ethnic differences in utilisation which cannot be accounted for by conventional determinants can only be explained by recourse to these more specific factors. Nevertheless, understanding the latter provides an important context for examining ethnic patterns in the utilisation of care, and it is these factors which form the subject of this chapter.

On the demand side, they include:

- health beliefs and knowledge

- knowledge of and attitudes to health services

- social structure.

Relevant supply side factors are:

- distribution of health care resources

- racism in service delivery

- quality of care.

Health beliefs and knowledge

Beliefs and knowledge about health and disease may differ between ethnic groups. The precise impact of any such differences on the utilisation of services is likely to be complex. In particular, a singular and determinate relationship between beliefs and actual behaviour is seldom likely to be found. For example, Bhopal notes that among the sample of South Asians which he studied in Glasgow, "Asian remedies were used before, with and after Western medicine" (1986b, p.103). Moreover, he found no correlation between the extent of belief in or use of South Asian medicine and patterns of general practice consultation. Nevertheless, an understanding of the context within which people think about and use health services is clearly important in considering how services may be used. The discussion below summarises some of the main studies which have examined this question.

Perhaps the most striking finding from most studies is the degree of broad congruence with the Western 'medical model' of disease exhibited by minority groups (Bhopal, 1986a,b; Bowes and Domokos, 1993; Currer, 1986; Donovan, 1986; Howlett et al., 1992), and a general confidence in the precepts of Western medicine. It is possible that respondents tend to under-report beliefs which they may feel are regarded as quaint or superstitious, but the weight of the evidence from the studies cited above – employing a variety of methodologies – does not support the notion that health beliefs among minority ethnic groups might be such as to dissuade them from using NHS services.

Some interesting findings have nevertheless emerged from these studies. Donovan (1986) conducted in-depth interviews and life histories of thirty Caribbean and South Asian Londoners, who were mainly born abroad. She found that some of her informants had quite extensive personal theories of disease and treatment which were 'incorrect' by the standards of orthodox medicine; an example is the theory among some South Asians of health as a consequence of the bodily balance between 'hot' and 'cold', a humoral lay theory common in a number of societies (Manderson, 1987). Some of the Caribbean informants expressed doubt that smoking was damaging to health, and several South Asians entertained similar doubts about obesity. In addition, many of Donovan's South Asian informants were confused about healthy diets, apparently having absorbed health education messages about the supposed dangers of traditional South Asian diets. If true more generally, all of these findings may be of relevance in devising improved strategies of health education.

Most of Donovan's informants of both ethnic origins reported experience of racism, believing this to be relevant to their health experience. One of the Caribbean women attributed her hypertension and diabetes to the experience of racism at her workplace. Most of the informants exhibited a considerable degree of fatalism about illness. In the words of one Caribbean informant:

> I don't worry about no sickness because what is written is written. Even when I myself became ill, I never moaned, I never grumbled because we don't buy sickness, it just comes
>
> (Donovan, 1986, p.115).

For present purposes, the significance of these findings is difficult to determine in the absence of comparison with the majority population, since health beliefs among the latter may depart from 'orthodoxy' in equal measure. A comparison of this sort is found in the work of Howlett *et al.* (1992), who analysed responses to the national *Health and Lifestyle Survey*. The researchers attempted to determine ethnic patterns in the concepts of health and illness causation revealed in the survey. They described their findings as exploratory, given the poor nature of the survey's ethnicity variable. Nevertheless, they were able to examine the health beliefs revealed by 129 'Asians' and 94 'Afro-Caribbeans' in comparison to samples of whites matched for age, gender, social class, marital status, employment, education and region of residence. Key findings included the following:

- Afro-Caribbeans and whites were more likely to describe health in terms of strength and fitness, whereas Asians were more likely to conceive of it functionally, in relation to the ability to perform everyday activities.

- Fewer Afro-Caribbeans and Asians than whites linked improved health over the last generation to better health care or improved standards of living.

- More Afro-Caribbeans and Asians than whites regarded health as a matter of luck, whereas more whites regarded ill health as the fault of the individual.

- Fewer Afro-Caribbeans and Asians than whites regarded stress as a cause of disease; similarly, fewer viewed smoking and alcohol as causes of illness.

The researchers suggested that the apparently more fatalistic attitudes of people from minority ethnic groups – encompassing a lack of emphasis on both voluntary behaviour and external factors – related to a perceived lack of control over their lives which, they argued, may in turn be a consequence of racism. In this respect, their results are consistent with Donovan's ethnographic findings. Functional definitions of health were also found by Fong and Watt (1994) in their study of a Chinese population.

A study among the South Asian – predominantly Punjabi – population of Glasgow sought more direct information about knowledge concerning specific diseases and practices. Bhopal (1986a) interviewed 65 South Asian people chosen randomly from the records of a general practice. Like Donovan, he found that his informants' knowledge was rooted in the Western 'medical model' and that they were generally scornful of many traditional South Asian beliefs, but that many were poorly informed about health issues, particularly older people and those who were less familiar with the English language (the two groups often coinciding). In particular, he found poor knowledge about risk factors for CHD, the dangers of alcohol and lead-based *surma* cosmetics, maintaining health in pregnancy, and malaria prophylaxis. Informants displayed better knowledge about rickets, perhaps as a result of the 'Stop Rickets' campaign (see Chapter 7). In another paper based on the same sample, Bhopal (1986b) examined the interactions between 'traditional' and Western health beliefs more closely. He found there to be a broad general awareness of traditional systems of medicine, and some use of it, particularly herbal preparations for common minor ailments. There was also some use of *hakims*, but mainly on trips to the subcontinent and for chronic illnesses; only 6 per cent of respondents reported a preference for South Asian medicine. Moreover, as Koo (1987) has pointed out, a preference for traditional medicine does not necessarily imply its routine use as an alternative to orthodox treatment.

An exception to the general pattern of congruence with the 'medical model' appears to exist among Traveller Gypsies. Taylor (1991) describes the existence of strong ritual beliefs about contamination among Gypsies which lead them to reject many health interventions. This is compounded by a broader rejection of non-Gypsy mores. Quoting an ethnographic study conducted among Gypsies, Taylor suggests that they often take note of health workers' beliefs and then deliberately adopt inverse ones. Nevertheless, according to Taylor, the nature of contamination beliefs is such that some use is made of maternity and child health services, even though they are not always provided in a convenient fashion. Her account provides an interesting example of how service use may be affected by health beliefs in ways which are unsuspected by the providers of care.

In addition to specific health beliefs it is possible that different cultural norms regarding the definition and nature of illness may also affect the use of services. This is in keeping with the discussion of Kleinman's (1987) work in Chapter 3, which suggested that illness can be not only mediated but substantially created within cultural contexts. For example, a Canadian study by Anderson *et al.* (1989) showed how responses to chronic childhood sickness or disability are mediated by an 'ideology of normalisation' among white families which seeks to re-define the child as healthy. By contrast, migrant Chinese families were less likely to subscribe to such an ideology, partly through lack of material resources and shared cultural meanings in negotiating health care, but also because of greater cultural acceptance of the 'deviance' of ill-health. The cultural context within which illness is viewed and the availability of an acceptable 'sick role' may be of some significance in the way that individuals interact with services.

A study by Krause (1989) among Punjabis in Britain, which investigated the experience of 'sinking heart' (for which there is no precise Western equivalent), is an interesting illustration of this point. If health beliefs differ in subtle ways from medical orthodoxy, confusion and frustration may result for both parties in the dialogue between doctor and patient, particularly where it may in any case be complicated by communication difficulties and ethnic stereotyping. Thus, negative attitudes to health care may be formed on the basis of poor coincidence with health beliefs.

Although different cultural norms and the impact of health beliefs on attitudes to care are probably unlikely to deform overall ethnic patterns of health care utilisation, such processes are clearly liable to affect the experience of health and health care in different ethnic groups. There is considerable scope for examining this question in terms of the interaction between material and cultural explanations discussed in Chapter 4. A key question is the extent to which these norms change with length of residence, and within subsequent locally born generations.

Health services: knowledge and attitudes

As well as being important in its own right, understanding the degree of knowledge displayed by ethnic groups of the services available to them and their attitudes to these services can help to explain patterns of service use, although knowledge and attitudes clearly involve supply side as well as demand side factors. This section examines evidence about:

- Knowledge of primary and preventive services among minority ethnic groups

- The factors affecting their choice of GP

- Their attitudes to and satisfaction with health services.

Looking first at knowledge of primary and preventive services, the evidence suggests that levels of GP registration are high among all ethnic groups, generally exceeding 90 per cent (Donovan, 1986; Johnson et al., 1983; MORI, 1993; Watt et al., 1993). In their West Midlands study, Johnson et al. (1983) found that South Asian and Caribbean patients were less likely than whites to refer themselves directly to hospital services, generally awaiting referral from their GP. This, they inferred, may partially explain the higher levels of GP consultation which they found. A rare study of a Chinese population in Hull also found a heavier reliance on the GP alone as the point of contact with the health service, and fewer interactions with other health professionals compared to a matched sample of whites (Watt et al., 1993).

In other areas of primary and preventive service provision, lower levels of utilisation are generally mirrored by less knowledge of these services. For example, Donaldson (1986) found a low degree of knowledge about services such as meals-on-wheels and home helps among elderly South Asian people in Leicester. Atkin et al. (1989) produced similar results, and found that elderly people reported they would use health services more frequently if they knew more about them, although work in Glasgow by McFarland et al. (1989) suggested that minority ethnic elders had low expectations of services. Hek (1991) found little knowledge of district nursing services among South Asian elders in Bristol. Watt et al. (1993) found that a smaller proportion of Chinese people in Hull had heard of preventive health programmes such as anti-smoking, immunisations, blood pressure checks and breast and cervical screening; moreover, fewer thought them desirable. Firdous and Bhopal (1989) found both less knowledge and less sophisticated kinds of knowledge about health topics such as cervical smears and breast self-examination among South Asian than among white maternity patients in Glasgow. This is in keeping with another Leicester study by McAvoy and Raza (1988). Naish *et al.* (1994) found that women from several ethnic groups in East London were keen to take up cervical screening services; their low uptake largely reflected perceived administrative and communication barriers. On the other hand, Hoare *et al.* (1992) found population mobility and return visits to the country of origin to be the dominant reasons underlying non-attendance for breast screening among South Asian women in Manchester, although perceptions of its irrelevance or apprehension about the procedure were also mentioned. By contrast, the young Caribbean mothers interviewed by Larbie (1985) displayed considerable knowledge of postnatal community-based services and, despite mixed experiences of satisfaction with the care provided and some scepticism about the role of health visitors and other professionals, some women expressed a need for levels of support from these services which were not readily forthcoming.

Overall, then, the GP is if anything an even more crucial point of contact with health services for people from minority ethnic populations than is the case for the majority population. Several studies, unfortunately confined only to South Asian populations, have investigated the factors affecting the choice of GP and their implications for the success of the doctor-patient relationship. Two main themes have been addressed: whether difficulties of language and communication exist, affecting the choice of a white or a South Asian GP, and whether problems exist for women in consulting with a male GP.

The relevant research has produced widely differing results. Earlier studies in the West Midlands suggested that the key determinant of GP choice was proximity, and that factors such as the ethnicity of the GP were less important (Jain *et al.*, 1985; Johnson *et al.*, 1983), although clearly there is considerable coincidence between areas of South Asian residence and the availability of South Asian GPs. Some more recent studies also suggest that difficulties in communication may not be a major problem. For example, Rashid and Jagger (1992) found that only 6 per cent of a sample of South Asian patients in Leicester found it difficult to explain their symptoms in English. Indeed, in many respects they reported fewer obstacles to communication than in an age-matched sample of whites. In Bristol, Pilgrim *et al.* (1993) found that although people who did not speak fluent English reported additional problems with GP consultations, these problems were not always as severe as might have been expected: less than half of the respondents who said their English was 'slight or none at all' reported that it was impossible for them to contact the GP on the telephone.

On the other hand, considerable problems in English fluency have been reported among elderly South Asians in Leicester (Donaldson, 1986) and South Asians, particularly Pakistanis, in Bradford (Ahmad *et al.*, 1989c). Both studies found poorer fluency among women than among men. The Bradford study, conducted in a practice with a white female and a South Asian male GP, found that inability to speak English was significantly associated with greater consultation with the male South Asian GP by both males and females. A later study by the same authors found that South Asian patients in general tended to consult more often with the South Asian doctor (Ahmad *et al.*, 1991a), a result consistent with Donovan's (1986) study in London in which she found that most, although not all, of her South Asian informants preferred to see a South Asian GP. Where this option is not available, it may be that a successful consultation is less likely, particularly where language difficulties are involved. Wright (1983), for example, found that GP perceptions of 'trivial complaining' among South Asian patients may largely arise from difficulties in communication.

Differences in English fluency may be expected between men and women and between age groups within particular minority ethnic populations on the basis of education and social background. Clearly, differences also exist between distinct South Asian populations; the work cited above may be indicative of the fact that Pakistanis in Bradford predominantly originating from the rural Mirpur district are less advantaged than the population of Leicester, which has a significant proportion of Gujarati Hindus of East African origin. Thus, although language difficulties may often not be a particularly severe problem in general – and can be expected to diminish over time – their significance for particular populations or groups within populations cannot be ignored.

Turning to the gender of the GP, it is often suggested that a generally greater sense of 'modesty' among South Asian – particularly Muslim – women makes them more reluctant to consult with a male doctor where physical, and especially vaginal, examination may be involved (Wright, 1983). On the face of it, this is not entirely supported by the empirical evidence, which suggests that most South Asian women consult with male doctors and relatively few (10-30 per cent) express a preference for a woman (Jain et al., 1985; Pilgrim et al., 1993; Rashid and Jagger, 1992). However, in her questionnaire of GPs in London, Wright (1983) found that problems with the physical examination of women were commonly reported. Similarly, Ahmad et al. (1989c) found in their Bradford study that 62 per cent of Pakistani women said they would object to being examined by a male GP, even though the majority of them did in fact consult with one.

This finding raises the possibility that 'linguistic concordance' is more important than gender, and that "the embarrassment caused by examination by the male doctor may be offset by the potential benefit from improved doctor-patient communication" (Ahmad et al. 1989c, p.155). Nevertheless, the researchers suggest that this phenomenon may be resulting in the under-reporting of gynaecological conditions among Pakistani women. Further research, preferably in practices containing white and South Asian GPs of both sexes, is warranted. However, it would appear that although problems of consultation with male GPs may sometimes be overstated, it remains a serious issue, particularly for Muslim women, and "it is probable that some women are tolerating unacceptable consultations because of the linguistic need to consult an Asian doctor" (Ahmad et al., 1989c, p.155). This underlines the broader point that the availability of doctors from the same ethnic group does not remove all the problems that people from minority ethnic populations may experience in seeking health care (Atkin and Rollings, 1993). Certainly, the notion that people from particular ethnic groups should always have a doctor from the same ethnic group may be flawed in several respects.

There is little research in Britain about ethnic patterns in attitudes to specific aspects of care. US research has documented the existence of ethnic differences in perceived barriers to care for emotional and behavioural problems, which can be accounted for by differences both in the stigma attached to seeking care and in access to services (Takeuchi et al., 1988). Research of this sort in Britain would certainly be warranted. There is some evidence of differences in preferred modes of treatment. For example, some researchers have found that Caribbean patients appear to exhibit a greater disliking for pills in comparison to liquid medicines (Donovan, 1986; Morgan and Watkins, 1988), perhaps in keeping with the use of traditional Caribbean 'tonic' treatments (Thorogood, 1993). Morgan and Watkins (1988) examined beliefs and responses to medication in an age- and class-controlled sample of white and Caribbean hypertensive patients in South London, finding that compliance with the drug regimen was much poorer among the Caribbean informants. The reasons for this were fear of long-term effects, feeling 'all right', and fear of mixing the drugs with alcohol. Morgan and Watkins argued that the Caribbean informants were "engaged in a continuous process of monitoring their condition and the effects of taking or 'leaving off' the tablets" (1988, p.571), noting the relative success of orthodox and alternative remedies in alleviating their hypertension and its symptoms. Significantly, the informants tended not to confide in their GPs about their behaviour, fearing the doctor's ridicule. Thus, although non-compliance is often attributed to poor communication or lack of understanding on the patient's part, Morgan and Watkins show that in this case it relates to a more complex process of 'negotiation' with the health care system.

Turning finally to evidence about the satisfaction of people from minority ethnic populations with the services they receive, relatively few systematic and large-scale studies have been undertaken. The discussion below summarises the findings of some of the main existing studies.

Levels of satisfaction with health services – particularly GP services – are generally high for both the majority and minority ethnic populations. Nevertheless, in a general analysis of the factors associated with satisfaction with health services, based on some 8,000 responses to a household survey, Judge and Solomon (1993) found that people who were 'non-white' were less likely to be satisfied with the running of the NHS and with in-patient – but not out-patient – services, even after controlling for other relevant factors.

Pilgrim *et al.* (1993) provide a detailed account of attitudes to GP services among minority ethnic populations in Bristol. They found ethnic and gender differences in terms of satisfaction with different aspects of consultation, such as whether there were opportunities to ask questions, whether information about diagnosis was given and so on. No clear pattern emerged, except perhaps that lower levels of satisfaction were generally expressed by 'Far East Asian' (ie. Chinese and Vietnamese) people, but overall levels of satisfaction were high. Similarly, a survey in East London found generally high levels of satisfaction, but a greater proportion of minority ethnic respondents felt that the time allotted them for the consultation was too short (MORI, 1993). Interestingly, a greater proportion also felt that they had not received proper treatment unless they had received medication.

Despite this general picture, Pilgrim *et al.* make the following caveat upon their findings:

respondents found it difficult to answer these questions … [they] did not feel they were in a position to criticise a service which was freely available and some drew favourable comparisons with inferior health services which they had experienced in the past … the respondents were reluctant to make critical comments in response to the interview questions but described unsatisfactory experiences of health services when the interview had finished
(1993, p.47).

These sentiments are echoed by Donovan (1986), who suggests that positive responses to questions asking directly about satisfaction conceal more complex experiences which deeper questioning can elicit. She found that although most of her Caribbean informants who had used health services reported themselves to be generally satisfied, many remained critical of the services they had received, and the men were at particular pains to avoid doctors if at all possible. In general, the Caribbean informants were more distrustful of health services than the South Asian ones, a fact which Donovan attributed in part to the shorter length of residence in Britain of most of the South Asian informants. In similar vein, Larbie (1985) reports the widespread existence of suspicion among Caribbean mothers that the role of health visitors and social workers was to 'check up on you' and that their children would be taken into statutory care if the mothers were perceived to be looking after them poorly.

Little research exists on ethnic patterns in satisfaction with acute services. Donovan (1986) found that most of her informants who had experienced acute care reported satisfaction with it. A study by Madhok *et al.* (1992) examined the attitudes of South Asian and other in-patients to non-clinical aspects of their care, finding them to be similar in most respects, although some of the South Asians experienced greater problems with food, language and interpretation and the availability of same-sex doctors. Melia *et al.* (1991) studied consumer attitudes to maternity care and discovered that 'non-Caucasian' women expressed a greater preference for longer periods of hospital stay, even after controlling for factors such as employment status, parity and availability of home support. McGovern and Hemmings (1994) undertook a follow-up study of the attitudes of 'second generation' Caribbean and white patients and their relatives with a first-admission diagnosis of schizophrenia at a Birmingham hospital five to ten years after first admission. In view of the contentious nature of schizophrenia diagnosis within the Caribbean population (see Chapter 3) higher levels of dissatisfaction among these patients were expected. It was found that they and their relatives were significantly more likely to perceive services as racist, and to advocate the need for more black staff and black day centres for after-care. However, although they expressed lower levels of satisfaction with most domains of care, these differences did not reach statistical significance. In general the results provided little evidence for substantial ethnic differences in satisfaction with care received, an interesting finding in the light of the broader debate about mental health and minority ethnic populations. It is possible that these findings reflect lower levels of expectation about the quality of care among the black respondents. Nevertheless, the results provide an interesting counterpoint to some of the broader literature on the minority ethnic experience of mental health services.

In conclusion, the evidence arguably suggests that attitudes to and satisfaction with health services do not differ vastly between the minority and majority ethnic populations. However, some important differences do appear to exist between particular populations, as revealed by the work of Ahmad *et al.* (1989c) among Pakistanis in Bradford. Significant age and gender differences are also apparent, and the available evidence suggests that health professionals should pay greater attention to promoting knowledge about primary and preventive services among minority ethnic populations. At the same time, much of the evidence described above must be interpreted cautiously, since it is possible that opinions are expressed relative to different reference points between populations in such a way that the findings mask greater underlying differences in experiences of health care. Expressed opinions may differ markedly from behaviour, and it is difficult to make firm conclusions in the absence of detailed knowledge about the perceived constraints within which such opinions are expressed. Thus, continuous and careful attention should be paid to ensuring that services are not provided in such a way as to obstruct their appropriate use by people from minority ethnic populations.

Social structure

Patterns of kinship, residence, gender relations and social interaction vary within and between ethnic groups. These may have a direct impact on health and the experience of illness, but it is also possible that such differences may independently affect patterns of health service utilisation. In pursuing this argument, there is a considerable danger of invoking stereotypes of minority ethnic 'culture' little supported by empirical evidence. For example, it is sometimes suggested that ethnic differences in utilisation of mental health services arise from the greater stigma attached to mental illness within Caribbean populations and from networks of social support within the South Asian population which 'keep mental illness in the family' (see discussions in Beliappa, 1991; Lipsedge, 1993; Littlewood, 1986). There is little compelling evidence for this. Although it may hold true for certain cases, blanket assertions of the importance of such phenomena as general explanations for ethnic patterns in utilisation are generally unconvincing.

Nevertheless, there is some evidence that family patterns may be important in explaining service use. For example, Donaldson (1986) showed that low uptake of a number of community services by elderly South Asians living in Leicestershire may be a consequence of different patterns of informal home care (although see Gunaratnam (1993a) for an alternative view). Research has cast doubt on the simple stereotype of South Asian elders living in large and supportive 'extended' families (Bhalla and Blakemore, 1981), but it appears to be the case that greater levels of domestic support are often available to South Asian elders than the white population (Mays, 1983). However, the opposite appears to be the case among Caribbean elders. Moreover, it cannot be assumed that such findings are static; patterns of social interaction are highly varied and there is some evidence of changes in intergenerational relationships upon migration (Mays, 1983; McFarland et al., 1989). Nor is it the case that family carers from minority ethnic populations do not themselves require support from statutory services (Atkin et al., 1989; McFarland et al., 1989).

Different patterns of informal home care have also been reported in the USA, where research has shown that white people are more likely to use nursing homes for long-term care of the elderly, whereas black people are more likely to rely upon informal home care, even after controlling for age, gender, income and health status. Headen (1992) tested an economic model to predict the observed ethnic difference in the mix of informal and nursing home care, finding essentially that the benefits forgone by devoting time to caring for elderly relatives among blacks were outweighed by the financial cost of supporting them in a nursing home, whereas the opposite was the case for whites. Thus, a phenomenon which appears to arise from the 'cultural' fact that black families place a stronger emphasis on informal care may in fact arise largely because of ethnic differences in patterns of family access to the labour market and/or services independently of income. Worobey and Angel (1990) found similar reasons underlying the typically higher degree of residence of elderly and disabled black and Hispanic women with their children in the USA, in comparison to the white population. Here, there is considerable scope for extending general feminist discussions of gender relations in 'racialised' societies (see, for example, Barrett and McIntosh, 1985; Bryan et al., 1985; Carby, 1982; Wilson, 1978) into more sustained analysis of women's roles and circumstances in terms of their implications for family health.

In summary, while it would be wrong to deny a role for social structure altogether in mediating ethnic patterns of service use, research of the sort undertaken by Headen underlines the need to view the effects of social structure and material or economic circumstances on patterns of utilisation as interactive rather than separate (see also Chapter 4).

The distribution of health care resources

Turning now to supply side factors, the physical proximity of health care facilities and their ease of use for local residents are fundamental determinants of access to care. It is widely stated that such facilities are often more fully provided in wealthier areas where the need for them is less, a view famously promulgated by Tudor Hart (1971) in his 'inverse care law'. In view of the substantial concentration of most minority ethnic populations in relatively deprived urban areas in Britain, it is possible that an inverse care law may be operating which reduces their access to and utilisation of care compared to the majority population overall, simply by virtue of their patterns of residence. However, Powell (1990) has argued that the empirical evidence for the existence of an inverse care law is poor, and although several investigations into the distribution of NHS resources have made passing reference to the needs of minority ethnic groups (McNaught, 1988), studies with a specific ethnic dimension have not been undertaken.

At a crude level, hospital resources in Britain are concentrated in urban areas, where the majority of people from minority ethnic groups live, while primary care resources are fairly evenly distributed throughout the country (King's Fund, 1992). However, primary care is probably the more significant aspect of the service for present purposes and there is some evidence that access to primary care in urban areas, particularly London, is poorer than elsewhere, and is of lower quality (Boyle and Smaje, 1993). A study by the GLC Health Panel noted that there was a:

> broad correlation between areas where ethnic minority communities have settled and the areas where primary health care problems are at their most intense: single-handed GPs working from inadequate premises, often without the support of a primary health care team

(1985, p.11).

Similarly, research in Leicester described in Chapter 2 found poor perinatal outcomes among South Asian women to be significantly associated with registration with GPs not on the obstetric list (Clarke et al., 1988; Clarke and Clayton, 1983). This illustrates the potential importance of such issues, although it does not in itself establish a causal link between GP quality and perinatal outcome.

Regardless of the putative impact of the overall distribution of NHS resources on ethnic differences in access, it is possible that more subtle effects exist at the local level on the basis of the mix of services provided as well as patterns of residence, transport connections and so on. US research has indicated how policy changes in the distribution of resources and the mix of care available can exert a major influence on ethnic patterns of utilisation (Swanson et al., 1993). Such issues await more detailed investigation in Britain.

Racism in service delivery

In considering the possible impact of racism on service delivery, it is useful to distinguish between several forms in which it may occur:

- *Direct racism,* where a health worker treats a person less favourably simply by virtue of the latter's ethnicity.

- *Indirect or institutional racism,* where, although ostensibly services are provided equally to all people, the form in which they are provided inevitably favours particular groups at the expense of others.

- *Ethnocentrism,* whereby inappropriate assumptions are made about the needs of people from minority ethnic groups on the basis of the majority experience.

The distinctions between these forms should not be overemphasised since, from the point of view of minority ethnic service users, they all result in discriminatory treatment. Racism has usefully been defined as 'prejudice plus power' (see Atkin and Rollings, 1993), and it is precisely the lack of power to contest majority assumptions and prejudices which lends racism its force in the experience of health care for many people from minority ethnic populations. Nevertheless, the distinctions are useful in emphasising that racism is not a unitary phenomenon, and that its significance may lie as much in how the interactions between health professionals and minority ethnic service users are shaped by broader social assumptions as by the existence of direct prejudice.

In spite of this, most accounts of racism in health service delivery focus either upon instances of direct discrimination (see, for example, Kushnick, 1988; Larbie, 1985; Pilgrim *et al.*, 1993; Wilson, 1978), or more general discussions which argue that racism is a pervasive feature of British society and institutions, not least the NHS (see, for example, Ahmad, 1992b; Black Health Workers and Patients Group, 1983; Bryan *et al.*, 1985; Torkington, 1991). Attempts to show precisely *how* racism shapes the interactions between NHS staff and minority ethnic users and the implications of this for patterns of service use or outcome are less common. One exception, discussed in Chapter 3, is the work of Roland Littlewood and his co-authors, whose studies in transcultural psychiatry provide a sustained analysis of how ethnocentrism among professionals shapes the experience of mental health services by minority ethnic users. The remainder of this section summarises several studies in other areas of service provision which address issues of this sort.

Bowler (1993) used ethnographic techniques to investigate the attitudes of midwives to their patients of South Asian origin, and to examine how these attitudes shaped their interactions. In keeping with other sociological accounts of health care, she found that the midwives employed stereotypes of different patient groups which affected the type of care they offered and the way they chose to offer it. Although such a practice is not necessarily wholly inappropriate, Bowler showed that the midwives' stereotypes of South Asian women were generally negative in character, intersecting with but autonomous from other patient stereotypes, such as class-based ones. In particular, the South Asian women's generally poor command of English led to stereotypes of lack of intelligence and rudeness. The midwives also tended to view the women as both uncompliant and exploitative in their relationship with the NHS, as attention-seeking and over-fussy, and as lacking a 'normal maternal instinct'.

Bowler demonstrated how these stereotypes arose – often in quite subtle ways – through communication barriers and through pre-existing cultural stereotypes. They both caused and were compounded by the South Asian women's inability to negotiate the kind of 'sick role' which the midwives expected. Bowler showed how this reduced the quality of the care the women received, but the overall impact of this on utilisation and outcomes was beyond the scope of her study.

A number of studies have examined the attitudes of GPs to minority ethnic patients (Ahmad *et al.*, 1991b; Fenton, 1989; Wright, 1983), although once again the focus is mainly on people of South Asian origin. These studies produced broadly similar results, finding that GPs generally perceived South Asian patients to consult more frequently, and often with more trivial complaints, to require longer consultations and to be less compliant. Ahmad *et al.* found that such attitudes were, if anything, more common among South Asian GPs than white GPs, a fact they attributed either to the 'internalisation' of dominant medical values or to the age and training of the GPs in question.

The appropriate interpretation of these studies is hard to determine. None of them were able to compare the GPs' attitudes with independent measurement of the 'true' prevalence of the behaviours in question, clearly a difficult undertaking. Ahmad *et al.* (1991b) placed their findings in a less positive light than the other studies, suggesting in essence that the social distance between the GPs and their South Asian patients shaped the more negative attitudes which they displayed. Wright emphasised a gulf of culture and communication between GPs and patients in somewhat more neutral terms:

> *The overwhelming impression … is of general practitioners puzzled by the influx of Asians to their practices, aware of considerable problems of management and yet unable or unwilling to make appropriate adjustments*
> (1983, p.103).

Fenton (1989) interprets his findings, based on discussions with Bristol GPs, in a more positive light. Although in his view they tended to underestimate the problems facing minority ethnic patients, this could be seen in the light of their wish to emphasise inner-city environments as a health problem for all of their patients, rather than singling out minority ethnic patients in particular as constituting a problem.

In summary, the studies cited above indicate that although direct racism is certainly present in the delivery of health care to minority ethnic populations, more complex problems also arise through difficulties of communication and ethnocentrism, which may also result in less satisfactory service provision. Moreover, as Kushnick (1988) argues, well-meaning attempts to correct these deficiencies within a multicultural framework can be counterproductive, since they may reinforce stereotypes of ethnic difference. At the same time, the inability of health care workers to provide adequate care does not always reflect insensitivity at an individual level, but rather the assumptions implicit in the very institutional structure within which they must operate (Anderson *et al.*, 1991).

Few broader attempts to examine the nature of institutional racism exist. Indeed, as Knowles (1991) has suggested, there is little conceptual clarity as to the meaning of institutional racism in concrete terms. Examples are often cited such as the failure of health authorities to provide information about services in appropriate media, so that minority ethnic populations are disadvantaged in terms of their ability to make use of them (CRE, 1992). This undoubtedly occurs. For example, a survey of health authorities by Donaldson and Odell (1984) found that only about 30 per cent of authorities with more than 500 South Asian residents provided any special services for South Asians or in-service training for staff, and nearly 30 per cent provided no health education programmes targeted at their South Asian population. Clearly, the lack of knowledge and poor uptake of certain preventive services among minority ethnic populations highlighted earlier in the chapter is not simply a demand side issue.

Despite being hampered by the lack of readily available local information, many health authorities have made attempts to identify gaps or deficiencies in service provision (see, for example, Derbyshire FPC, 1988; MORI, 1993). However, in the absence of more detailed local study it is difficult to determine the success of these efforts or the broader significance of continuing discriminatory practice in shaping the experience of health care among minority ethnic groups.

Quality of care

Very little published research exists on ethnic differences in the quality of clinical care, although this may change with the introduction of routine ethnic monitoring and the increasing emphasis in the reformed NHS of the 1990s on the measurement of clinical outcomes.

Research by Shaukat et al. (1993) examined the clinical features, risk factors and referral delay of South Asian and non-South Asian patients referred to a regional cardiothoracic centre. Controlling for age, gender and extent of coronary disease, they found a significant difference in mean referral delay between white patients (7 months) and South Asians (17 months). Although the authors acknowledged the possibility of GP referral bias, they preferred to invoke – on the not entirely convincing basis of high overall referral rates among GPs with large South Asian populations – demand side factors in explaining the delay, such as a reluctance among South Asians to seek hospital treatment or a lifestyle which avoids angina-provoking exercise.

Hawthorne (1990) found that glycaemic control in a sample of South Asian diabetics attending a hospital clinic in Nottingham was typically poorer than in a matched white sample. This might have arisen from the quality of education about diet and secondary risks, which appeared to have been poorer in the South Asian sample. Nutritional advice in particular appeared to be inappropriate to the kind of diets and food preparation arrangements to which the South Asians adhered.

Parsons and Day (1992) evaluated the impact on birth outcomes of the availability of health advocates to women from minority ethnic groups during their maternity care in East London. Although their study contained certain methodological weaknesses, they found that women who had had contact with an advocate experienced significantly better obstetric outcomes in terms of length of antenatal stay, spontaneous onset of labour and normal vaginal delivery than women who had had no such contact. They suggested that these differences could have arisen as a result of an improved quality of contact between health professionals and women from minority ethnic populations achieved by the advocates. Health advocacy is discussed further in Chapter 7.

Research in the USA has examined at a more detailed level ethnic differences in clinical procedures and outcomes. For example, Whittle et al. (1993) have shown that, even after controlling for other relevant factors, white people admitted to Veterans' Administration (VA) hospitals with cardiovascular disease are more likely to undergo invasive surgical procedures than black people. Restricting the study to VA hospitals effectively controls for insurance status, which may affect utilisation in the USA, although it also biases the sample to some extent. Another VA-based study by Peterson et al. (1994) produced similar results, showing that black people admitted following myocardial infarction were significantly less likely to receive a variety of treatments, even after controlling for age, severity of infarction, co-morbidity and hospital location and technology. A study by Kahn et al. (1994) examined differences in the quality of care – measured across a number of dimensions – for black and low-income people, unfortunately failing to distinguish between the two groups. Poorer quality of care was found for the disadvantaged groups for each category of hospital examined, but since these groups typically received care in higher-quality urban teaching hospitals there was no overall difference in quality of care. Similarly, Escarce *et al.* (1993) found that elderly black people received fewer interventions than whites in 32 common surgical procedures, and that these differences were heightened in rural areas. Research of this sort may be of some interest in Britain, in view of the similarities between the two countries in the geographical distribution of both hospital resources and minority ethnic groups.

Other US research has documented poorer survival of kidney transplants among black people (Butkus *et al.*, 1992), ethnic differences in pain management for a given severity of trauma (Todd *et al.*, 1994), and excess mortality (age-adjusted mortality rates and years of potential life lost) among black people in a number of 'sentinel' conditions such as cervical cancer, asthma and appendicitis, which are normally preventable given timely and appropriate medical intervention (Schwartz *et al.*, 1990; Woolhandler *et al.*, 1985). Schwartz *et al.* (1990) found that the excess mortality arose from higher case-fatality rates rather than greater incidence which, they argued, was suggestive of poorer access to or utilisation of care. Similarly, Otten *et al.* (1990) examined the determinants of excess mortality among black people in the USA. Using a national survey, and controlling for the distribution of known risk factors within the populations and for socioeconomic status on the basis of income, they found that nearly a third of the excess remained unexplained.

The implications of these studies for the availability and quality of care are rather unclear, except insofar as they all provide 'conspicuous evidence of considerable inequalities' (Wolinsky *et al.*, 1989), which are likely to stem in part at least from poorer treatment and/or poorer access. Clearly, the issues in Britain may well be rather different. However, these studies at least establish the relevance of examining ethnic differences in clinical process and outcome.

7 Ethnicity and health policy

Introduction

19565   108.27

This chapter takes a step back from examining specific aspects of the health and health care experience of minority ethnic populations to consider more broadly policy-making in the health sector which has attempted to address their health care needs. Although this approach runs the risk of emphasising what has been 'done to' minority ethnic populations at the expense of what has been 'done by' them, it is probably fair to say that health policy-making on ethnic issues historically has been characterised by top-down and often centrally led operational modes. Although a number of important initiatives in areas such as sickle cell disorder and mental health services have stemmed directly from the activities of minority ethnic led groups (Stubbs, 1993), the extent to which the locus of power in setting the policy agenda has shifted from formal organisational structures is questionable.

To provide a context within which to examine the relevant issues, the chapter begins with a brief outline of the broader political environment which frames the policy process, drawing in particular upon analyses of the role of 'race' in public policy. This is followed by two sections which respectively examine how policy problems have been defined in the health sector and critically evaluate specific policy initiatives which have attempted to address the health needs of minority ethnic populations. The final section describes broader critical analyses of the policy-making process, distinguishing in particular between liberal and radical critiques of the *status quo*.

Figure 7.1 provides a chronology of some of the major relevant events. Although far from comprehensive, it attempts to pick out the key themes with which policy-makers have engaged. Given the political realities of ethnic divisions in British society, it is scarcely surprising that many of the policies detailed in the figure reflect a process-oriented, managerialist agenda at some distance from practical issues in the delivery of care. Indeed, the effectiveness of practical attempts to improve services for minority ethnic populations has received relatively little systematic evaluation. Thus, one of the aims of this chapter is to provide a critical context within which the assumptions and likely consequences of particular policy initiatives can be examined.

The policy context

Commentators writing from different perspectives across the field of social policy broadly concur that government policy in response to the large-scale postwar Commonwealth migrations it had substantially encouraged was initially characterised by a *laissez faire* phase in which no special attention was paid to the new minority groups, despite accumulating evidence of discrimination and inequality (Daniel, 1968; Nanton, 1992; Sivanandan, 1976; Smith, 1987; Williams, 1989; Young, 1983). Indeed, writers such as Sivanandan and Smith have argued that it was the very 'race neutrality' of public policy that contributed significantly to the entrenchment of inequality. However, from the mid-1960s onwards the *laissez faire* phase was supplanted by more explicit, if unfocused, policy attention. Nanton (1992) identifies two subsequent phases. First, he suggests that assimilationist

Figure 7.1 **Ethnicity and health policy**

Year	Event	
1965	Commonwealth Immigrants White Paper	Suggested that immigrants placed a burden on health services, that Regional Hospital Boards needed to consider immigrants in hospital building programmes and that the NHS should employ immigrant community nurses.
	Letter to Medical Officers of Health and GPs	Encouraged local efforts to prevent and treat TB among immigrants.
1976	Health Circular (25)	Regional Health Authorities asked to consult Community Relations Councils in appointing Community Health Council (CHC) members.
1977	Asians in Britain Project	DHSS, King's Fund and National Extension College established a project to produce educational and training material for South Asian people and NHS staff.
1978	Health Circular (36)	Outlined implications of 1976 Race Relations Act for NHS.
1980	Yellowlees Report	Examined immigrant health, concluding that - with the main exception of TB - there was no evidence to suggest immigrants were more or less healthy than the general population.
	Black Report	Commented briefly on race and ethnicity as dimensions of inequalities in health.
	Short Report	Recommended health authorities to make 'positive efforts to seek out pregnant women in minority groups'.
	Multi-ethnic Women's Health Project	City & Hackney CHC established project pioneering the concept of the 'health advocate'.
1981	Stop Rickets Campaign	DHSS formally established campaign - administered by the Save the Children Fund - arising out of earlier health education efforts among the South Asian population.
1981	Health Circular (6)	Suggested that DHAs had 'suitable' representation from ethnic minorities among their members.
1983	Health Circular (6)	Suggested ethnic minority interests should be considered in arrangements for care in the community and joint finance, where appropriate.
1984	Asian Mother and Baby Campaign	DHSS established campaign - along similar lines to Stop Rickets - in 16 DHAs to improve antenatal and postnatal care and the sensitivity of the services provided. 'Linkworkers' pioneered.
	Health Circular (19)	Suggested FPCs consider 'ethnic origin' in membership nominations.
1985	Haringey DHA appointed ethnic adviser	The first such appointment in the NHS.
1986	Equal Opportunities Task Force	DHSS part funded a King's Fund Task Force to help health authorities develop equal opportunities policies and address equality of opportunity more generally.
1987	NHS Management Seminar	Minister for Health hosted NHS seminar on ethnic minority health.
	Black Health Forum	National Community Health Resource established Forum as a network for community workers in black health issues.
1988	Routine sickle cell/ thalassaemia screening	Brent DHA first health authority to introduce routine screening. The government reviewed its sickle cell/thalassaemia policy.
	Action Not Words	NAHA produced a 'strategy to improve health services for black and minority ethnic groups', which the government endorsed.

Figure 7.1 **Continued**

Year	Event	
1989	Ethnic Health Adviser	Department of Health appointed a special adviser on ethnic minority health.
	Department of Health Continuing Fund	£500,000 fund established for project work on the health of minority ethnic populations.
1990	NHS and Community Care Act	NHS reforms required purchasers to assess the health needs of their local populations and to consult with them.
	Department of Health/ King's Fund Grants	Department of Health funded three projects at the King's Fund Centre to examine ethnic dimensions in mental health, carer issues and purchasing. The King's Fund awarded four DHAs with grants to examine purchasing issues.
	Departmental Working Group	Established in the Department of Health to examine health and ethnicity issues.
1991	Patient's Charter	Introduced to make NHS more 'user friendly'.
	SHARE	Department of Health funded King's Fund Centre to develop an information exchange on health and race issues.
	Primary Care Code of Practice	Secretary of State for Health launched voluntary code drawn up by Commission for Racial Equality.
	NHS Contracts and Racial Equality	CRE publishes guide to contracting for health authorities.
1992	Chief Medical Officer's Report	Devoted a chapter to minority ethnic health issues.
	Health of the Nation White Paper	The government's health strategy identified people from minority ethnic populations as a 'special group' with a number of particular needs.
	Guidelines on patients' spiritual needs	NHS Management Executive issued guidelines on spiritual needs of patients from different faiths.
1993	King's Fund Grants	Grants provided to 4 statutory/voluntary partnerships to improve access to health and social care for people from minority ethnic populations.
	Checklist Health and Race	King's Fund Centre produced a checklist for managers on improving services for minority ethnic populations.
	Ethnic Health Unit	Established for a period of 3 years by the Department of Health to encourage research and support health purchasers and providers in improving access to health services for minority ethnic populations.
	Ethnicity and Health	Department of Health published a 'guide for the NHS' as part of its *Health of the Nation* initiative and Ethnic Health Unit launch.
	Equality Across the Board	NAHAT/King's Fund Centre published Department of Health funded report and recommendations on increasing minority ethnic non-executive NHS membership.
	Ethnic Minority Staff in the NHS	Secretary of State for Health launched 8-point action plan to achieve equitable representation of minority ethnic groups at all levels in the NHS (including professional staff groups), to reflect the ethnic composition of the local population.

policies were developed, which Saggar (1993) has called the 'liberal settlement', since it commanded bipartisan political support and attempted to defuse the politics of race by promoting 'racial harmony'. Nanton argues that this phase was in turn replaced by more pluralist notions of integration in public policy, which recognised the distinctive and persistent character of different ethnic identities.

Few would dispute the validity of this as an empirical account of the trajectory in 'race' policy. However, not everyone would accept its implicit view of a trend towards greater progressiveness in recognising the distinctive character of ethnic identity. On the one hand, writers such as Stubbs (1993) and Williams (1989) point out how change has arisen to some extent through the efforts of minority ethnic groups to have their own concerns incorporated into the policy process. On the other, it has been suggested that the changes in the policy agenda are fairly superficial, representing nothing more than window dressing in the face of earlier policy failures and mounting ethnic tension (Sivanandan, 1976). For example, it could be argued that the *laissez faire* phase was not sustainable in the face of evidence on widespread discrimination in housing and employment and rising ethnic conflict, but the policy response was to locate the 'problems' in the fact of immigration itself, a response echoed in health policy by the emphasis on 'port health', in which the main concern is to prevent the importation of illness by immigrants (Johnson, 1993). Similarly, assimilationist policies largely rest upon the assumption that indigenous cultural behaviours are uniquely appropriate, and that the 'disadvantage' faced by minority ethnic groups can be substantially banished simply by encouraging greater inter-ethnic understanding. From a more radical standpoint, a number of writers have argued that the 'welfare' arm of the state is little less coercive in its encounter with minority ethnic populations than the judicial and immigration systems (Black Health Workers and Patients Group, 1983; Bryan *et al.*, 1985). Moreover, even if it is possible to identify a more recent policy trend in recognising ethnic difference and attempting to tackle ethnic inequality, it is far from clear what concrete agenda will emerge, or indeed whether one is likely to do so. As Saggar has commented in the case of local government:

> there is virtually no such thing as 'race policy' in British local government. Instead, there is a situation which broadly approximates to the sub-issue network stage of policy formulation. This situation can be described as a 'race policy environment', a term which almost certainly overstates the scale of coherence involved....the search for a discrete 'race policy' has been riddled with difficulties in the absence of a stable constellation of interests to sustain such a policy area

(1993, p.43).

Sustained analysis of the health sector at this kind of structural level has, as yet, failed to emerge. It is possible that the 'race policy environment' within the health sector may differ substantially from the situation in local government since, unlike the latter, health agencies have no statutory obligation to address racial discrimination and promote equal opportunities, and operate within a different constitutional framework. Nevertheless, the three policy changes identified by Solomos (1989) as a consequence of local government's statutory responsibilities – ethnic monitoring, equal opportunities in employment practices and the promotion of communication with minority ethnic populations – have also been prominent concerns within the health sector. Indeed, the themes and debates outlined above can all usefully be applied to health policy issues. Certainly, Nanton's three phases provide a convenient device with which to examine the formulation of health policy, and can be discerned in the events described in Figure 7.1. However, rather than forming distinct approaches separable through time, they may be better viewed as different but overlapping strands of policy-making. Thus, early concerns identified in the figure with the prevalence of infectious disease among immigrants reflect 'port health' thinking, which is nevertheless still a prominent concern (Bhopal, 1988). From the mid-1970s, in keeping with the assimilationist model, policy efforts focused more upon increasing representation from minority ethnic groups among health authority membership, and to a lesser extent on increasing knowledge about health services among people from minority groups, a theme which has persisted into the 1990s, along with a number of initiatives in the 'pluralist' mode, such as the appointment of 'ethnic advisers' locally, the NAHA (1988) report *Action Not Words*, and the recent creation of an Ethnic Health Unit at the Department of Health.

Interest in ethnicity as a dimension of health inequalities has also developed in recent years. The Black and Short Reports (Townsend and Davidson, 1992; House of Commons, 1980) first drew attention to the issue in the early 1980s, and subsequent research outlined in this review has documented, albeit in piecemeal fashion, the extent of ethnic inequalities in health. As with the more general debate on health inequalities, governments have been slow to turn scholarly interest into public policy, although there were tentative signs of progress in the *Health of the Nation* White Paper (Johnson, 1992a).

Neither ethnic nor socioeconomic inequalities in health can be divorced from the broader context of housing, employment and other currents of public policy. However, in the case of minority ethnic groups these inequalities are potentially exacerbated by government policies which restrict immigration and deny or restrict welfare benefits to many migrants (Amin and Oppenheim, 1992; Gordon and Newnham, 1985). Analysis of the relationship between health policy and other areas of public policy-making has received little systematic attention, although Ahmad (1992b), Kushnick (1988) and McNaught (1988) have usefully drawn attention to the significance of broader policies and ideologies in framing the 'race policy environment' for health.

In a discussion which focuses specifically upon 'race' policy, it is easy to overlook how little importance is attached to ethnic issues in health policy-making more generally. Ethnicity merits barely a mention in textbook accounts of health policy in Britain (Ham, 1992; Harrison *et al.*, 1990; Small, 1989). In broader policy frameworks, it typically receives attention only as a proxy indicator for need or deprivation in resource allocation instruments such as the Jarman 'underprivileged area' index and the Personal Social Services allocation formula. Even within the specific field of policies aimed at minority ethnic groups, a glance at Figure 7.1 reveals few initiatives with secure long-term funding, a problem which also appears to prevail at the local level (Bellamy, 1994). This situation of an inchoate and contested 'race policy environment' within the broader context of a neglected ethnic dimension in health policy-making provides an important background against which to consider the specific policy initiatives examined in subsequent sections.

Defining the problem in the health sector

Discussion of minority ethnic issues in the health sector has been dominated by two kinds of question. The first concerns the existence of local structures within health agencies – on both the commissioning and the providing sides – to enable an ethnic dimension to be built into the formulation of policy. The second has been concerned more directly with the nature of service provision itself, and has questioned the extent to which available services are appropriate to the needs of users from minority ethnic populations. This section examines each of these debates in turn.

The politics of local decision-making about minority ethnic health remain somewhat obscure since, in contrast to more general analyses of policy-making in the NHS (Harrison et al., 1990), there are no detailed comparative studies at the local level. One of the few writers to have undertaken empirical research in this area is McNaught (1988), who studied the formation of West Lambeth Health Authority's 'race policy' in the early 1980s, describing the tortuous process of community consultation and policy development which produced it. According to McNaught, this policy had a rather inconclusive impact in practical terms on the delivery of services. He contrasted this with its apparent coherence in documents promulgated by the District Management Team. McNaught employed Alford's (1975) theory of 'structural interests' to argue that minority health issues were essentially coopted by the Management Team to serve the health authority's interests in the context of the constraints upon its budget arising from the national implementation of the Resource Allocation Working Party's recommendations, although he suggested that the influence of two local 'product champions' and the impact of the 1981 Brixton riots also helped to raise the profile of minority ethnic issues. His study indicates the extent to which the success of local policy-making, in the absence of strong central direction, is at the mercy of committed local managers and the drift of broader health policy concerns.

In contrast, McNaught's (1987) study of community health initiatives (CHIs) is noticeably more positive. CHIs are rather loosely defined, but generally refer either to neighbourhood- or community-based health projects run by community workers, health professionals or volunteers, or to broader advocacy, self-help or resource projects. McNaught describes projects as diverse as a London black women's group which arose to campaign in relation to a parliamentary Bill prohibiting female circumcision, the Sickle Cell Disease Society, and groups in Bradford and Liverpool whose aims were respectively to raise the profile of health issues among local ethnic organisations, and to lobby the health authority about minority ethnic health.

It is worth making three points in relation to McNaught's account of CHIs. First, CHIs tend to focus on issues which have generally escaped mainstream NHS attention. In this sense they can intersect productively with the NHS, subject to the caveats implicit in McNaught's West Lambeth work. Certainly, the value of 'partnerships' between statutory and voluntary organisations is increasingly recognised, albeit that this in turn raises complex questions about the appropriate role of voluntary bodies as service providers on the one hand and campaigning organisations on the other. Second, in this regard it could be argued that CHIs may to some extent compensate for the traditional lack of NHS accountability to its client groups, but – like other voluntary groups – they have generally adopted their own bureaucratic structures within the confines of Britain's political institutions. Herein lies a danger of assuming that 'community groups' necessarily are the sovereign representatives of minority ethnic interests. Moreover, partnership models may represent merely the mediation of continued disadvantage, particularly since they tend to be based on relationships of unequal power between partners, operate at a short-term level with insecure funding, and possibly allow statutory service providers to assume that the voluntary sector is able to manage minority ethnic issues without any need for internal change themselves (Atkin and Rollings, 1993). Charges of the 'ghettoisation' of minority ethnic health interests in the hands of 'experts' have some force in this respect (Bryan *et al.*, 1985).

This leads to the third point that, paradoxically, the very success of the NHS as a public institution may impede local strategies of community development and empowerment for health, such as those pioneered in North America (McKnight, 1985; Schorr, 1988). For example, McNaught describes the experiences of a US black inner-city community which:

> took control of its local hospital as part of a community empowerment strategy. When community members realised that this did not lead to improved health, they looked at the major causes of hospital admissions and took action ... rounding up stray dogs ... having traffic patterns ... altered to improve road safety
>
> (1987, p.62).

In Britain, the greater centralisation of local control into elected and appointed authorities, in which it may be harder for minority ethnic representatives to articulate an independent voice, rather precludes such approaches (Jacobs, 1985; McNaught, 1987). However, regardless of the merits of the political traditions in either country, the example is at least illustrative of the complexity involved in developing local policies for minority ethnic health. Moreover, as McNaught (1988) has argued, the process of local policy development has often been sporadic, of low priority and undertaken in ignorance of similar efforts being made elsewhere.

Turning to the second set of issues, it is often suggested that many of the services provided by the NHS are inappropriate to the needs of minority ethnic populations (Ahmad, 1993b; Bhopal, 1991; 1988). This encompasses two distinct points:

- The health issues typically highlighted as being of special relevance to particular ethnic groups are often of less significance than other issues which are ignored.

- The methods by which health issues are brought to the attention of minority groups are inappropriate, and interventions are therefore often unsuccessful.

In Chapter 4 it was argued that an inappropriate focus on the presumed differences or even deficiencies of minority cultures is implicit in a number of studies. Many of these concerns are also entrenched in the provision of services, with the likely result that attention is deflected from more pressing needs. For example, Bhopal and Donaldson (1988) have documented how health education materials aimed at minority ethnic groups have been disproportionately dominated by 'traditional generalisations' about nutrition, infection, and maternal and child health. By contrast, they found little information on chronic diseases, accessing health services, smoking and alcohol. Fertility control has been another common theme, notoriously so in the debate about the excessive prescription of the drug Depo-Provera to women from minority ethnic populations (Bryan *et al.*, 1985).

In the field of health education at least, more recent research has shown that the picture painted by Bhopal and Donaldson may be beginning to change, although major gaps persist (Bhatt and Dickinson, 1992). However, as Bhopal has commented more recently:

Lost time needs to be made up. It seems incredible, looking back, that while attention focused on the 'specific problems' of ethnic minority groups … an epidemic of coronary heart disease was sweeping through the South Asian community and was the underlying cause of up to 50 per cent of deaths. Why did this go unnoticed?

(1993, p.5).

A focus on the inappropriately identified 'special needs' of minority ethnic populations may therefore hinder the development of services which address their 'true' needs. Of clear relevance here is the distinction drawn by Bhopal (1988) between the epidemiological focus on relative risk and the public health focus on absolute risk. To the extent that the former has influenced the policy agenda, it may be that service providers place an inordinate emphasis upon ethnic differences rather than commonalities. However, the path between research focus and service provision is not a wholly determinate one. Indeed, it has been argued that some services, such as sickle cell screening and treatment, are not adequately provided to minority ethnic populations precisely because they *can* be identified as relating to the special needs of minority groups (see page 128).

Notwithstanding the correct mix of services, it has also been argued – not least by a former health minister, Tony Newton – that in order to be effective, services must be delivered in appropriate ways:

It is not necessarily a case of providing extra or special services but where appropriate of considering different ways of providing existing services

(Department of Health and Social Security, 1988, p.2).

Few would demur at this suggestion, but there has been relatively little systematic evaluation of what it means in practice. There is a growing body of literature within both multicultural and anti-racist frameworks which attempts to educate health professionals and managers into thinking about the issues involved in delivering services to multiethnic populations (see, for example, Mares *et al.*, 1985; McAvoy and Donaldson, 1990; NAHA, 1988). However, most research attention has focused on four areas:

• Language and communication

• Linkworkers and advocates

• Prevention and health promotion/education

• Transcultural medicine.

Issues of language and communication have been discussed elsewhere in this book. Although they do not present a major problem for many ethnic groups, they do constitute severe obstacles to care for particular subpopulations, perhaps most obviously among women and elderly people from certain South Asian populations. Medical interviews conducted via interpreters are probably less likely to yield successful outcomes, particularly where the interpreter is not a professional, is not fluent in both languages or is a relative or child of the patient, since all of these are likely to result in greater levels of either wilful or unwitting mistranslation (Ahmad *et al.*, 1989c; Ebden *et al.*, 1988). Donaldson and Odell (1984) showed that most health authorities relied upon such informal channels for dealing with communication difficulties across the entire range of their services. A poorer service may be the result.

The use of linkworkers and advocates is one of the better-evaluated areas of service provision for minority ethnic groups (Bahl, 1990; Hicks and Hayes, 1991; Hoare *et al.*, 1994; Rocheron, 1991). It is examined in some detail in the following section. Here, it is simply worth noting that although most commentators are agreed upon the potential – if not always the actual – benefits of such schemes, broader doubts exist about the models of health service delivery implicit in them.

Turning to health promotion and education, it was suggested above that the emphasis of health promotion materials for minority ethnic populations may be misplaced. Bhopal (1991) argues that health educators often believe the health education needs of minority ethnic groups are different from those of the majority, but that the relevant techniques are not, whereas in reality the opposite is often the case. For example, McAvoy and Raza (1991) show how unusual interventions like targeted home visiting and video production can be more successful in increasing the uptake of preventive services than traditional written materials, even when translated into appropriate languages. Lee (1994) describes how a proactive approach to preventive screening in general practice, based upon household-by-household invitation, can improve the uptake of services and detection of illness among Bangladeshi families in London. Indeed, as Bhopal and White (1993) point out, even though the uptake of routine preventive screening among minority ethnic populations is generally lower than in the white population, research studies involving community-based screening typically achieve comparable response rates from both minority and majority populations. They suggest that this discrepancy arises because in the latter case special efforts are made to target minority groups in appropriate ways. This has clear policy implications, yet it is not always easy to determine the optimal form of intervention, since health professionals often lack the appropriate information about:

> *the community's views and aspirations; on their reactions to and intuitions regarding proposed methods, actors and settings; and on the effects of interventions, not only in terms of changes in the target behaviour, knowledge or ill health, but also in terms of their effects on wider social and cultural aspects of the community's life*
>
> (Bhopal and White, 1993, p.149).

Nevertheless, they argue that more effective future activity can be delivered through the flexible application of rational planning principles and local intelligence-gathering skills which better enable health promoters to determine their population's real rather than professionally-determined needs. Hawthorne (1994) also emphasises the complexity of the pathways by which health education messages may or may not be incorporated into behaviour, stressing the need for understanding among professionals of the cultural (and, one might add, material) constraints faced by individuals in acting upon them, and the need for good knowledge of the local population, so that elementary mistakes are not made in preparing health education materials which undermine their persuasiveness. In similar vein, Nickens stresses the need for flexibility among health educators in recognising the realities of social differentiation:

> *the ... advertising industry has been quick to understand and exploit the segmentation of markets using a complex mix of demographic factors, designing specifically tailored messages for each segment of the market. The health community should use the expertise of the advertising industry as it begins to think seriously about how to influence health behaviour*
>
> (1990, p.138).

Transcultural medicine adopts a much broader focus, suggesting that in order to understand and 'negotiate' the illnesses of people from minority ethnic populations, health professionals need to understand illness in the context of other cultures and appreciate the cultural specificity of their own concepts of health and society. This thinking has perhaps been most fully developed in the field of transcultural psychiatry – even if only as a critique of the methods still dominant in its parent discipline – but it has also been advocated for the provision of social services (Ballard, 1979) and for general practice and primary care (Huby and Salkind, 1989). At one end of the spectrum such approaches are broadly multicultural in nature, and often imply little more than urging health professionals to display greater cultural sensitivity in delivering services to people from minority ethnic populations than has often hitherto been the case. However, more radical critiques – particularly where combined with political and historical analysis of racism – suggest that orthodox medicine is fundamentally incapable of delivering appropriate services to minority ethnic groups, since it is deeply immured in the network of dominant social institutions which oppress them (Ahmad, 1993b). It is perhaps hardly surprising that the former position – despite its possible shortcomings – has had more to say on the practicalities of the interactions between health professionals and minority ethnic patients.

Developing specific initiatives

Having discussed in fairly general terms the kinds of issues which health policy-makers face, we now turn to five particular areas of policy attention, varying in their degree of specificity, as exemplars of some of the issues which have arisen in developing policy responses to the perceived needs of minority ethnic populations. They are as follows:

- Contracting for minority ethnic health in the reformed NHS

- Minority ethnic representation in NHS non-executive membership

- The introduction of ethnic monitoring of service use

- The use of linkworkers and advocates in health education campaigns

- Service delivery for sickle cell disorders.

These have been chosen to illustrate the range of structural issues that arise in attempting to address the problems discussed in the previous section, and which can both enable and impede the formulation of appropriate policy.

The NHS reforms

The emphasis on contracting for the needs of the local population in the reformed NHS of the 1990s has provoked considerable interest among those concerned with minority ethnic health issues (Bahl, 1993; Johnson, 1992a; Rathwell, 1991). In addition, the recognition in *The Health of the Nation* of ethnic differences in patterns of health, and the emphasis in the Patient's Charter on respect for privacy, dignity and 'religious and cultural beliefs' (Department of Health, 1991) have been viewed as overdue indications that policy-makers are taking the heterogeneous needs of patients seriously (Johnson, 1992b). Clearly, it is too early to assess the extent to which the reforms have facilitated better provision for people from minority ethnic populations, but in theory they provide the opportunity for more innovative and flexible approaches to provision, such as allowing purchasers leverage to demand services which better address the health needs of local minority ethnic populations, or through contracting in partnership with the voluntary sector (Jeyasingham, 1992; Rathwell, 1991). On the other hand, much depends upon the behaviour of purchasers, and there is a danger both that the needs of minority ethnic populations will be seen as tangential to key priorities and that the geographic distribution of minority ethnic groups will lead to a residualisation of their needs in newly emerging structures of health care provision, perhaps especially in community care (Ahmad, 1992b; Doyle et al., 1994; Rathwell, 1991; Walker and Ahmad, 1993).

In an attempt to explore ways of building an enduring minority ethnic dimension into the mainstream contracting process, the King's Fund, in association with the Department of Health, awarded grants to four purchasing authorities in 1990. The projects focused on different aspects of contracting for a variety of services, but were generally concerned with involving minority ethnic populations through consultation in needs assessment and service development, setting and monitoring quality standards in contracts with particular reference to minority ethnic populations, and in developing new services and improving existing ones to cater better for people from such populations. It would appear that these projects succeeded in raising the profile of minority ethnic issues in the contracting process and drew attention to a number of issues in access to and utilisation of services (Mohammed, 1993). It is questionable whether they provide generalisable models of policy-making for minority ethnic groups, but the early indications are that they have charted useful territory in attempting to operationalise the new emphasis on user-sensitive purchasing. Indeed, in the face of the heterogeneity of minority ethnic health needs, the relative devolvement of the purchasing process and the dominance of professional models in priority setting (Stubbs, 1993), the likely success of attempts to formalise the process of purchasing for minority ethnic health remains uncertain (but see Fulop and Jewkes, 1992; Gunaratnam, 1993b).

Non-executive membership

Figure 7.1 (see page 115) indicated that concern about the adequate representation of people from minority ethnic populations in the non-executive membership of NHS organisations has been expressed for some time. A recent report emphasises the continuing need to address this issue in the reformed NHS, underscoring its argument with the startling figures that only four out of 530 trust and health authority chairs, and only 45 out of some 1,500 trust and regional non-executives, are from minority ethnic populations (NAHAT and King's Fund Centre, 1993).

The representational role of NHS non-executives is somewhat unclear, and there is no statutory obligation for them to reflect the concerns of all sections of the local population. However, it is apparent from the figures quoted above that the composition of client populations is not currently reflected within most NHS organisations, and that both the NHS and its patients are therefore likely to suffer from the denial of the skills and insights that greater minority ethnic non-executive membership would bring. The NAHAT/King's Fund report identifies some of the current obstacles to more effective recruitment, and calls for national and local action to address the issue.

Clearly, such action is an essential step in guaranteeing proper participation for people from minority ethnic groups in public institutions. From another perspective, however, important questions remain about the likely success of these individuals in re-focusing NHS attention on minority ethnic health issues. As Saggar (1993) has argued, in the absence of a stable and committed constellation of interests, agreed 'race' policies may not emerge. Thus, membership may not in itself achieve significant change, and few commentators have explicitly charted the kinds of initiatives that minority ethnic non-executives might productively pursue.

Ethnic monitoring

Recording the ethnicity of service users as part of routine NHS data collection, when combined with population denominators from census data, can provide information on ethnic patterns in local service utilisation. Such management information can assist in planning services for minority ethnic populations and identifying gaps in provision (Karmi and Horton, 1992). For this reason, following the introduction of ethnic monitoring in education and social services, the Department of Health has proposed to introduce ethnic monitoring in the NHS. Originally, it was intended that it be introduced across the whole of the service by April 1993, but its implementation has been subject to considerable delay during further consultation. It has recently been announced that ethnic monitoring will be introduced in April 1995 as a mandatory part of the contract minimum data set for all providers, but for in-patients only (NHS Executive, 1994). This will involve asking patients to indicate their ethnicity from a list replicating the ethnic categories employed in the 1991 Census, with the aim that health authorities:

> should assess whether all sections of the population are gaining equal access to NHS hospital services, whether the services are appropriate, and what services should be provided in the future
>
> (NHS Executive, 1994, p.2).

Relatively little detailed attention has been paid to how the information yielded by ethnic monitoring can best be used for these purposes. Karmi and Horton (1992) identify a number of institutional obstacles which might obstruct the flow of data to the relevant people, suggesting the need for it to be properly integrated into the decision-making process. Others have questioned the utility of large-scale data collection in the absence of clearly formulated hypotheses about the relevant ethnic health issues (Ahmad and Sheldon, 1991). In this respect, ethnic monitoring raises many of the broader issues about ethnic data collection discussed in Chapter 1. Are the ethnic categories employed sufficiently sensitive to enable meaningful policy development? Will the mere collection of statistics be a substitute for a managerial commitment to action? Certainly, the routine production of ethnic statistics can easily lead to the 'mindless empiricism' feared by Ahmad and Sheldon. Moreover, ethnic monitoring alone does not necessarily enable managers to identify the precise factors underlying patterns of service usage which require policy attention (Heath, 1991). On the other hand, as Chapter 5 showed, there is a dearth of useful information on ethnic patterns of utilisation, and particularly of health outcomes. To the extent that ethnic monitoring might help correct these deficiencies and encourage health authorities to confront the health needs of their local minority populations, its introduction may achieve positive results. As Heath (1991) points out, in order to be useful ethnic monitoring, like any form of audit, needs the cycle to be completed with the implementation of relevant policy. This requires appropriate frameworks within which to interpret and act upon ethnic monitoring data.

Linkworkers and advocates: the Stop Rickets and Asian Mother and Baby Campaigns

Concern about rickets and poor perinatal health among South Asian populations towards the end of the 1970s led the Department of Health to establish two successive health education campaigns in the early 1980s. The Stop Rickets Campaign and the later Asian Mother and Baby Campaign (AMBC) ran for 18 months and three years respectively. They had much in common, sharing the same director, the same management structure and a broadly similar approach. Both campaigns initiated community-based health education programmes among the relevant populations, advising on appropriate lifestyles and use of health services. In addition, the AMBC attempted to improve the quality of the maternity services provided to South Asian women, pioneering the use of linkworkers. These were South Asian women, generally of similar background to the maternity patients, who had also experienced maternity care. Their role was:

> to interpret, to explain the health care system, to encourage the uptake of services, to escort women to appointments and generally to act as a bridge between the…women and the health care professionals
>
> (Hicks and Hayes, 1991, p.90).

Both campaigns reported considerable success, particularly in improving knowledge among the South Asian population and in improving the quality of communication between health professionals and South Asian women (Bahl, 1990; Stop Rickets Campaign, 1983). A 50 per cent increase in the uptake of antenatal services associated with the AMBC was reported in one health authority (Bahl, 1990). Despite these practical successes, the campaigns have been criticised on a number of grounds from a more structural point of view (Parsons *et al.*, 1993; Rocheron, 1991). First, it is argued that they largely ignored deprivation and racism, concentrating instead on a 'cultural' model of improving communication between health professionals and the client group. As Rocheron points out in the case of the AMBC, such an approach:

> runs the risk, in the long term, of remaining tangential to the complex causes which determine higher perinatal mortality rates among some groups of Asian women
>
> (1991, p.189).

Moreover, the underlying principle of both campaigns in acting to change individual behaviour towards majority norms is questionable both politically, (Rocheron, 1991) and in terms of accepted health promotion practice (Rose, 1992; Syme, 1986), which places the emphasis on structural change to make healthy lifestyle choices easier. Certainly, the decision in the Stop Rickets Campaign to emphasise individual behavioural change rather than recommending fortification of chapatti flour with vitamin D has been criticised in the light of the policy to fortify margarine with vitamin D, which had previously been adopted to prevent rickets in the majority population (Donovan, 1984), although this decision has been defended on practical grounds (Stop Rickets Campaign, 1983). Nevertheless, research by Stephens *et al.* (1981) indicated that health education had had little impact on dietary intake of vitamin D among South Asians in Rochdale, leading the investigators to ask 'is encouragement enough?'.

The Stop Rickets Campaign and the AMBC have been characterised as consensus-making processes which, by attempting to improve communication between health professionals and clients, adopted a model of internal 'cultural' change within both the patient and the professional groups. However, by constituting South Asian women as a special client group, they may unwittingly have inculcated stereotypes of 'black pathology' (Rocheron, 1991). At the same time, their impact on health outcomes has not been the focus of significant attention. Indeed, the model of 'cultural change' within the professional group may obscure more pressing problems of access to health services which typically obtain in the deprived inner-city areas where the majority of South Asian people live.

The enduring legacy of the AMBC has been the concept of the linkworker. Linkworkers continue to be employed by many health authorities to improve communication between professionals and patients (predominantly South Asian women) in a number of clinical settings. However, in a survey of several health authorities, Hicks and Hayes (1991) found that authorities typically:

• Lacked knowledge about the extent of need for the linkworker service

• Lacked knowledge about languages spoken locally

• Failed to advertise the linkworker service to the relevant populations

• Did not provide the service out of working hours.

This led them to conclude that:

> *if Linkworker provision is seen as a valuable commodity in enhancing equal opportunities in health care, then the service needs to be systematised. If it is perceived to be of little demonstrable value, then it should be scrapped. In either case, some clear policy decisions are required*
>
> (1991, p.89).

The use of linkworkers to increase the uptake of breast screening by women of Pakistani and Bangladeshi origin in Oldham is one of the few policies in the area of ethnic health to have been evaluated through a randomised controlled trial. Hoare *et al.* (1994) found that there were no significant differences in the uptake of screening between a group of women receiving a visit from trained linkworkers, who provided information about the screening service and encouraged attendance, and a control group who received no visit. It is possible that any potential effect was diminished by 'contamination' of the control group through informal transfer of information from the intervention group. Nevertheless, in contrast to earlier studies which pointed to the efficacy of personal contact in improving the uptake of cervical screening (McAvoy and Raza, 1991), the study calls into question the utility of diffuse strategies of community intervention employing linkworkers, and underlines the point made by Hicks and Hayes about the need for a more systematic approach to their deployment.

An alternative model, arising out of work in City and Hackney Health Authority in the early 1980s, is that of the health advocate. In some respects this is a similar role to that of the linkworker, but here the emphasis is on the advocate as a 'watchguard' of the client's interests who "ensures that the right questions are asked and the right information given" (Rocheron, 1991, p.191). Cornwell and Gordon (1984) further describe the development of the advocate concept at City and Hackney as based in a 'community supportive' rather than 'community oppressive' model, in which the advocate's primary accountability is to the minority ethnic population rather than to health care professionals. It therefore provides a less internal and less consensual model of organisational change than that implicit in the linkworker scheme. Nevertheless, as with the AMBC, the project – which again focused principally on maternity care – inevitably placed considerable emphasis on developing understanding and communication between professionals and users. An unusual feature of the project is the extent to which it has been evaluated in terms of its impact on birth outcomes (Parsons and Day, 1992). Although it is difficult to apportion the extent to which improvements over time were a direct result of the project, as Chapter 6 showed, there is some evidence that advocacy in City and Hackney has had a tangible positive effect on birth outcomes (see page 112).

Sickle cell disorders

As it was suggested in Chapter 3, SCDs are of relatively minor importance in terms of their contribution to the overall burden of ill health among minority ethnic populations, but since they predominantly affect these populations the provision of services for sufferers has assumed some political significance as a test of the willingness in the NHS to address minority ethnic health issues. Despite the fact that SCDs are severe chronic diseases requiring considerable clinical and social support, "a coordinated effort to organise comprehensive care for SCD has never taken off" (Brozovic et al., 1989, p. 103). There are a number of SCD centres based in health facilities around the country, together with some 20 districts which have an SCD counsellor or development officer (Anionwu, 1993). However, Anionwu suggests that provision is in general *ad hoc* and patchy. An earlier survey by the Runnymede Trust contrasted this with the provision of services for genetic diseases which predominantly affect white people:

> *If phenylketonuria with an estimated incidence of about 10-12 cases in London every year can be covered by a central newborn screening and follow-up programme...then sickle cell disease, with at least 4,000 sufferers in Britain, must be offered equal treatment*

(quoted in Anionwu, 1989, p.128).

The need for coordinated acute and community services to address the needs of SCD sufferers, and the absence of such provision except in a few areas such as Brent, has been a consistent theme in writings on the subject in recent years (Anionwu, 1993; Brozovic et al., 1989; Franklin, 1988; Prashar et al., 1985; Sickle Cell Society, 1983). These writings suggest that treatment could be developed along the same model used for the care of haemophiliacs, with a centrally sponsored programme of antenatal diagnosis, community screening and counselling upon request, genetic counselling and liaison between haematologists, paediatricians and community-based health professionals, as well as education of other staff likely to come into contact with sufferers.

Another area of concern is the lack of appropriately formulated contraceptive advice given to women suffering from SCDs. Although unwanted pregnancies are particularly undesirable for these women, use of oral contraceptives is contraindicated since it can cause thrombosis and painful crises. Research by Howard et al. (1993) suggests a lack of consensus among health professionals about the relevant sorts of advice and support to provide.

Overall, the latest indications are that although the Department of Health supports the development of comprehensive SCD care within the NHS and the introduction of antenatal and neonatal screening, priorities for service development will be left in the hands of individual commissioning authorities (Department of Health, 1994). While it could be argued that this is in keeping with the logic of new structures of NHS provision and the more flexible application of child health surveillance practices, it is scarcely surprising that the historic lack of attention to SCD in comparison to other inherited diseases has been perceived as indicative of, at best, complacency and, at worst, racism (Franklin, 1988). It is worth noting that the failure to promote coordinated care for the 'special needs' of minority ethnic populations is not restricted to SCDs alone. For example, although tuberculosis is often identified as an important health issue among most minority ethnic groups, Hardie and Watson (1993) have shown that there is little provision of screening and treatment at the district health authority level.

Critiques of policy-making

This chapter has indicated that health policies specifically designed to address minority health issues are, in keeping with broader currents of public policy, of relatively recent origin. Most analysts agree that policy-making has been piecemeal and lacking in coherence, a view which Figure 7.1 (page 115) arguably confirms. This has been compounded by the continued lack of secure long-term funding for minority ethnic health issues. Recently, such issues have assumed somewhat greater importance in health service thinking, and a more consistent policy agenda has developed in the Department of Health, reflected in new initiatives such as the creation of an Ethnic Health Unit and the introduction of ethnic monitoring. Nevertheless, a strong case could still be made that 'ethnic pluralism' in health policy-making remains marginal at both national and local levels.

At the same time, among those who are concerned with policy development for minority ethnic health there is little consensus about the best way forward. Two strands of policy critique can be discerned. First, 'liberal' arguments suggest that the main problem has been the invisibility to policy attention of minority ethnic populations and their particular needs; in constituting minority ethnic populations as a special client group, some of these problems can be rectified, in the same way that policies have been developed to improve services for other special groups, such as the elderly and mentally ill. Thus, White and Bhopal (1993) call for a national strategy of health promotion for minority ethnic populations; Johnson (1992a) cautiously welcomes the recognition of ethnic groups in *The Health of the Nation;* Bahl (1993) emphasises the need to train health professionals and provide information about minority ethnic groups; and a number of authors argue that increasing NHS accountability to its users is a key issue (Bahl, 1993; Mohammed, 1993; Johnson, 1992b). Implicit in most of these arguments is the view that improving access to appropriate health care is the key issue.

A more radical strand is suspicious of such approaches, arguing that by constituting the health of people from minority ethnic populations as a subject of special character, it is the people from these populations themselves who are made into the 'problem'. The focus on 'special needs' engenders unhelpful approaches and terminologies – 'Asian rickets' being a good example of the latter (Goel *et al.*, 1981) – while missing the importance of neglected common needs, such as CHD among South Asians (Bhopal, 1993). Moreover, the emphasis on special needs elides the significance of racism and systematic socioeconomic disadvantage in determining the health of minority ethnic groups. Writers espousing this view (see, for example, Ahmad, 1992c; Baxter and Baxter, 1988; Donovan, 1984; Kushnick, 1988; Rocheron, 1991; Torkington, 1983) display varying degrees of confidence in the ability of the NHS to adjust to minority health issues, but generally locate the possibilities for change outside the bureaucratic process.

An examination of Figure 7.1 would suggest that, in so far as either strand of critique has successfully contributed to policy development, liberal approaches have been predominant. Although this may be expected on the grounds that they are clearly less threatening to the political *status quo*, it is probably also true to say that the radical critique has had relatively little to say in concrete terms about how policy *ought* to be developed. For example, Baxter and Baxter (1988) point to the structural causation of poor health among minority ethnic populations and argue convincingly of the need for community participation in policy development. However, in describing the nature of such participation they identify little more than "the active participation of people from ethnic minority communities on existing committees" (1988, p.569). Having identified the insuperable racialisation of existing structures, it is perhaps difficult realistically to propose anything other than revolutionary change.

In this sense, the radical critique has much in common with neo-Marxist analyses of the welfare state which, as Harrison *et al.* (1990) argue, have successfully demonstrated how broader socioeconomic and ideological forces structure the provision of welfare, but have engaged less successfully with an empirical agenda of policy analysis to specify – in this case – better services for minority ethnic populations. Perhaps inevitably, propositions for liberal, incremental change are more easily accepted and implemented. Nevertheless, the radical critique provides an important reminder of the dangers of taking too limited a view of the circumstances that affect the health of people from minority ethnic populations.

In view of the substantial doubts that remain about the appropriate way even to understand ethnic patterns of health and health care, it is scarcely surprising that a concrete policy agenda has failed to emerge. Moreover, policy responses in one area of welfare provision must be considered in the context of the active reproduction of minority ethnic disadvantage elsewhere in British society and politics. Clearly, however, policy-making is not a unitary phenomenon, and it would be misleading to suggest that practical policies have not been developed at the central and local levels to help improve the health of minority ethnic populations. In fact, Saggar's (1993) concept of a 'race policy environment', in which stakeholders from different and often competing positions contest the formulation of policy, provides a useful summation of the fractured progress of the development of policies for minority ethnic health.

Conclusion

As the previous chapters have shown, there is an extensive literature documenting many aspects of the health experience of minority ethnic populations. Yet some quite fundamental questions remain unclear, not only because they have not been adequately researched but also because of a lack of consensus about how they *should* be researched, and how appropriate policies should accordingly be developed. These concluding remarks briefly highlight some of the questions which need to be addressed.

Three key issues requiring more sustained analytical attention can be identified. These are:

- A need for theoretically informed empirical research to fill major gaps in understanding of the health and health care of minority ethnic populations. This entails both gaining better knowledge about particular ethnic groups, and in gaining new kinds of knowledge about all groups.

- A need to disentangle the various mechanisms underlying ethnic patterns in health experience.

- A need to engage in wider discussion about appropriate policies within the health sector to improve the health of minority ethnic populations, and a need to consider how such policies can be systematically implemented.

The remainder of the chapter comments briefly on each of these points in turn.

A striking point about existing knowledge of ethnic patterns in health experience is its incompleteness. Very little is known at all about many ethnic groups: the Irish, Chinese, Sri Lankans, South and East Europeans, 'Arabs', Caribbean Asians, Gypsies and the long-established African/Caribbean populations in several port cities spring to mind. On a slightly different conceptual level, the experience of people with 'mixed' ethnic origin also needs to be better documented.

Some of these problems may relate in part to ambiguities about the definition of ethnicity in comparison to 'race', which complicate questions about the proper object of analysis in ethnic studies (see Chapter 1). It may also relate to the small size of the relevant populations or their invisibility in official statistics. However, even among some major 'black' populations, there is a dearth of empirical analysis. Indeed, as Stubbs (1993) has pointed out, most research has focused upon South Asian to the exclusion of Caribbean and African populations. Extending existing knowledge of the less frequently examined minority ethnic populations is not only important from a simple, empirical perspective, but may also be important in understanding causal mechanisms. It is noteworthy, for example, that the Irish population in Britain has a health profile which differs distinctively from both the majority white population and other minority populations. As Mays has commented:

some of the most instructive insights into the nature of the relation between ethnic group membership and health can be derived from the study of the Irish population in Britain. Their history shows that despite strong cultural similarity, differences in material circumstances and health between the Irish and the 'host' population are still visible after more than a century, sustained by the complex interaction of selective migration, discrimination and a disadvantageous position in the labour market. This suggests that the differences seen in the black population will not rapidly evaporate and are not fundamentally cultural in origin
(1994, p.67).

Moving from gaps in knowledge of groups to gaps in the kind of knowledge, an excessive reliance upon mortality data is apparent in the literature. Apart from the usual biases which this introduces, such a reliance is arguably even more problematic among minority ethnic groups in view of their typically younger age structure. At the same time, research interest in the health of minority ethnic elders is in its infancy. The 'triple jeopardy' described by Norman (1985) of old age, racism and inaccessible services will undoubtedly form an increasingly prominent issue in service provision which so far has been inadequately addressed. Other sociodemographic factors cutting across ethnic categories also require greater attention. For example, although several important qualitative studies have examined aspects of women's health, both men's health as a gendered issue and gender differences in health experience within minority ethnic groups have received scant attention (Krieger and Fee, 1994). Similarly, the significance of socioeconomic status both within and across minority ethnic groups has been examined with little subtlety. More important, perhaps, is the substantial lack of either reliable data or sophisticated research attention to ethnic patterns in the use of health services, and – in contrast to a burgeoning American literature – the outcomes of health interventions.

Bhopal (1991; 1989) has identified two of the obstacles to producing more productive and comprehensive research. First, as it was suggested in Chapter 2, there is a need for more careful distinctions to be made between relative and absolute incidence of illness, the latter being most relevant to health service planning. Second:

most research … has been undertaken by researchers whose main interest is in one … disorder. They seek a new perspective on that disorder; the ethnic minority angle is peripheral. In the future, more research needs to be done by researchers whose main interest is in ethnic minorities and their health; the disorder being peripheral

(1989, p.3).

Certainly, the important body of epidemiological research into the aetiology of specific disorders among ethnic groups needs to be complemented by research with a broader concern for the general health of minority ethnic populations.

Turning to the issue of ethnicity itself, there is a need for more careful discussion of the meaning of ethnicity as an explanatory variable in empirical health research. Given the relative poverty of the empirical record, a simple step forward would be for researchers to be more explicit about their understanding of ethnicity and their operationalisation of the concept. This must be accompanied by clear hypotheses which lead to proper adjustment – where appropriate – for confounding variables, such as morbidity in the case of utilisation studies, and socioeconomic status in aetiological enquiry, although much remains to be learned about how to achieve the latter effectively with specific reference to minority ethnic groups.

More fundamentally, however, researchers must begin to disentangle the multiple impact of the various possible explanatory factors outlined in Chapter 4 upon the health of ethnic groups. Some important theoretical discussions have begun to address this issue from a range of viewpoints (Andrews and Jewson, 1993; Cooper and David, 1986; Kleinman, 1987; LaVeist, 1994; Senior and Bhopal, 1994; Sheldon and Parker, 1992; Stubbs, 1993; D. Williams et al., 1994). In doing so, it is important that identification of the relevant mechanisms is kept separate from critical analysis of the politics of ethnicity and health. To be sure, research does not exist in a political vacuum. Indeed, writers such as Ahmad (1993b), Stubbs (1993) and Donovan (1984) have convincingly shown that claims of value neutrality in much research on the health of minority ethnic populations – particularly that which focuses upon minority 'culture' – are spurious. Yet, as Stubbs (1993) points out, it is insufficient simply to replace the 'catch-all' category of culture with another one, say, of racism. If racism has a direct impact upon health, *how* does it do so? Similarly, is it sufficient to locate ethnic differences in health within socioeconomic differences between populations, or is attention required to the particular experience of social and economic conditions within and between ethnic groups?

Such questions indicate above all the need for careful strategies of empirical research which address the dynamic and interactive nature of the social factors associated with ethnic patterns of health experience. Although writers such as D. Williams *et al.* (1994) have begun to chart in exemplary fashion how such empirical insights can be built up into persuasive multifactorial accounts of the determinants of minority ethnic health experience, it is probably true to say that theoretical efforts of this sort have so far exceeded empirical ones. Nevertheless, as this review has shown, a good deal of empirical work has already been undertaken in epidemiology (Ramaiya *et al.*, 1991), historical sociology and demography (Williams, 1994a,b; 1992), ethnography (Donovan, 1986; Dressler, 1993) and geography (LaVeist, 1993; Robinson, 1987) which has helped considerably to refine understanding of how the social ascription of ethnicity is associated with health experiences.

Clearly, however, better knowledge of the causes of poor health among minority ethnic groups is not a sufficient condition for tackling them. Indeed, perhaps in some circumstances research can serve to mystify the effects of poverty and racism, or be used as a substitute for action. Here, the critique of health policy mentioned above, and examined in Chapter 7, provides a useful context within which to debate the formulation of appropriate policy (see, for example, Ahmad, 1992c; Williams, 1989). It has demonstrated the need to understand ethnicity as a pervasive social fact which structures individual experience, in contrast to the way it has typically received attention from policy makers, whereby:

> the emphasis has been to identify a particular issue and to concentrate effort on that issue at the cost of all other health needs. The effects of this approach have been to marginalise Black people's health needs to a limited number of conditions and issues, as well as to remove any need to develop new approaches that will bring about structural and organisational change
>
> (Mohammed, 1993, p.1).

It was argued in Chapter 7 that policy-making is indeed beginning to move towards a wider conception of the health needs of minority ethnic populations. However, it was also suggested that there is a lack of both knowledge and agreement about how this wider conception can be translated into practical policy initiatives. Policy analysis in the health sector appears to have absorbed the contrasting positions of broader multiculturalist and anti-racist policy debates, along with the attendant weaknesses of both positions. Although, far from being a 'problem', the health of most minority ethnic groups compares favourably with the general population, it is important to recognise that major societal obstacles exist to the development of an equitable opportunity structure in health and welfare across ethnic groups. Thus, while an increasingly sophisticated research literature exists which is beginning to provide the basis for the development of knowledge-based health policy interventions, what is now required is a much broader – and much more difficult – political debate about how these interventions can be made to work.

Bibliography

W. Ahmad (1994), 'Consanguinity and related demons: science and racism in the debate on consanguinity and birth outcome', in C. Samson and N. South (1994).

W. Ahmad (1993a), *'Race' and Health in Contemporary Britain,* Open University Press, Buckingham.

W. Ahmad (1993b), 'Making black people sick; 'race', ideology and health research', in W. Ahmad (1993a), pp. 11-33.

W. Ahmad (1993c), 'Introduction', in W. Ahmad (1993a), pp. 1-7.

W. Ahmad (1992a), *The Politics of 'Race' and Health,* Race Relations Research Unit, Bradford.

W. Ahmad (1992b), ' "Race", disadvantage and discourse: contextualising black people's health', in W. Ahmad (1992a), pp. 7-38.

W. Ahmad (1992c), 'The maligned healer: the 'hakim' and western medicine', *New Community,* Vol. 18, No. 4, pp. 521-536.

W. Ahmad and T. Sheldon (1991), 'Race' and statistics', *Radical Statistics Newsletter,* Vol. 48, pp. 27-33.

W. Ahmad, E. Kernohan and M. Baker (1991a), 'Patients' choice of general practitioner: importance of patients' and doctors' sex and ethnicity', *British Journal of General Practice,* Vol. 41, pp. 330-331.

W. Ahmad, M. Baker and E. Kernohan (1991b), 'General practitioners' perceptions of Asian and non-Asian patients', *Family Practice,* Vol. 8, No. 1, pp. 52-56.

W. Ahmad, E. Kernohan and M. Baker (1989a), 'Health of British Asians; a research review', *Community Medicine,* Vol. 11, No. 1, pp. 49-56.

W. Ahmad, E. Kernohan and M. Baker (1989b), 'Influence of ethnicity and unemployment on the perceived health of a sample of general practice attenders', *Community Medicine,* Vol. 11, No. 2, pp. 148-156.

W. Ahmad, E. Kernohan and M. Baker (1989c), 'Patients' choice of general practitioner: influence of patients' fluency in English and the ethnicity and sex of the doctor', *Journal of the Royal College of General Practitioners,* Vol. 39, pp. 153-155.

W. Ahmad, E. Kernohan and M. Baker (1988), 'Alcohol and cigarette consumption among white and Asian general practice patients', *Health Education Journal,* Vol. 47, No. 4, pp. 128-129.

M. Alderson (1983), *An Introduction to Epidemiology,* Macmillan, Basingstoke.

H. Aldrich, J. Cater, T. Jones, D. McEvoy and P. Velleman (1986), 'Asian residential concentration and business development: an analysis of shop-keepers' customers in three cities', *New Community,* Vol. 13, No. 1, pp. 52-64.

R. Alford (1975), *Health Care Politics,* University of Chicago Press, Chicago.

T. Allen (1994), *The Invention of the White Race,* Verso, London.

R. Alwash and M. McCarthy (1988), 'Accidents in the home among children under 5: ethnic differences or social disadvantage', *British Medical Journal,* Vol. 296, pp. 1450-1453.

K. Amin and C. Oppenheim (1992), *Poverty in Black and White,* Child Poverty Action Group/Runnymede Trust, London.

B. Anderson (1991), *Imagined Communities: Reflections on the Origins and Spread of Nationalism,* Verso, London.

J. Anderson, C. Blue and A. Lau (1991), 'Women's perspectives on chronic illness: ethnicity, ideology and restructuring of life', *Social Science and Medicine,* Vol. 33, No. 2, pp. 101-113.

J. Anderson, H. Elfert and M. Lai (1989), 'Ideology in the clinical context: chronic illness, ethnicity and the discourse on normalisation', *Sociology of Health and Illness,* Vol. 11, No. 3, pp. 253-278.

A. Andrews and N. Jewson (1993), 'Ethnicity and infant deaths: the implications of recent statistical evidence for materialist explanations', *Sociology of Health and Illness,* Vol. 15, No. 2, pp. 137-156.

C. Aneshensel (1992), 'Social stress: theory and research', *Annual Review of Sociology,* Vol. 18, pp. 15-38.

E. Anionwu (1993), 'Sickle cell and thalassaemia: community experiences and official response', in W. Ahmad (1993b), pp. 76-95.

E. Anionwu (1989), 'Running a sickle cell centre: community counselling', in J. Cruikshank and D. Beevers (1989), pp 123-135.

M. Anwar (1990), 'Ethnic classifications, ethnic monitoring and the 1991 Census', *New Community,* Vol. 16, No. 4, pp. 607-615.

M. Anwar (1979), *The Myth of Return: Pakistanis in Britain,* Heinemann, London.

C. Armstead, K. Lawler, G. Gorden, J. Cross and J. Gibbons (1989), 'Relationship of racial stressors to blood pressure responses and anger expression in black college students', *Health Psychology,* Vol. 8, No. 5, pp. 541-556.

K. Atkin and J. Rollings (1993), *Community Care in a Multi-Racial Britain: A Critical Review of the Literature,* HMSO, London.

K. Atkin, E. Cameron, F. Badger and H. Evers (1989), 'Asian elders' knowledge and future use of community social and health services', *New Community,* Vol.15, No.3, pp.439-445.

J. Ayaniyan (1994), 'Race, class and the quality of medical care', *Journal of the American Medical Association,* Vol. 271, No. 15, pp. 1207-1208.

J. Ayaniyan (1993), 'Heart disease in black and white', *New England Journal of Medicine,* Vol. 329, No. 9, pp. 656-658.

C. Bagley (1971), 'The social aetiology of schizophrenia in immigrant groups', *International Journal of Social Psychiatry,* Vol. 17, pp. 292-304.

V. Bahl (1993), 'Development of a black and ethnic minority health policy at the Department of Health', in A. Hopkins and V. Bahl (1993), pp. 1-9.

V. Bahl (1990), 'Results of the Asian Mother and Baby Campaign', *Midwife, Health Visitor and Community Nurse,* Vol. 23, No. 2, pp. 60-62.

D. Baker, R. Illsley and D. Vagero (1993), 'Today or in the past? The origins of ischaemic heart disease', *Journal of Public Health Medicine*, Vol. 15, No. 3, pp. 243-248.

M. Baker, R. Bandaranayake and M. Schweiger (1984), 'Differences in rate of uptake of immunisation among ethnic groups', *British Medical Journal*, Vol. 288, pp. 1075-1078.

R. Balarajan (1991), 'Ethnic differences in mortality from ischaemic heart disease and cerebrovascular disease in England and Wales', *British Medical Journal*, Vol. 302, pp. 560-564.

R. Balarajan and V. Raleigh (1993), *Ethnicity and Health: A Guide for the NHS*, Department of Health, London.

R. Balarajan and L. Bulusu (1990), 'Mortality among immigrants in England and Wales, 1979-83', in M. Britton (1990), pp. 103-121.

R. Balarajan and V. Raleigh (1990), 'Variations in perinatal, neonatal, postneonatal and infant mortality by mother's country of birth, 1982-85', in M. Britton (1990), pp. 123-137.

R. Balarajan and B. Botting (1989), 'Perinatal mortality in England and Wales: variations by mother's country of birth', *Health Trends*, Vol. 21, pp. 79-84.

R. Balarajan and P. Yuen (1986), 'British smoking and drinking habits: variations by country of birth', *Community Medicine*, Vol. 8, No. 3, pp. 237-239.

R. Balarajan, V. Raleigh and P. Yuen (1991), 'Hospital care among ethnic minorities in Britain', *Health Trends*, Vol. 23, No. 3, pp. 90-93.

R. Balarajan, V. Raleigh and B. Botting (1989a), 'Sudden infant death syndrome and postneonatal mortality in immigrants in England and Wales', *British Medical Journal*, Vol. 298, pp. 716-720.

R. Balarajan, V. Raleigh and B. Botting (1989b), 'Mortality from congenital malformations in England and Wales: variations by mother's country of birth', *Archives of Disease in Childhood*, Vol. 64, pp. 1457-1462.

R. Balarajan, P. Yuen and V. Raleigh (1989c), 'Ethnic differences in general practitioner consultations', *British Medical Journal*, Vol. 299, pp. 958-960.

R. Balarajan, L. Bulusu, A. Adelstein and V. Shukla (1984), 'Patterns of mortality among migrants to England and Wales from the Indian subcontinent', *British Medical Journal*, Vol. 289, pp. 1185-1187.

R. Ballard (1992), 'New clothes for the emperor? The conceptual nakedness of the race relations industry in Britain', *New Community*, Vol. 18, No. 3, pp. 481-492.

R. Ballard (1979), 'Ethnic minorities and the social services', in V. Khan (1979a), pp. 146-164.

D. Barker (1991), 'The foetal and infant origins of inequalities in health in Britain', *Journal of Public Health Medicine*, Vol. 13, No. 2, pp. 64-68.

R. Barker and M. Baker (1990), 'Incidence of cancer in Bradford Asians', *Journal of Epidemiology and Community Health*, Vol. 44, pp. 125-129.

M. Barrett and M. McIntosh (1985), 'Ethnocentrism and socialist-feminist theory', *Feminist Review*, No. 20, pp. 23-47.

C. Baxter and D. Baxter (1988), 'Racial inequalities in health: a challenge to the British National Health Service', *International Journal of Health Services*, Vol. 18, No. 4, pp. 563-571.

A. Beattie, M. Gott, L. Jones and M. Sidell (1993), *Health and Wellbeing: A Reader*, Macmillan, Basingstoke.

L. Becker, B. Han, P. Meyer, F. Wright, K. Rhodes, D. Smith, J. Barrett and CPR Chicago Project (1993), 'Racial differences in the incidence of cardiac arrest and subsequent survival', *New England Journal of Medicine*, Vol. 329, No. 9, pp. 600-606.

J. Beliappa (1991), *Illness or Distress? Alternative Models of Mental Health*, Confederation of Indian Organisations, London.

M. Bellamy (1994), 'Taking forward an ethnicity and health programme in a Health Agency', Paper presented to a workshop on sharing initiatives to improve the health of ethnic groups, Health Education Authority, 17th January 1994.

M. Benzeval, K. Judge and C. Smaje (in press), 'Beyond race, class and ethnicity: deprivation and health in Britain', *Health Services Research*.

M. Benzeval and K. Judge (1993), *The Development of Population-Based Need Indicators from Self-Reported Health Care Utilisation Data*, King's Fund Institute, London.

M. Benzeval, K. Judge and M. Solomon (1992), *The Health Status of Londoners: A Comparative Perspective*, King's Fund, London.

A. Bhalla and K. Blakemore (1981), *Elders of the Minority Ethnic Groups*, AFFOR, Birmingham.

A. Bhat, R. Carr-Hill and S. Ohri (1988) *Britain's Black Population*, Gower, Aldershot.

A. Bhatt and R. Dickinson (1992), 'An analysis of health education materials for minority communities by cultural and linguistic group', *Health Education Journal*, Vol. 51, No. 2, pp. 72-77.

R. Bhopal (undated), *Setting Priorities for Health Care for Ethnic Minority Groups*, Department of Epidemiology and Public Health, University of Newcastle upon Tyne.

R. Bhopal (1993), 'The coronary heart disease epidemic in 'South Asians'', *SHARE Newsletter*, No. 6, pp. 4-5.

R. Bhopal (1991), 'Health education and ethnic minorities', *British Medical Journal*, Vol. 302, p. 1338.

R. Bhopal (1989), 'Future research on the health of ethnic minorities – back to basics: a personal view', *Ethnic Minorities Health: A Current Awareness Bulletin*, Vol. 1, No. 3, pp. 1-3.

R. Bhopal (1988), 'Health care for Asians: conflict in need, demand and provision', in *Equity: a Pre-requisite for Health*, Proceedings of the 1987 Summer Scientific Conference of the Faculty of Community Medicine.

R. Bhopal (1986a), 'Asians' knowledge and behaviour on preventive health issues: smoking, alcohol, heart disease, pregnancy, rickets, malaria prophylaxis and surma', *Community Medicine*, Vol. 8, No. 4, pp. 315-321.

R. Bhopal (1986b), 'The inter-relationship of folk, traditional and Western medicine within an Asian community in Britain', *Social Science and Medicine*, Vol. 22, No. 1, pp. 99-105.

R. Bhopal and M. White (1993), 'Health promotion for ethnic minorities: past present and future', in W. Ahmad, (1993b), pp. 137-166.

R. Bhopal and L. Donaldson (1988), 'Health education for ethnic minorities: current provision and future directions', *Health Education Journal*, Vol. 47, No. 4, pp. 137-140.

R. Bhopal and A. Samim (1988), 'Immunization uptake of Glasgow Asian children: paradoxical benefit of communication barriers', *Community Medicine*, Vol. 10, No. 3, pp. 215-220.

R. Bhopal, P. Phillimore and H. Kohli (1991), 'Inappropriate use of the term 'Asian': an obstacle to ethnicity and health research', *Journal of Public Health Medicine*, Vol. 13, No. 4, pp. 244-246.

M. Bhrolchain (1990), 'The ethnicity question for the 1991 Census: background and issues', *Ethnic and Racial Studies*, Vol. 13, No. 4, pp. 542-567.

J. Black (1985a), 'The difficulties of living in Britain', *British Medical Journal*, Vol. 290, pp. 615-617.

J. Black (1985b), 'Contact with the health services', *British Medical Journal*, Vol. 290, pp. 689-690.

J. Black (1985c), 'Asian families I: cultures', *British Medical Journal*, Vol. 290, pp. 762-764.

J. Black (1985d), 'Asian families II: conditions that may be found in the children', *British Medical Journal*, Vol. 290, pp. 830-833.

J. Black (1985e), 'Families from the Mediterranean and the Aegean', *British Medical Journal*, Vol. 290, pp. 923-925.

J. Black (1985f), 'Afro-Caribbean and African families', *British Medical Journal*, Vol. 290, pp. 984-988.

J. Black (1985g), 'Chinese and Vietnamese families', *British Medical Journal*, Vol. 290, pp. 1063-1065.

Black Health Workers and Patients Group (1983), 'Psychiatry and the corporate state', *Race and Class*, Vol. 15, No. 2, pp. 49-64.

K. Blakemore (1982), 'Health and illness among the elderly of minority ethnic groups living in Birmingham: some new findings', *Health Trends*, Vol. 14, pp. 69-72.

K. Blakemore and M. Bonham (1994), *Age, Race and Ethnicity: A Comparative Approach*, Open University Press, Buckingham.

D. Blane, G. Davey Smith and M. Bartley (1993), 'Social selection: what does it contribute to social class differences in health?', *Sociology of Health and Illness*, Vol. 15, pp. 1-15.

M. Blaxter (1990), *Health and Lifestyles*, Tavistock/Routledge, London.

M. Bone, A. Bebbington and G. Nicolaas (1994), *Pilot Study (1) on the Use of Healthy Active Life Expectancy Measures*, PSSRU Discussion Paper 1047/2, Personal Social Services Research Unit, Canterbury.

A. Bonnett (1993), 'Forever 'white'? Challenges and alternatives to a 'racial' monolith', *New Community*, Vol. 20, No. 1, pp. 173-180.

H. Booth (1988), 'Identifying ethnic origin: the past, present and future of official data production', in A. Bhat *et al.* (1988), pp. 237-266.

J. Bornat, C. Pereira, D. Pilgrim and F. Williams (1993), *Community Care: A Reader*, Macmillan, Basingstoke.

P. Bourdieu (1977), *Outline of a Theory of Practice*, Cambridge University Press, Cambridge.

A. Bowes and T. Domokos (1993), 'South Asian women and health services: a study in Glasgow', *New Community*, Vol. 19, No. 4, pp. 611-626.

I. Bowler (1993), ''They're not the same as us': midwives' stereotypes of South Asian descent maternity patients', *Sociology of Health and Illness*, Vol. 15, No. 2, pp. 157-178.

S. Boyle and C. Smaje (1993), *Primary Health Care in London: Quantifying the Challenge*, King's Fund Institute, London.

S. Bradley and E. Friedman (1993), 'Cervical cytology screening: a comparison of uptake among 'Asian' and 'non-Asian' women in Oldham', *Journal of Public Health Medicine*, Vol. 15, No. 1, pp. 46-51.

F. Brancati, J. Whittle, P. Whelton, A. Seidler and M. Klag (1992), 'The excess incidence of diabetic end-stage renal disease among blacks', *Journal of the American Medical Association*, Vol. 268, No. 21, pp. 3079-3084.

British Medical Journal (1992), 'Are doctors from ethnic minorities discriminated against?', *British Medical Journal*, Vol. 304, p. 1513.

M. Britton (1990), *Mortality and Geography: A Review in the Mid-1980s*, OPCS, Series DS No. 9, London.

C. Brown (1984), *Black and White Britain: The Third PSI Survey*, Gower, Aldershot.

D. Brown, L. Gary, A. Greene and N. Milburn (1992), 'Patterns of social affiliation as predictors of depressive symptoms among urban blacks', *Journal of Health and Social Behavior*, Vol.33, pp.242-253.

M. Brozovic, S. Davies and J. Henthorn (1989), 'Haematological and clinical aspects of sickle cell disease in Britain', in J. Cruickshank and D. Beevers (1989), pp. 103-113.

I. Bruegel (1989), 'Sex and race in the labour market', *Feminist Review*, No. 32, pp. 49-68.

B. Bryan, S. Dadzoe and S. Scafe (1985), *The Heart of the Race: Black Women's Lives in Britain*, Virago, London.

S. Bundey, H. Alam, A. Kaur, S. Mir and R. Lancashire (1991), 'Why do UK-born Pakistani babies have high perinatal and neonatal mortality rates?', *Paediatric and Perinatal Epidemiology*, Vol. 5, pp. 101-114.

S. Bundey, H. Alam, A. Kaur, S. Mir and R. Lancashire (1990), 'Race, consanguinity and social features in Birmingham babies: a basis for prospective study', *Journal of Epidemiology and Community Health*, Vol. 44, pp. 130-135.

A. Burke (1984), 'Racism and psychological disturbance among West Indians in Britain', *International Journal of Social Psychiatry*, Vol. 30, pp. 50-68.

D. Butkus, E. Meydrech and S. Raju (1992), 'Racial differences in the survival of cadaveric renal allografts', *New England Journal of Medicine*, Vol. 327, No. 12, pp. 840-845.

CCCS (Centre for Contemporary Cultural Studies) (1982), *The Empire Strikes Back: Race and Racism in 70s Britain*, Hutchinson, London.

CRE (Commission for Racial Equality) (1992), *Race Relations Code of Practice in Primary Health Care Services*, CRE, London.

S. Calder, G. Anderson, W. Harper and P. Gregg (1994), 'Ethnic variation in epidemiology and rehabilitation of hip fracture', *British Medical Journal*, Vol.309, pp.1124-1125.

H. Carby (1982), 'White woman listen! Black feminism and the boundaries of sisterhood', in CCCS (1982), pp. 212-235.

L. Carpenter and I. Brockington (1980), 'A study of mental illness in Asians, West Indians and Africans living in Manchester', *British Journal of Psychiatry*, Vol. 137, pp. 201-205.

B. Centerwall (1984), 'Race, socioeconomic status and domestic homicide: Atlanta, 1971-1972', *American Journal of Public Health*, Vol. 74, pp. 813-815.

N. Chaturvedi and P. McKeigue (1994), 'Methods for epidemiological surveys of ethnic minority groups', *Journal of Epidemiology and Community Health*, Vol. 48, pp. 107-111.

L. Chitty and R. Winter (1989), 'Perinatal mortality in different ethnic groups', *Archives of Disease in Childhood*, Vol. 64, pp. 1036-1041.

I. Chrystie, S. Palmer, A. Kenney and J. Banatvala (1992), 'HIV seroprevalence among women attending antenatal clinics in London', *Lancet*, Vol. 339, p. 364.

T. Clark, N. Richards, D. Adu and J. Michael (1993), 'Increased prevalence of dialysis-dependent renal failure in ethnic minorities in the West Midlands', *Nephrology, Dialysis, Transplantation*, Vol. 8, pp. 146-148.

M. Clarke and D. Clayton (1983), 'Quality of obstetric care provided for Asian immigrants in Leicestershire', *British Medical Journal*, Vol. 286, pp. 621-623.

M. Clarke, D. Clayton, E. Mason and J. MacVicar (1988), 'Asian mothers' risk factors for perinatal death – the same or different?', *British Medical Journal*, Vol. 297, pp. 384-387.

R. Cochrane (1977), 'Mental illness in immigrants to England and Wales: an analysis of mental hospital admissions 1971', *Social Psychiatry*, Vol. 12, pp. 25-35.

R. Cochrane and S. Bal (1989), 'Mental hospital admission rates of immigrants to England: a comparison of 1971 and 1981', *Social Psychiatry and Psychiatric Epidemiology*, Vol. 24, pp. 2-11.

R. Cochrane and S. Bal (1987), 'Migration and schizophrenia: an examination of five hypotheses', *Social Psychiatry*, Vol. 22, pp. 181-191.

R. Cochrane and M. Stopes-Roe (1981a), 'Social class and psychological disorder in natives and immigrants to Britain', *International Journal of Social Psychiatry*, Vol. 27, pp. 173-82.

R. Cochrane and M. Stopes-Roe (1981b), 'Psychological symptom levels in Indian immigrants to England – a comparison with native English', *Psychological Medicine*, Vol. 11, pp. 319-327.

W. Cockerham (1990), 'A test of the relationship between race, socioeconomic status and psychological distress', *Social Science and Medicine*, Vol. 31, No. 12, pp. 1321-1326.

A. Coldman, T. Braun and R. Gallagher (1988), 'The classification of ethnic status using name information', *Journal of Epidemiology and Community Health*, Vol. 42, pp. 390-395.

J. Comaroff (1985), *Body of Power, Spirit of Resistance*, University of Chicago Press, Chicago.

R. Cooper and R. David (1986), 'The biological concept of race and its application to public health and epidemiology', *Journal of Health Politics, Policy and Law*, Vol. 11, No. 1, pp. 97-116.

R. Cope (1989), 'The compulsory detention of Afro-Caribbeans under the Mental Health Act', *New Community*, Vol. 15, No. 3, pp. 343-356.

J. Cornwell and P. Gordon (1984), *An Experiment in Advocacy: The Hackney Multi-Ethnic Women's Health Project*, King's Fund Centre, London.

Coronary Prevention Group (1986), *Coronary Heart Disease and Asians in Britain*, CPG/Confederation of Indian Organisations, London.

J. Cox and S. Bostock (1989), *Racial Discrimination in the Health Service*, Penrhos, Newcastle-under-Lyme.

T. Craig, A. Goodman and G. Haugland (1982), 'Impact of DSM-III on clinical practice', *American Journal of Psychiatry*, Vol.139, pp.922-925.

J. Cruickshank (1993), 'The challenge for the Afro-Caribbean community of controlling stroke and hypertension', in North East and North West Thames RHA (1993), pp. 27-42.

J. Cruickshank (1989a), 'Continuing rarity of ischaemic heart disease in Afro-Caribbeans in the West Indies and the UK, and in West Africa', in J. Cruickshank and D. Beevers (1989), pp. 264-266.

J. Cruickshank (1989b), 'An outline of cerebrovascular and renal disease', in J. Cruickshank and D. Beevers (1989), pp. 266-268.

J. Cruickshank (1989c), 'The natural history of blood pressure in black populations in the West Indies, West Africa and the UK: a comparison with the USA', in J. Cruickshank and D. Beevers (1989), pp. 268-279.

J. Cruickshank (1989d), 'Diabetes: contrasts between peoples of black (West African), Indian and white European origin', in J. Cruickshank and D. Beevers (1989), pp. 289-304.

J. Cruickshank and D. Beevers (1989), *Ethnic Factors in Health and Disease*, Wright, Sevenoaks.

J. Cruickshank, S. Jackson, L. Bannan, D. Beevers, M. Beevers and V. Osbourne (1983), 'Blood pressure in black, white and Asian factory workers in Birmingham', *Postgraduate Medical Journal*, Vol. 59, pp. 622-626.

J. Cruickshank, D. Beevers, V. Osbourne, R. Haynes, J. Corlett and S. Selby (1980), 'Heart attack, stroke, diabetes, and hypertension in West Indians, Asians and whites in Birmingham, England', *British Medical Journal*, Vol. 281, p. 1108.

C. Currer (1986), 'Concepts of mental well- and ill-being: the case of Pathan mothers in Britain', in C. Currer and M. Stacey (1986), pp. 181-198.

C. Currer and M. Stacey (1986), *Concepts of Health, Illness and Disease*, Berg, Oxford.

W. Daniel (1968), *Racial Discrimination in England*, Penguin, Harmondsworth.

G. Davey Smith and A. Phillips (1992), 'Confounding in epidemiological studies: why 'independent' effects may not be all they seem', *British Medical Journal*, Vol. 305, pp. 757-759.

Department of Health (1993), *Report of a Working Party of the Standing Medical Advisory Committee on Sickle Cell, Thalassaemia and Other Haemoglobinopathies*, HMSO, Crown Copyright, London.

Department of Health (1992), *On the State of the Public Health*, HMSO, London.

Department of Health (1991), *The Patient's Charter*, HMSO, London.

Department of Health (1988), *Third Report of the Sub-committee on Nutritional Surveillance: Executive Summary*, Report on health and social subjects No. 33, HMSO, London.

Department of Health and Social Security (1988), *Ethnic Minority Health: A Report of a Management Seminar*, DHSS, Crown Copyright, London.

Derbyshire FPC (1988), *Raising the Issues: A Review of Service Provision for the Ethnic Minorities*, Derbyshire FPC, Derby.

L. Diggs (1992), 'Intracranial haemorrhage in blacks as compared with whites', *New England Journal of Medicine*, Vol. 327, p. 568.

V. Dominguez (1977), 'Social classification in Creole Louisiana', *American Ethnologist*, Vol. 4, No. 4, pp. 589-602.

C. Donaldson and K. Gerard (1993), *Economics of Health Care Financing: The Visible Hand*, Macmillan, Basingstoke.

L. Donaldson (1986), 'Health and social status of elderly Asians: a community survey', *British Medical Journal*, Vol. 293, pp. 1079-1082.

L. Donaldson and D. Clayton (1984), 'Occurrence of cancer in Asians and non-Asians', *Journal of Epidemiology and Community Health*, Vol. 38, pp. 203-207.

L. Donaldson and A. Odell (1984), 'Planning and providing services for the Asian population', *Journal of the Royal Society of Health*, Vol. 104, pp. 199-202.

L. Donaldson and J. Taylor (1983), 'Patterns of Asian and non-Asian morbidity in hospitals', *British Medical Journal*, Vol. 286, pp. 949-951.

J. Donovan (1986), *We Don't Buy Sickness, It Just Comes*, Gower, Aldershot.

J. Donovan (1984), 'Ethnicity and health: a research review', *Social Science and Medicine*, Vol. 19, No. 7, pp. 663-670.

Y. Doyle (1991), 'A survey of the cervical screening service in a London district, including reasons for non-attendance, ethnic responses and views on the quality of the service', *Social Science and Medicine*, Vol. 32, No. 8, pp. 953-957.

Y. Doyle, P. Moffatt and S. Corlett (1994), 'Coping with disabilities: the perspective of young adults from different ethnic backgrounds in inner London', *Social Science and Medicine*, Vol. 38, No. 11, pp. 1491-1498.

W. Dressler (1993), 'Type A behavior: contextual effects within a southern black community', *Social Science and Medicine*, Vol. 36, No. 3, pp. 289-295.

W. Dressler (1988), 'Social consistency and psychological distress', *Journal of Health and Social Behaviour*, Vol. 29, pp. 79-91.

K. Dunnell (1993), 'Sources and nature of ethnic health data', in North East and North West Thames RHA, (1993).

E. Durkheim (1952), *Suicide: A Study in Sociology*, Routledge and Kegan Paul, London.

P. Ebden, O. Carey, A. Bhatt and B. Harrison (1988), 'The bi-lingual consultation', *Lancet*, i, p. 347.

S. Ebrahim, N. Patel, M. Coats, C. Grieg, J. Gilley, C. Bangham and S. Stacey (1991), 'Prevalence and severity of morbidity among Gujarati Asian elders: a controlled comparison', *Family Practice*, Vol. 8, No. 1, pp. 57-62.

R. Ecob and R. Williams (1991), 'Sampling Asian minorities to assess health and welfare', *Journal of Epidemiology and Community Health*, Vol. 45, pp. 93-101.

J. Escarce, K. Epstein, D. Colby and J. Schwartz (1993), 'Racial differences in the elderly's use of medical procedures and diagnostic tests', *American Journal of Public Health*, Vol. 83, No. 7, pp. 948-954.

A. Farooqi (1993), 'How can family practice improve access to health care for black and ethnic minority patients?', in A. Hopkins and V. Bahl (1993), pp. 57-62.

G. Feder, T. Vaclavik and A. Streetly (1993), 'Traveller Gypsies and childhood immunization: a study in east London', *British Journal of General Practice*, Vol. 43, pp. 281-284.

J. Feehally, A. Burden, J. Mayberry, C. Probert, M. Roshan, A. Samanta and K. Woods (1993), 'Disease variations in Asians in Leicester', *Quarterly Journal of Medicine*, Vol. 86, pp. 263-269.

S. Fenton (1989), 'Racism is harmful to your health', in J. Cox and S. Bostock (1989), pp. 15-26.

S. Fenton (1985), *Race, Health and Welfare*, University of Bristol (Department of Sociology), Bristol.

S. Fenton and A. Sadiq (1993), *The Sorrow in My Heart: Sixteen Asian Women Speak About Depression*, Commission for Racial Equality, London.

S. Fernando (1992), 'Roots of racism in psychiatry', *Open Mind*, Vol. 59, October/November, pp. 10-11.

S. Fernando (1991), *Mental Health, Race and Culture*, Macmillan, Basingstoke.

R. Firdous and R. Bhopal (1989), 'Reproductive health of Asian women: a comparative study with hospital and community perspectives', *Public Health*, Vol. 103, pp. 307-315.

C. Fong and I. Watt (1994), 'Chinese health behaviour: breaking barriers to better understanding', *Health Trends*, Vol. 26, No. 1, pp. 14-15.

M. Foucault (1979), *Discipline and Punish: The Birth of the Prison*, Penguin, Harmondsworth.

M. Foucault (1967), *Madness and Civilisation: A History of Insanity in the Age of Reason*, Tavistock, London.

J. Fox (1990), 'Social class, mental illness and social mobility: the social selection-drift hypothesis for serious mental illness', *Journal of Health and Social Behavior*, Vol.31, pp.344-353.

K. Fox and L. Shapiro (1988), 'Heart disease in Asians in Britain', *British Medical Journal*, Vol. 297, pp. 311-312.

E. Francis (1993), 'Psychiatric racism and social police: black people and the psychiatric services', in W. James and C. Harris (1993), pp. 179-205.

I. Franklin (1988), 'Services for sickle cell disease: unified approach needed', *British Medical Journal*, Vol. 296, p. 592.

P. Fryer (1984), *Staying Power: The History of Black People in Britain*, Pluto, London.

N. Fulop and R. Jewkes (1992), 'Background information', *Health Service Journal*, 5th March 1992, pp. 28-29.

A. Furnham and S. Bochner (1986), *Culture Shock: Psychological Reactions to Unfamiliar Environments*, Routledge, London.

GLC Health Panel (1985), *Ethnic Minorities and the National Health Service in London*, GLC, London.

S. Gillam, B. Jarman, P. White and R. Law (1989), 'Ethnic differences in consultation rates in urban general practice', *British Medical Journal*, Vol. 299, pp. 953-957.

D. Gillies, G. Lealman, K. Lumb and P. Congdon (1984), 'Analysis of ethnic influence on stillbirths and infant mortality in Bradford 1975-81', *Journal of Epidemiology and Community Health*, Vol. 38, pp. 214-217.

P. Gilroy (1990), 'The end of anti-racism', *New Community*, Vol. 17, No. 1, pp. 71-83.

P. Gilroy (1987), *There Ain't No Black in the Union Jack,* Hutchinson, London.

N. Glazer and K. Young (1983), *Ethnic Pluralism and Public Policy,* Lexington/Heinemann, London.

G. Glover (1989), 'Psychiatric hospital admissions in North London', in J. Cruickshank and D. Beevers (1989), pp. 200-203.

I. Godsland (1994), 'Insulin resistance in hypertension', *Lancet,* Vol. 344, pp. 1018-1019.

K. Goel, S. Campbell, R. Logan, E. Sweet, A. Attenburrow and G. Arneil (1981), 'Reduced prevalence of rickets in Asian children in Glasgow', *Lancet,* ii, pp. 405-407.

J. Goering (1993), 'Reclothing the emperor while avoiding ideological polarisation: a comment on Roger Ballard's essay', *New Community,* Vol. 19, No. 2, pp. 336-347.

P. Gordon and A. Newnham (1985), *Passport to Benefits? Racism in Social Security,* Child Poverty Action Group/Runnymede Trust, London.

S. Gould (1981), *The Mismeasure of Man,* Penguin, Harmondsworth.

S. Gould (1977), *Ever Since Darwin: Reflections in Natural History,* Penguin, Harmondsworth.

R. Griffiths, M. White and M. Stonehouse (1989), 'Ethnic differences in birth statistics from central Birmingham', *British Medical Journal,* Vol. 298, pp. 94-95.

Y. Gunaratnam (1993a), 'Breaking the silence: Asian carers in Britain', in J. Bornat *et al.* (1993), pp. 114-123.

Y. Gunaratnam (1993b), *Checklist Health and Race: A Starting Point for Managers on Improving Services for Black Populations,* King's Fund, London.

M. Haan, G. Kaplan and T. Camacho (1987), 'Poverty and health: prospective evidence from the Alameda County Study', *American Journal of Epidemiology,* Vol. 125, No. 6, pp. 989-998.

D. Halpern (1993), 'Minorities and mental health', *Social Science and Medicine,* Vol. 36, No. 5, pp. 597-607.

C. Ham (1992), *Health Policy in Britain: The Politics and Organisation of the National Health Service,* Macmillan, Basingstoke.

M. Haour-Knipe and F. Dubois-Arber (1993), 'Minorities, immigrants and HIV/AIDS epidemiology: concerns about the use and quality of data', *European Journal of Public Health,* Vol. 3, No. 4, pp. 259-263.

R. Hardie and J. Watson (1993), 'Screening migrants at risk of tuberculosis', *British Medical Journal,* Vol. 307, pp. 1539-1540.

J. Harland, M. White, R. Bhopal, S. Raybould, K. Alberti and B. Harrington (1994), 'Identifying a representative sample of UK Chinese for epidemiological research', Paper presented to the 38th Annual Scientific Meeting of the UK Society for Social Medicine, Leeds 14-16th September 1994.

G. Harrison (1993), 'Psychiatric disorders in ethnic groups: the nature of the evidence', in North East and North West Thames RHA (1993), pp. 62-71.

G. Harrison, D. Owens, A. Holdon, D. Neilson and D. Bood (1988), 'A prospective study of severe mental disorder in Afro-Caribbean patients', *Psychological Medicine,* Vol. 18, No. 3, pp. 434-57.

S. Harrison, D. Hunter and C. Pollitt (1990), *The Dynamics of British Health Policy,* Unwin Hyman, London.

G. Hart and A. Durante (1991), 'A review of the behavioural research on drug users and gay men from the VII International Conference on AIDS, Florence 1991', *Health Education Journal,* Vol. 50, No. 4, pp. 174-178.

I. Harvey, M. Williams, P. McGuffin and B. Toone (1990), 'The functional psychoses in Afro-Caribbeans', *British Journal of Psychiatry,* Vol. 157, pp. 515-522.

J. Haskey (1993), 'The ethnic group question in the 1991 Census', Paper presented at a conference, Using the 1991 Census ethnic group question in the OPCS Longitudinal Study, London, 24th May 1993.

K. Hawthorne (1994), 'Diabetes health education for British South Asians: a review of aims, difficulties and achievements', *Health Education Journal,* Vol. 53, pp. 309-321.

K. Hawthorne (1990), 'Asian diabetics attending a British hospital clinic: a pilot study to evaluate their care', *British Journal of General Practice,* Vol. 40, pp. 243-247.

H. Hazuda, S. Haffner, M. Stern and C. Eifler (1988), 'Effects of acculturation and socioeconomic status on obesity and diabetes in Mexican Americans', *American Journal of Epidemiology,* Vol. 128, No. 6, pp. 1289-1301.

H. Hazuda, P. Comeaux, M. Stern, S. Haffner, C. Eifler and M. Rosenthal (1986), 'A comparison of three indicators for identifying Mexican Americans in epidemiological research', *American Journal of Epidemiology,* Vol. 123, No. 1, pp. 96-111.

A. Headen (1992), 'Time costs and informal social support as determinants of differences between black and white families in the provision of long-term care', *Inquiry,* Vol. 29, pp. 440-450.

I. Heath (1991), 'Ethnic monitoring in general practice', *British Journal of General Practice,* Vol. 41, No. 349, pp. 310-11.

G. Hek (1991), 'Contact with Asian elders', *Journal of District Nursing,* December 1991, pp. 13-15.

C. Helman (1990), *Culture, Health and Illness,* Wright, London.

A. Henley and C. Taylor (1981), *Asians in Britain: Recording and Using Asian Names,* DHSS/King's Fund, London.

C. Hennekens and J. Buring (1987), *Epidemiology in Medicine,* Little Brown, Boston.

C. Henry (1992), 'Understanding the underclass: the role of culture and economic progress', in J.Jennings (1992), pp.67-86.

F. Hickling (1991), 'Psychiatric hospital admission rates in Jamaica, 1971 and 1988', *British Journal of Psychiatry,* Vol. 159, pp. 817-821.

C. Hicks and L. Hayes (1991), 'Linkworkers in antenatal care: facilitators of equal opportunities in health provision or salves for the management conscience?', *Health Services Management Research,* Vol. 4, No. 2, pp. 89-93.

A. Hill (1989), 'Molecular markers of ethnic groups', in J. Cruickshank and D. Beevers (1989), pp. 25-31.

T. Hoare (1993), 'Screening for breast cancer', in North East and North West Thames RHA (1993), pp. 84-89.

T. Hoare, C. Thomas, A. Biggs, M. Booth, S. Bradley and E. Friedman (1994), 'Can the uptake of breast screening by Asian women be increased? A randomized controlled trial of a linkworker intervention', *Journal of Public Health Medicine,* Vol. 16, No. 2, pp. 179-185.

T. Hoare, C. Johnson, R. Gorton and C. Alberg (1992), 'Reasons for non-attendance for breast screening by Asian women', *Health Education Journal*, Vol. 51/4, pp. 157-161.

A. Hopkins and V. Bahl (1993), *Access to Health Care for People from Black and Ethnic Minorities*, Royal College of Physicians, London.

House of Commons (1980), *Perinatal and Neonatal Mortality: Second Report of the Social Services Committee*, House of Commons Paper 663-1 (Session 1979-80), HMSO, London (The Short Report).

R. Howard, C. Lillis and S. Tuck (1993), 'Contraceptives, counselling and pregnancy in women with sickle cell disease', *British Medical Journal*, Vol. 306, pp. 1735-1737.

B. Howlett, W. Ahmad and R. Murray (1992), 'An exploration of white, Asian and Afro-Caribbean peoples' concepts of health and illness causation', *New Community*, Vol 18, No. 2, pp. 281-292.

G. Huby and M. Salkind (1989), 'General medical practice in a multicultural and multiracial environment: report from a multidisciplinary casework seminar', *Health Trends*, Vol. 21, pp. 86-88.

L. Hughes and J. Cruickshank (1989), 'Ischaemic heart disease in people of Indian subcontinent origin', in J. Cruickshank and D. Beevers (1989), pp. 257-263.

D. Hull (1979), 'Migration, adaptation and illness: a review', *Social Science and Medicine*, Vol. 13A, pp. 25-36.

B. Ineichen (1987), 'The mental health of Asians in Britain: a research note', *New Community*, Vol. 14, pp. 136-141.

P. Jackson (1987), *Race and Racism: Essays in Social Geography*, Allen and Unwin, London.

S. Jackson, L. Bannan and D. Beevers (1981), 'Ethnic differences in respiratory disease', *Postgraduate Medical Journal*, Vol. 57, pp. 777-778.

B. Jacobs (1985), 'Private initiative and community responsibility: a strategy for the black community', *Public Administration*, Vol. 63, pp. 309-325.

S. Jacobson (1987), 'Cholesterol oxides in Indian ghee: possible cause of unexplained high risk of atherosclerosis in Indian immigrant populations', *Lancet*, ii, pp. 656-658.

C. Jain, N. Naryan, K. Naryan, L. Pike, M. Clarkson, I. Cox and J. Chatterjee (1985), 'Attitudes of Asian patients in Birmingham to general practitioner services', *Journal of the Royal College of General Practitioners*, Vol. 35, pp. 416-418.

W.James (1993), 'Migration, racism and identity formation: the Caribbean experience in Britain', in W.James and C.Harris (1993), pp.231-287.

W. James and C. Harris (1993), *Inside Babylon: The Caribbean Diaspora in Britain*, Verso, London.

C. Jayawardena (1980), 'Culture and ethnicity in Guyana and Fiji', *Man*, Vol. 15, No. 3, pp. 430-450.

R. Jenkins (1986), 'Social anthropological models of inter-ethnic relations', in J. Rex and D. Mason (1986), pp. 170-186.

J. Jennings (1992), *Race, Politics and Economic Development: Community Perspectives*, Verso, London.

M. Jeyasingham (1992), 'Acting for health: ethnic minorities and the Community Health Movement', in W. Ahmad (1992a), pp. 143-157.

S. Jivani (1986), 'Asian neonatal mortality in Blackburn', *Archives of Disease in Childhood*, Vol. 61, pp. 510-512.

M. Johnson (1993), 'Equal opportunities in service delivery: responses to a changing population?', in W. Ahmad (1993b), pp. 182-198.

M. Johnson (1992a), 'Health and social services', *New Community*, Vol. 18, No. 4, pp. 611-618.

M. Johnson (1992b), 'Health and social services', *New Community*, Vol. 18, No. 2, pp. 316-325.

M. Johnson, M. Cross and S. Cardew (1983), 'Inner-city residents, ethnic minorities and primary health care', *Postgraduate Medical Journal*, Vol. 59, pp. 664-667.

J. Jones (1981), 'How different are human races?', *Nature*, Vol. 293, pp. 188-190.

T. Jones (1993), *Britain's Ethnic Minorities*, Policy Studies Institute, London.

K. Judge and M. Solomon (1993), 'Public opinion and the National Health Service: patterns and perspectives in consumer satisfaction', *Journal of Social Policy*, Vol. 22, No. 3, pp. 299-327.

K. Kahn, M. Pearson, E. Harrison, K. Desmond, W. Rogers, L. Rubenstein, R. Brook and E. Keeler (1994), 'Health care for black and poor hospitalized medicare patients', *Journal of the American Medical Association*, Vol. 271, No. 15, pp. 1169-1174.

N. Kaplan (1994), 'Ethnic aspects of hypertension', *Lancet*, Vol. 344, pp. 450-452.

G. Karmi and C. Horton (1992), *Guidelines for the Implementation of Ethnic Monitoring in Health Service Provision*, North East and North West Thames Regional Health Authorities, London.

R. Kessler and H. Neighbors (1986), 'A new perspective on the relationships among race, social class and psychological distress', *Journal of Health and Social Behaviour*, Vol. 27, pp. 107-115.

V. Khan (1979a), *Minority Families in Britain: Support and Stress*, Macmillan, London.

V. Khan (1979b), 'Migration and social stress: Mirpuris in Bradford', in V. Khan (1979a), pp. 36-57.

M. King, E. Coker, G. Leavey, A. Hoare and E. Johnson-Sabine (1994), 'Incidence of psychotic illness in London: comparison of ethnic groups', *British Medical Journal*, Vol.309, pp.1115-1119.

King's Fund (1992), *London Health Care 2010: Changing the Future of Health Care in the Capital*, King's Fund, London.

A. Kleinman (1987), 'Anthropology and psychiatry: the role of culture in cross-cultural research on illness', *British Journal of Psychiatry*, Vol. 151, pp. 447-454.

T. Knight, Z. Smith, J. Lockton, P. Sahota, A. Bedford, M. Toop, E. Kernohan and M. Baker (1993), 'Ethnic differences in risk markers for heart disease in Bradford and implications for preventive strategies', *Journal of Epidemiology and Community Health*, Vol. 47, pp. 89-95.

C. Knowles (1991), 'Afro-Caribbeans and schizophrenia: how does psychiatry deal with issues of race, culture and ethnicity?', *Journal of Social Policy*, Vol. 20, No. 2, pp. 173-190.

H. Kohli (1989), 'A comparison of smoking and drinking among Asian and white schoolchildren in Glasgow', *Public Health*, Vol. 103, pp. 433-439.

L. Koo (1987), 'Concepts of disease causation, treatment and prevention among Hong Kong Chinese: diversity and eclecticism', *Social Science and Medicine*, Vol. 25, No. 4, pp. 405-417.

I. Krause (1989), 'Sinking heart: a Punjabi communication of distress', *Social Science and Medicine*, Vol. 29, No. 4, pp. 563-575.

N. Krieger (1990), 'Racial and gender discrimination: risk factors for high blood pressure?', *Social Science and Medicine*, Vol. 30, No. 12, pp. 1273-1281.

N. Krieger and E. Fee (1994), 'Man-made medicine and women's health: the biopolitics of sex/gender and race/ethnicity', *International Journal of Health Services*, Vol. 24, No. 2, pp. 265-283.

Z. Kurtz (1993), 'Better health for black and ethnic minority children and young people', in A. Hopkins and V. Bahl (1993), pp. 63-92.

L. Kushnick (1988), 'Racism, the National Health Service, and the health of black people', *International Journal of Health Services*, Vol. 18, No. 3, pp. 457-470.

Lancet (1992), 'Hypertension in black and white', *Lancet* (editorial), Vol. 339, pp. 28-29.

Lancet (1991), 'Consanguinity and health', *Lancet* (editorial), Vol. 338, pp. 85-86.

J. Larbie (1985), *Black Women and the Maternity Services*, Health Education Council/National Extension College, London.

J. Last (1988), *A Dictionary of Epidemiology*, Oxford University Press, Oxford.

T. LaVeist (1994), 'Beyond dummy variables and sample selection: what health services researchers ought to know about race as a variable', *Health Services Research*, Vol. 29, No. 1, pp. 1-16.

T. LaVeist (1993), 'Segregation, poverty and empowerment: health consequences for African Americans', *Milbank Quarterly*, Vol. 71, No. 1, pp. 41-64.

E. Lawrence (1982a), 'In the abundance of water the fool is thirsty: sociology and black 'pathology'', in CCCS (1982), pp. 95-142.

E. Lawrence (1982b), 'Just plain common sense: the 'roots' of racism', in CCCS (1982), pp. 47-94.

E. Lee (1994), 'General practice screening clinic for Bangladeshi families', *British Journal of General Practice*, Vol. 44, pp. 268-270.

M. Lee, N. Borhani and L. Kuller (1990), 'Validation of reported myocardial infarction mortality in blacks and whites', *Annals of Epidemiology*, Vol. 1, No. 1, pp. 1-12.

K. Leech (1989), *A Question in Dispute: The Debate about an 'Ethnic' Question in the Census*, Runnymede Trust, London.

J. Levin (1994), 'Religion and health: is there an association, is it valid, and is it causal?', *Social Science and Medicine*, Vol. 38, No. 11, pp. 1475-1482.

G. Lewis, C. Croft-Jeffreys and A. David (1990), 'Are British psychiatrists racist?', *British Journal of Psychiatry*, Vol. 157, pp. 410-415.

M. Lipsedge (1993), 'Mental health: access to care for black and ethnic minority people', in A. Hopkins and V. Bahl (1993), pp. 169-185.

J. Little and A. Nicoll (1988), 'The epidemiology and service implications of congenital and constitutional anomalies in ethnic minorities in the United Kingdom', *Paediatric and Perinatal Epidemiology*, Vol. 2, pp. 161-184.

R. Littlewood (1992), 'Psychiatric diagnoses and racial bias: empirical and interpretative approaches', *Social Science and Medicine*, Vol. 34, No. 2, pp. 141-149.

R. Littlewood (1986), 'Ethnic minorities and the Mental Health Act', *Bulletin of the Royal College of Psychiatrists*, Vol. 10, pp. 306-308.

R. Littlewood and M. Lipsedge (1989), *Aliens and Alienists*, Unwin Hyman, London.

R. Littlewood and S. Cross (1980), 'Ethnic minorities and psychiatric services', *Sociology of Health and Illness*, Vol. 2, pp. 194-201.

M. Lock (1994), 'Interrogating the human genome project', *Social Science and Medicine*, Vol. 39, No. 5, pp. 603-606.

E. Logue and D. Jarjoura (1990), 'Modeling heart disease mortality with census tract rates and social class mixtures', *Social Science and Medicine*, Vol. 31, pp. 545-550.

M. Loney, R. Bocock, J. Clarke, A. Cochrane, P. Graham and M. Wilson (1991), *The State or the Market: Politics and Welfare in Contemporary Britain*, Sage, London.

M. Loring and B. Powell (1988), 'Gender, race and DSM-III: a study of the objectivity of psychiatric diagnostic behavior', *Journal of Health and Social Behavior*, Vol.29, pp.1-22.

A. Lowy, K. Woods and J. Botha (1991), 'The effects of demographic shift on coronary heart disease mortality in a large migrant population at high risk', *Journal of Public Health Medicine*, Vol. 13, No. 4, pp. 276-280.

MORI (1993), *East London Health: Research Study Conducted for City and East London FHSA*, MORI, London.

MRC Tuberculosis and Chest Diseases Unit (1985), 'National survey of notifications of tuberculosis in England and Wales in 1983', *British Medical Journal*, Vol. 291, pp. 658-661.

C. MacArthur, M. Lewis and E. Knox (1993), 'Comparison of long-term health problems following childbirth among Asian and Caucasian mothers', *British Journal of General Practice*, Vol. 43, pp. 519-522.

S. Macintyre (1986), 'The patterning of health by social position in contemporary Britain: directions for sociological research', *Social Science and Medicine*, Vol. 23, No. 4, pp. 393-415.

S. Macintyre, S. Maciver and A. Sooman (1993), 'Area, class and health: should we be focusing on places or people?', *Journal of Social Policy*, Vol. 22, No. 2, pp. 213-234.

R. Madhok, R. Bhopal and R. Ramaiah (1992), 'Quality of hospital service: a study comparing 'Asian' and 'non-Asian' patients in Middlesborough', *Journal of Public Health Medicine*, Vol. 14, No. 3, pp. 271-279.

L. Manderson (1987), 'Hot-cold food and medical theories: overview and introduction', *Social Science and Medicine*, Vol. 25, No. 4, pp. 329-330.

P. Mares, A. Henley and C. Baxter (1985), *Health Care in Multiracial Britain*, Health Education Council/National Extension College, Cambridge.

K. Markides (1989), *Aging and Health: Perspectives on Gender, Race, Ethnicity and Class*, Sage, London.

M. Marmot (1989), 'General approaches to migrant studies: the relation between disease, social class and ethnic origin', in J. Cruickshank and D. Beevers (1989), pp. 12-17.

M. Marmot, A. Adelstein and L. Bulusu (1984), *Immigrant Mortality in England and Wales: 1970-1978,* (OPCS Studies on Population and Medical Subjects: No. 47), HMSO, London.

M. Marmot, G. Rose, M. Shipley and P. Hamilton (1978), 'Employment grade and coronary heart disease in British civil servants', *Journal of Epidemiology and Community Health,* Vol. 32, pp. 244-249.

D. Mason (1990), 'A rose by any other name …?: categorisation, identity and social science', *New Community,* Vol. 17, No. 1, pp. 123-133.

H. Mather and H. Keen (1985), 'The Southall diabetes survey: prevalence of known diabetes in Asians and Europeans', *British Medical Journal,* Vol. 291, pp. 1081-1084.

B. Mayall (1991), 'Researching childcare in a multi-ethnic society', *New Community,* Vol. 17, No. 4, pp. 553-568.

N. Mays (1994), ' "Race" and health in contemporary Britain' (Review), *British Medical Journal,* Vol. 309, p. 67.

N. Mays (1983), 'Elderly South Asians in Britain: a survey of relevant literature and themes for future research', *Ageing and Society,* Vol. 3, No. 1, pp. 71-97.

B. McAvoy and R. Raza (1991), 'Can health education increase the uptake of cervical smear testing among Asian women?', *British Medical Journal,* Vol. 302, pp. 833-836.

B. McAvoy and L. Donaldson (1990), *Health Care for Asians,* Oxford University Press, Oxford.

B. McAvoy and R. Raza (1988), 'Asian women: (i) contraceptive knowledge, attitudes and usage (ii) contraceptive services and cervical cytology', *Health Trends,* Vol. 20, pp. 11-14.

A. McCormick and M. Rosenbaum (1990), *1981-1982 Morbidity Statistics from General Practice, Third National Study: Socioeconomic Analysis,* Series M85, No. 2, HMSO, London.

E. McFarland, M. Dalton and D. Walsh (1989), 'Ethnic minority needs and service delivery: the barriers to access in a Glasgow inner-city area', *New Community,* Vol.15, No.3, pp.405-415.

D. McGovern (1989), 'Ethnic factors in psychoses: a picture from Birmingham, UK', in J. Cruickshank and D. Beevers (1989), pp. 190-194.

D. McGovern and P. Hemmings (1994), 'A follow-up of second generation Afro-Caribbeans and white British with a first admission diagnosis of schizophrenia: attitudes to mental illness and psychiatric services of patients and relatives', *Social Science and Medicine,* Vol. 38, No. 1, pp. 117-127.

D. McGovern and R. Cope (1991), 'Second generation Afro-Caribbeans and young whites with a first admission diagnosis of schizophrenia', *Social Psychiatry and Psychiatric Epidemiology,* Vol. 26, pp. 95-99.

D. McGovern and R. Cope (1987), 'First psychiatric admission rates of first and second generation Afro-Caribbeans', *Social Psychiatry,* Vol. 22, pp. 139-149.

P. McKeigue (1993), 'Coronary heart disease and diabetes in South Asians', in North East and North West Thames RHA (1993), pp. 43-54.

P. McKeigue (1992), 'Coronary heart disease in Indians, Pakistanis and Bangladeshis: aetiology and possibilities for prevention', *British Heart Journal,* Vol. 67, pp. 341-342.

P. McKeigue, B. Shah and M. Marmot (1991), 'Relation of central obesity and insulin resistance with high diabetes prevalence and cardiovascular risk in South Asians', *Lancet,* Vol. 337, pp. 382-386.

P. McKeigue, G. Miller and M. Marmot (1989), 'Coronary heart disease in South Asians overseas: a review', *Journal of Clinical Epidemiology,* Vol. 42, No. 7, pp. 597-609.

P. McKeigue, M. Marmot, Y. Syndercombe Court, D. Cottier, S. Rahman, R. Riemersma (1988), 'Diabetes, hyperinsulinaemia and coronary risk factors in Bangladeshis in East London', *British Heart Journal,* Vol. 60, pp. 390-396.

P. McKeigue, M. Marmot, A. Adelstein, S. Hunt, M. Shipley, S. Butler, R. Riemersma and P. Turner (1985), 'Diet and risk factors for coronary heart disease in Asians in northwest London', *Lancet,* ii, pp. 1086-1090.

J. McKnight (1985), 'Health and empowerment', *Canadian Journal of Public Health,* May/June, pp. 37-38.

A. McNaught (1990), 'Organisation and delivery of care', in B. McAvoy and L. Donaldson (1990), pp. 31-39.

A. McNaught (1988), *Race and Health Policy,* Croom Helm, London.

A. McNaught (1987), *Health Action and Ethnic Minorities,* Bedford Square Press/NCHR, London.

T. Meade, M. Brozovic, R. Chakrabarti, A. Haines, W. North and Y. Stirling (1978), 'Ethnic group comparisons of variables associated with ischaemic heart disease', *British Heart Journal,* Vol. 40, pp. 789-795.

R. Melia, M. Morgan, C. Wolfe and A. Swan (1991), 'Consumers' views of the maternity services: implications for change and quality assurance', *Journal of Public Health Medicine,* Vol. 13, No. 2, pp. 120-126.

R. Melia, S. Chinn and R. Rona (1988), 'Respiratory illness and home environment of ethnic groups', *British Medical Journal,* Vol. 296, pp. 1438-1441.

K. Mercer (1986), 'Racism and transcultural psychiatry', in P. Millar and N. Rose (1986), pp. 112-142.

J. Merrill (1989), 'Attempted suicide by deliberate self-poisoning amongst Asians', in J. Cox and S. Bostock (1989), pp. 69-78.

R. Miles (1982), *Racism and Migrant Labour,* Routledge and Kegan Paul, London.

P. Millar and N. Rose (1986), *The Power of Psychiatry,* Polity Press, London.

T. Modood (1988), ''Black', racial equality and Asian identity', *New Community,* Vol. 14, No. 3, pp. 397-404.

S. Mohammed (1993), *User Sensitive Purchasing,* King's Fund Centre, London.

P. Moodley and G. Thornicroft (1988), 'Ethnic group and compulsory detention', *Medical Science Law,* Vol. 28, No. 4, pp. 324-328.

M. Morgan and C. Watkins (1988), 'Managing hypertension: beliefs and responses to medication among cultural groups', *Sociology of Health and Illness,* Vol. 10, No. 4, pp. 561-578.

NAHA (1988), *Action Not Words: A Strategy to Improve Health Services for Black and Minority Ethnic Groups,* NAHA, Birmingham.

NAHAT and King's Fund Centre (1993), *Equality Across the Board,* King's Fund Centre, London.

NHS Executive (1994), *Collection of ethnic group data for admitted patients,* Executive Letter EL(94)77, 30th September 1994.

J. Naish, J. Brown and B. Denton (1994), 'Intercultural consultations: investigation of factors that deter non-English speaking women from attending their general practitioners for cervical screening', *British Medical Journal,* Vol.309, pp.1126-1128.

P. Nanton (1992), 'Official statistics and problems of inappropriate ethnic categorisation', *Policy and Politics,* Vol. 20, No. 4, pp. 277-285.

V. Navarro (1990), 'Race or class versus race and class: mortality differentials in the United States', *Lancet,* Vol. 336, pp. 1238-1240.

V. Navarro (1989), 'Race or class, or race and class', *International Journal of Health Services,* Vol. 19, No. 2, pp. 311-314.

H. Nickens (1990), 'Health promotion and disease prevention among minorities', *Health Affairs,* Vol. 9, No. 2, pp. 133-143.

A. Nicoll and S. Logan (1989), 'Viral infections of pregnancy and childhood', in J. Cruickshank and D. Beevers (1989), pp. 95-102.

A. Nicoll, K. Bassett and S. Ulijaszek (1986), 'What's in a name?: accuracy of using surnames and forenames in ascribing Asian ethnic identity in English populations', *Journal of Epidemiology and Community Health,* Vol. 40, pp. 364-368.

K. Nikolaides, A. Barnett, A. Spiliopoulos and P. Watkins (1981), 'West Indian diabetic population of a large inner city diabetic clinic', *British Medical Journal,* Vol. 283, pp. 1374-1375.

A. Norman (1985), *Triple Jeopardy: Growing Old in a Second Homeland,* Centre for Policy on Ageing, London.

North East and North West Thames RHA (1993), *The Health of the Nation – the Ethnic Dimension: Proceedings of a National Conference held on 21 June 1993,* North East and North West Thames RHA, London.

OPCS (Office of Population Censuses and Surveys) (1994), *1991 Census User Guide No. 58: Undercoverage in Great Britain,* OPCS, Crown Copyright, London.

OPCS (1992), *1991 Census: Local Base Statistics,* OPCS, Crown Copyright, London.

O. Odugbesan and A. Barnett (1985), 'Asian patients attending a diabetic clinic', *British Medical Journal,* Vol. 290, pp. 1051-1052.

O. Odugbesan, B. Rowe, J. Fletcher, S. Walford and A. Barnett (1989), 'Diabetes in the UK West Indian community: the Wolverhampton survey', *Diabetic Medicine,* Vol. 6, pp. 48-52.

S. Ohri (1988), 'The politics of racism, statistics and equal opportunity: towards a black perspective' in A. Bhat *et al.* (1988), pp. 9-28.

C. Oppenheim (1990), *Poverty: The Facts,* Child Poverty Action Group, London.

M. Otten, S. Teutsch, D. Williamson and J. Marks (1990), 'The effect of known risk factors on the excess mortality of black adults in the United States', *Journal of the American Medical Association,* Vol. 263, No. 6, pp. 845-850.

D. Owen and A. Green (1992), 'Labour market experience and occupational change amongst ethnic groups in Great Britain', *New Community,* Vol. 19, No. 1, pp. 7-29.

P. Pacy (1989), 'Nutritional patterns and deficiencies', in J. Cruickshank and D. Beevers (1989), pp. 216-226.

L. Parsons and S. Day (1992), 'Improving obstetric outcomes in ethnic minorities: an evaluation of health advocacy in Hackney', *Journal of Public Health Medicine,* Vol. 14, No. 2, pp. 183-191.

L. Parsons, A. MacFarlane and J. Golding (1993), 'Pregnancy, birth and maternity care', in W. Ahmad (1993b), pp. 51-75.

H. Peach (1984), 'A critique of survey methods used to measure the occurrence of osteomalacia and rickets in the United Kingdom', *Community Medicine,* Vol. 6, pp. 20-28.

M. Pearson (1983), *Ethnic Minority Health Studies: Friend or Foe?,* Centre for Ethnic Minority Health Studies, Bradford.

H. Pedoe, D. Clayton, J. Morris, W. Brigden and L. McDonald (1975), 'Coronary heart attacks in East London', *Lancet,* ii, pp. 833-838.

E. Peterson, S. Wright, J. Daley and G. Thibault (1994), 'Racial variation in cardiac procedure use and survival following acute myocardial infarction in the Department of Veterans' Affairs', *Journal of the American Medical Association,* Vol. 271, No. 15, pp. 1175-1180.

A. Phizacklea (1984), 'A sociology of migratiion or 'race relations'? a view from Britain', *Current Sociology,* Vol. 32, No. 4, pp. 199-218.

S. Pilgrim, S. Fenton, T. Hughes, C. Hine and N. Tibbs (1993), *The Bristol Black and Ethnic Minorities Health Survey Report,* University of Bristol, Bristol.

M. Pirani, M. Yolles and E. Bassa (1992), 'Ethnic pay differentials', *New Community,* Vol. 19, No. 1, pp. 31-42.

A. Poerksen and D. Petitti (1991), 'Employment and low birth weight in black women', *Social Science and Medicine,* Vol. 33, No. 11, pp. 1281-1286.

M. Powell (1990), 'Need and provision in the National Health Service: an inverse care law?', *Policy and Politics,* Vol. 18, No. 1, pp. 31-37.

U. Prashar, E. Anionwu and M. Brozovic (1985), *Sickle Cell Anaemia – Who Cares?,* Runnymede Trust, London.

P. Rack (1990), 'Psychological and psychiatric disorders', in B. McAvoy and L. Donaldson (1990), pp. 290-303.

P. Rack (1982), *Race, Culture and Mental Disorder,* Tavistock, London.

J. Raftery, D. Jones and M. Rosato (1990), 'The mortality of first and second generation Irish immigrants in the UK', *Social Science and Medicine,* Vol. 31, No. 5, pp. 577-584.

V. Raleigh and R. Balarajan (1992), 'Suicide levels and trends among immigrants in England and Wales', *Health Trends,* Vol. 24, No. 3, pp. 91-94.

K. Ramaiya, A. Swai, D. McLarty, R. Bhopal and K. Alberti (1991), 'Prevalence of diabetes and cardiovascular disease risk factors in Hindu Indian subcommunities in Tanzania', *British Medical Journal,* Vol. 303, pp. 271-6.

A. Rashid and C. Jagger (1992), 'Attitudes to and perceived use of health care services among Asian and non-Asian patients in Leicester', *British Journal of General Practice,* Vol. 42, pp. 197-201.

T. Rathwell (1991), 'The NHS reforms and Britain's ethnic communities', *Ethnic Minorities Health: A Current Awareness Bulletin,* Vol. 3, No. 1, pp. 1-3.

T. Rathwell and D. Philips (1986), *Health, Race and Ethnicity,* Croom Helm, London.

J. Rex (1989), *The Ghetto and the Underclass: Essays on Race and Social Policy*, Gower, Aldershot.

J. Rex and D. Mason (1986), *Theories of Race and Ethnic Relations*, Cambridge University Press, Cambridge.

V. Robinson (1990), 'Roots to mobility: the social mobility of Britain's black population, 1971-87', *Ethnic and Racial Studies*, Vol. 13, No. 2, pp. 274-286.

V. Robinson (1987), 'Race, space and place: the geographical study of UK ethnic relations 1957-1987', *New Community*, Vol. 14, No. 1/2, pp. 186-197.

V. Robinson (1986), *Transients, Settlers and Refugees: Asians in Britain*, Clarendon Press, Oxford.

Y. Rocheron (1991), 'The Asian mother and baby campaign: the construction of ethnic minorities' health needs', in M. Loney *et al.* (1991), pp. 184-205.

P. Roderick, I. Jones, V. Raleigh, M. McGeown and N. Mallick (1994), 'Population need for renal replacement therapy in Thames regions: ethnic dimension', *British Medical Journal*, Vol.309, pp.1111-1114.

R. Rogers (1992), 'Living and dying in the USA: sociodemographic determinants of death among blacks and whites', *Demography*, Vol. 29, No. 2, pp. 287-303.

R. Rona, S. Chinn and W. Holland (1988), 'The national study of health and growth: nutritional status of children of ethnic minorities and inner city areas in England', in Department of Health (1988), pp. 7-8.

G. Rose (1992), *The Strategy of Preventive Medicine*, Oxford Medical Publications, Oxford.

S. Rose, R. Lewontin and L. Kamin (1984), *Not In Our Genes: Biology, Ideology and Human Nature*, Penguin, London.

B. Rushing, C. Ritter and R. Burton (1992), 'Race differences in the effects of multiple roles on health: longitudinal evidence from a national sample of older men', *Journal of Health and Social Behavior*, Vol.33, pp.126-139.

S. Saggar (1993), 'The politics of 'race policy' in Britain', *Critical Social Policy*, Vol. 37, pp. 32-51.

E. Said (1978), *Orientalism*, Vintage Books, New York.

C. Samson and N. South (1994), *Conflict and Consensus in Social Policy*, BSA/Macmillan, Basingstoke.

S. Sashidharan and E. Francis (1993), 'Epidemiology, ethnicity and schizophrenia', in W. Ahmad (1993a) pp. 96-113.

K. Schoendorf, C. Hogue, J. Kleinman and D. Rowley (1992), 'Mortality among infants of black as compared with white college-educated parents', *New England Journal of Medicine*, Vol. 326, No. 23, pp. 1522-1526.

L. Schorr (1988), *Within Our Reach: Breaking the Cycle of Disadvantage*, Anchor, New York.

E. Schwartz, V. Kofie, M. Rivo and R. Tuckson (1990), 'Black/white comparisons of deaths preventable by medical intervention: United States and the District of Columbia 1980-86', *International Journal of Epidemiology*, Vol. 19, No. 3, pp. 591-598.

R. Scribner and J. Dwyer (1989), 'Acculturation and low birthweight among Latinos in the Hispanic HANES', *American Journal of Public Health*, Vol. 79, No. 9, pp. 1263-1267.

Secretary of State for Health (1992), *The Health of the Nation*, Cm 1986, HMSO, London.

P. Senior and R. Bhopal (1994), 'Ethnicity as a variable in epidemiological research', *British Medical Journal*, Vol. 309, pp. 327-330.

N. Shaukat and J. Cruickshank (1993), 'Coronary artery disease: impact upon black and ethnic minority people', in A. Hopkins and V. Bahl (1993), pp. 133-146.

N. Shaukat, D. deBono, J. Cruickshank (1993), 'Clinical features, risk factors, and referral delay in British patients of Indian and European origin with angina matched for age and extent of coronary atheroma', *British Medical Journal*, Vol. 307, pp. 717-718.

T. Sheldon and H. Parker (1992), 'Race and ethnicity in health research', *Journal of Public Health Medicine*, Vol. 14, No. 2, pp. 104-110.

Sickle Cell Society (1983), *Sickle Cell Disease: The Need for Improved Services*, Sickle Cell Society, London.

D. Simmons, D. Williams and M. Powell (1989), 'Prevalence of diabetes in a predominantly Asian community: preliminary findings of the Coventry diabetes study', *British Medical Journal*, Vol. 298, pp. 18-21.

A. Sivanandan (1982), *A Different Hunger*, Pluto, London.

A. Sivanandan (1976), 'Race, class and the state: the Black experience in Britain', *Race and Class*, Vol. 17, No. 4, pp. 347-368.

N. Small (1989), *Politics and Planning in the National Health Service*, Open University Press, Buckingham.

S. Smith (1987), 'Residential segregation: a geography of English racism?' in P. Jackson (1987), pp. 25-49.

J. Solomos (1989), *Race and Racism in Contemporary Britain*, Macmillan, Basingstoke.

P. Sorlie, E. Rogot, R. Anderson, N. Johnson and E. Backlund (1992), 'Black-white mortality differences by family income', *Lancet*, Vol. 340, pp. 346-350.

C. Stack (1974), *All Our Kin: Strategies for Survival in a Black Community*, Harper and Row, New York.

W. Stephens, P. Klimiuk and S. Warrington (1981), 'Preventing vitamin D deficiency in immigrants: is encouragement enough?', *Lancet*, i, pp. 945-946.

Stop Rickets Campaign (1983), *Report of a Health Education Campaign*, Save the Children Fund/DHSS Working Group, London.

M. Storkey (1994), *London's Ethnic Minorities: One City Many Communities*, London Research Centre, London.

P. Stubbs (1993), ''Ethnically sensitive' or 'anti-racist'? Models for health research and service delivery', in W. Ahmad (1993b), pp. 34-47.

J. Swanson, C. Holzer and V. Ganju (1993), 'Hispanic Americans and the state mental hospitals in Texas: ethnic parity as a latent function of a fiscal incentive policy', *Social Science and Medicine*, Vol. 37, No. 7, pp. 917-926.

S. Syme (1986), 'Strategies for health promotion', *Preventive Medicine*, Vol. 15, pp. 492-507.

S. Syme, M. Marmot, H. Kagan and G. Rhoads (1975), 'Epidemiologic studies of CHD and stroke in Japanese men living in Japan, Hawaii and California: introduction', *American Journal of Epidemiology*, Vol. 102, pp. 477-480.

D. Takeuchi, P. Leaf and H. Kuo (1988), 'Ethnic differences in the perception of barriers to help-seeking', *Social Psychiatry and Psychiatric Epidemiology*, Vol. 23, pp. 273-280.

J. Taylor (1991), 'Health behaviour and beliefs', *Health Visitor,* Vol. 64, No. 7, pp. 223-224.

A. Teague (1993), 'Ethnic group: first results from the 1991 Census', *Population Trends,* No. 72, pp. 12-17.

P. Terry, J. Bissenden. R. Condie and P. Mathew (1985), 'Ethnic differences in congenital malformations', *Archives of Disease in Childhood,* Vol. 60, pp. 866-879.

V. Thomas and F. Rose (1991), 'Ethnic differences in the experience of pain', *Social Science and Medicine,* Vol. 32, No. 9, pp. 1063-1066.

N. Thorogood (1993), 'Caribbean home remedies and their importance for black women's health care in Britain', in A. Beattie *et al.* (1993), pp. 23-33.

N. Thorogood (1989), 'Afro-Caribbean women's experience of the health service', *New Community,* Vol.15, No.3, pp.319-334.

K. Todd, T. Lee and J. Hoffman (1994), 'The effect of ethnicity on physician estimates of pain severity in patients with isolated extremity trauma', *Journal of the American Medical Association,* Vol. 271, No. 12, pp. 925-928.

P. Torkington (1991), *Black Health: A Political Issue,* Catholic Association for Racial Justice, London.

P. Torkington (1983), *The Racial Politics of Health: A Liverpool Profile,* Merseyside Area Profile Group, Liverpool.

P. Townsend and N. Davidson (1992), *Inequalities in Health,* Penguin, Harmondsworth.

P. Townsend and D. Gordon (1989), 'What is enough? New evidence on poverty in Greater London allowing the definition of a minimum benefit', Memorandum of Evidence to the House of Commons Social Services Committee, August 1989.

J. Tudor Hart (1971), 'The inverse care law', *Lancet,* i, pp. 405-412.

N. Verma, S. Mehta, S. Madhu, H. Mather and H. Keen (1986), 'Prevalence of known diabetes in an urban Indian environment: the Darya Ganj diabetes survey', *British Medical Journal,* Vol. 293, pp. 423-424.

R. Walker and W. Ahmad (1993), 'Black elders and community care', *HFA 2000 News,* Spring, No. 22, pp. 19-21.

S. Wallman (1986), 'Ethnicity and the boundary process in context' in J. Rex and D. Mason (1986), pp. 226-245.

J. Walvin (1984), *Passage to Britain,* Penguin, Harmondsworth.

J. Watson (1977), *Between Two Cultures: Migrants and Minorities in Britain,* Basil Blackwell, Oxford.

I. Watt, D. Howel and L. Lo (1993), 'The health care experience and health behaviour of the Chinese: a survey based in Hull', *Journal of Public Health Medicine,* Vol. 15, No. 2, pp. 129-136.

A. Weissman (1990), '"Race-ethnicity': a dubious scientific concept', *Public Health Reports,* Vol. 105, No. 1, pp. 102-103.

P. Werbner (1987), 'Barefoot in Britain: anthropological research on Asian immigrants', *New Community,* Vol. 14, No. 1/2, pp. 176-181.

M. White and R. Bhopal (1993), 'Health promotion for ethnic minorities', *HFA 2000 News,* Spring, pp. 3-5.

M. Whitehead (1992), 'The health divide', in P. Townsend and N. Davidson (1992).

J. Whittle, J. Conigliaro, C. Good and R. Lofgren (1993), 'Racial differences in the use of invasive cardiovascular procedures in the department of Veterans' Affairs medical system', *New England Journal of Medicine,* Vol. 329, No. 9, pp. 621-627.

B. Williams (1994), 'Insulin resistance: the shape of things to come', *Lancet,* Vol. 344, pp. 521-524.

D. Williams, R. Lavizzo-Mourey and R. Warren (1994), 'The concept of race and health status in America', *Public Health Reports,* Vol. 109, No. 1, pp. 26-41.

D. Williams, D. Takeuchi and R. Adair (1992), 'Marital status and psychiatric disorder among blacks and whites', *Journal of Health and Social Behavior,* Vol.33, pp.140-157.

F. Williams (1989), *Social Policy: A Critical Introduction,* Polity Press, Cambridge.

R. Williams (1994a), 'Medical, economic and population factors in areas of high mortality: the case of Glasgow', *Sociology of Health and Illness,* Vol. 16, No. 2, pp. 143-181.

R. Williams (1994b), 'Britain's regional mortality: a legacy from disaster in the Celtic periphery?', *Social Science and Medicine,* Vol. 39, No. 2, pp. 189-199.

R. Williams (1993), 'Health and length of residence among South Asians in Glasgow: a study controlling for age', *Journal of Public Health Medicine,* Vol. 15, No. 1, pp. 52-60.

R. Williams (1992), 'The health of the Irish in Britain', in W. Ahmad (1992a), pp. 81-103.

R. Williams, R. Bhopal, K. Hunt (1994), 'Coronary risk in a British Punjabi population: comparative profile of non-biochemical factors', *International Journal of Epidemiology,* Vol. 23, No. 1, pp. 28-37.

R. Williams, R. Bhopal and K. Hunt (1993), 'Health of a Punjabi ethnic minority in Glasgow: a comparison with the general population', *Journal of Epidemiology and Community Health,* Vol. 47, pp. 96-102.

A. Wilson (1978), *Finding a Voice: Asian Women in Britain,* Virago, London.

M. Winkleby, D. Ragland and S. Syme (1988), 'Self-reported stressors and hypertension: evidence of an inverse association', *American Journal of Epidemiology,* Vol. 127, No. 1, pp. 124-133.

F. Wolinsky, B. Aguirre, L. Fann, V. Keith, C. Arnold, J. Niederhauer and K. Dietrich (1989), 'Ethnic differences in the demand for physician and hospital utilization among older adults in major American cities: conspicuous evidence of considerable inequalities', *Milbank Quarterly,* Vol. 67, Nos. 3-4, pp. 412-449.

S. Woolhandler, D. Himmelstein, R. Silber, M. Bader, M. Harnly and A. Jones (1985), 'Medical care and mortality: racial differences in preventable deaths', *International Journal of Health Services,* Vol. 15, No. 1, pp. 1-22.

J. Worobey and R. Angel (1990), 'Poverty and health: older minority women and the rise of the female-headed household', *Journal of Health and Social Behaviour,* Vol.31, pp.370-383.

C. Wright (1983), 'Language and communication problems in an Asian community', *Journal of the Royal College of General Practitioners,* Vol. 33, pp. 101-104.

K. Young (1983), 'Ethnic pluralism and the policy agenda in Britain', in N. Glazer and K. Young (1983), pp. 287-300.

Author index

Page references for first named author only

W. Ahmad 10, 12, 17, 20, 22, 25, 42,
44, 46, 49, 82, 83, 85, 89, 91, 98, 104,
105, 107, 110, 111, 118, 120, 121, 123,
124, 125, 130, 132
M. Alderson 23
H. Aldrich 31
R. Alford 119
T. Allen 15, 24
R. Alwash 75
K. Amin 30, 31, 84, 118
B. Anderson 17
J. Anderson 44, 86, 102, 111
A. Andrews 42, 84, 89, 132
C. Aneshensel 56
E. Anionwu 78, 128
M. Anwar 24, 27, 88
C. Armstead 47
K. Atkin 10, 103, 105, 108, 110, 120
J. Ayaniyan 43, 55

C. Bagley 65, 70, 71
V. Bahl 122, 123, 126, 129
D. Baker 45
M. Baker 91, 98
R. Balarajan 10, 35, 36, 37, 38, 39, 40,
41, 42, 49, 51, 52, 53, 54, 56, 58, 59,
62, 63, 72, 75, 76, 77, 91, 92, 94, 95
R. Ballard 18, 123
D. Barker 45, 55
R. Barker 63
M. Barrett 108
C. Baxter 130
L. Becker 55
J. Beliappa 68, 73, 108
M. Bellamy 118
M. Benzeval 25, 44, 46, 83, 91, 93, 96
A. Bhalla 108
A. Bhatt 120
R. Bhopal 11, 23, 25, 35, 48, 49, 51, 52,
58, 77, 82, 91, 98, 100, 102, 118, 120,
121, 122, 129, 132
M. Bhrolchain 22, 24
J. Black 48
Black Health Workers and Patients'
Group 33, 69, 74, 110, 117
K. Blakemore 47, 48, 93, 97
D. Blane 87
M. Blaxter 45, 46
M. Bone 44
A. Bonnett 11, 24
H. Booth 22, 23
P. Bourdieu 17

A. Bowes 97, 100
I. Bowler 43, 85, 110
S. Boyle 109
S. Bradley 91, 99
F. Brancati 61
British Medical Journal 84
M. Britton 35, 83
C. Brown 30
D. Brown 86
M. Brozovic 58, 78, 128
I. Bruegel 30
B. Bryan 49, 89, 108, 110, 117, 120
S. Bundey 42, 43
A. Burke 73
D. Butkus 113

CRE 111
S. Calder 47, 79
H. Carby 108
L. Carpenter 65, 68
B. Centerwall 83
N. Chaturvedi 81
L. Chitty 39, 42
I. Chrystie 75
T. Clark 61
M. Clarke 39, 41, 42, 43, 109
R. Cochrane 64, 65, 67, 68, 71, 73,
86, 87
W. Cockerham 70
A. Coldman 21
J. Comaroff 16, 71
R. Cooper 15, 16, 19, 26, 132
R. Cope 66, 69
J. Cornwell 127
Coronary Prevention Group 56, 83
T. Craig 68
J. Cruickshank 10, 54, 55, 58, 59, 60, 61
C. Currer 73, 74, 86, 100

W. Daniel 114
G. Davey Smith 34
Department of Health 10, 121, 123, 129
Derbyshire FPC 112
L. Diggs 58
V. Dominguez 16
C. Donaldson 91
L. Donaldson 47, 52, 63, 97, 103, 104,
108, 111, 121
J. Donovan 10, 16, 50, 77, 78, 79, 85,
86, 98, 100, 101, 102, 103, 104, 106,
107, 126, 130, 132, 133
Y. Doyle 44, 91, 99, 124

W. Dressler 47, 56, 73, 86, 87, 133
K. Dunnell 44, 45
E. Durkheim 71

P. Ebden 121
S. Ebrahim 47, 93, 97
R. Ecob 21, 32, 73, 81
J. Escarce 113

A. Farooqi 99
G. Feder 91, 98
J. Feehally 61
S. Fenton 47, 73, 74, 86, 111
S. Fernando 69, 74
R. Firdous 43, 48, 99, 104
C. Fong 49, 102
M. Foucault 69
J.Fox 67
K.Fox 55, 56
E. Francis 67, 69, 71, 85
I. Franklin 128, 129
P. Fryer 26
N. Fulop 124
A. Furnham 70, 88

S. Gillam 72, 73, 91, 97
D. Gillies 39
P. Gilroy 14, 15, 18, 70
GLC Health Panel 109
G. Glover 70
I. Godsland 57
K. Goel 129
J. Goering 18
P. Gordon 31, 118
S. Gould 13, 89
R. Griffiths 39
Y. Gunaratnam 108, 124

M. Haan 32
D. Halpern 73
C. Ham 118
M. Haour-Knipe 75
R. Hardie 129
J. Harland 21
G.Harrison 65, 66, 68
S.Harrison 118, 119, 130
G. Hart 75
I. Harvey 68, 69
J. Haskey 24
K. Hawthorne 112, 122
H. Hazuda 20, 86
A. Headen 108, 109

146

Subject index